The ABC of the projectariat

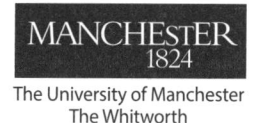

The University of Manchester
The Whitworth

Kuba Szreder

The ABC of the projectariat

Living and working in a
precarious art world

the **Whitworth**

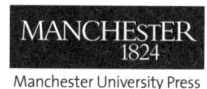

Manchester University Press

Co-published by Manchester University Press and the
Whitworth, The University of Manchester.

First published in 2021.

Manchester University Press, Oxford Road, Manchester
M13 9PL www.manchesteruniversitypress.co.uk

The Whitworth, Oxford Road, Manchester M15 6ER
www.whitworth.manchester.ac.uk

British Library Cataloguing-in-Publication Data
A catalogue record for this book is available from the
British Library

ISBN   978 1 5261 6132 1   paperback

Whitworth Manuals
Series Editors: Poppy Bowers and John Byrne
Commissioning Editor: Emma Brennan
Design: Textbook Studio / Vicky Carr
Printed by: Bell & Bain Ltd, Glasgow

Cover design: Textbook Studio / Vicky Carr, images by
Kuba Szreder, flag designs courtesy of Krzysztof Pyda
and Zofia Kofta.

Diagram on pp. 206-207 designed by Vicky Carr. The
motive on the flags of anti-fascist interdependence was
designed by Krzysztof Pyda in the context of the
anti-fascist street party organised in Warsaw in 2019.

Edited by Emma Brennan and Poppy Bowers

Preface

The *ABC of the projectariat* is a book about the life and work of the artistic projectariat, a group of people who do projects in order to make a living. The *ABC* talks about the fight and plight of these freelancers roaming the global networks of contemporary art – artists, curators, critics, academics, writers, technicians and assistants. To stay afloat they have to chase the flow of intermittent opportunities, which take the form of jobs, projects, commissions and assignments. The majority of projectarians do not own much beyond their own capacity to circulate, which is a precarious privilege in the globalised world, where the freedom of movement is denied to so many. Projectarians are torn between promises of unrestrained mobility and looming poverty, and the riskiness of their situation is only amplified by the global crisis caused by COVID-19.

In this book, I reverse-engineer the social machines that propel the circulation of artistic ideas, objects and bodies. Their basic tenets are discussed in sixty-six alphabetically ordered entries. But the *ABC* is not a dictionary or a lexicon. It does not pretend to represent a comprehensive list of ideas. Instead, it embraces contradictions – like the one between youthful enthusiasm and cut-throat competition – to create an interlinked mesh of references that mimics the distributed and ruptured patterns of living and working as a projectarian.

The book offers an uncompromising critique of the cruel economy of contemporary art, contrasted with a deep and non-judgemental understanding of the perils and attractions of artistic labour. Most importantly, it provides an outline of what practical action can be taken to change the situation of the projectariat for the better, through new modes of collective action aimed at overcoming the structural deficiencies of artistic networks.

I use the ABC format to show how the organisational vocabulary of the projectariat can either be structured in accordance with the syntax of networked power or rearranged by following the grammar of collective resistance. Using a system of hyperlinks (referenced as →) a reader can follow the path of → entrepreneurial → opportunists, who in pursuit of → independence have to → apply for everything, facing → burn-outs and → exclusion. Or, they can read into the collective modes of action of radicalised → art workers, who instead of pursuing → deadlines, → struggle for collective futures by building better social → time machines. This distributed structure highlights the inconsistencies, dissonances and contradictions experienced by so many projectarians on a daily basis. These tensions are identified as exciting sites of potential action and political intervention.

I hope that the *ABC* can serve as both a critical reader and a practical handbook that addresses the worries, pursuits, ambitions and struggles of projectarians worldwide, quite a few of whom are currently looking for ways to move beyond the structural conundrum of artistic networks, where nothing is certain except one's own precarity. To unpick the paradoxes of this position, the book assumes a viewpoint of the precarious workforce that mans the fluid assembly lines of artistic factories, flocks to mega-events, studies at art schools, works at gallery counters, curates exhibitions, facilitates audiences, makes art and writes applications. But first and foremost, these intermittent labourers make projects, one after another, and many at the same time. Following in the footsteps of Marx, this book analyses hierarchies, conflicts, means of exploitation and modes of resistance specific to their – supposedly fluid – universe by 'descending into the hidden abode' of networked production.

Rooted in the daily exertions of the artistic projectariat, the *ABC* has been long in the making. When Jack Kerouac was asked about the process of writing *On the Road* (1957), the manifesto of the beat-boomer generation, he quipped that it took him three weeks of writing and years of drifting. I wish the same could be said about this book, but now it takes more than three weeks to write an application to academic publishers. There are some similarities, though. The *ABC* emerged from two decades of being on the move – chasing the networked flows and doing far too many intermittent projects. Thus, it could be read as a logbook of my years in artistic circulation, where everything moves but nothing ever changes, a theoretically infused diary of networked labour, spiced up with practical examples and everyday anecdotes.

This book – despite addressing the rootless space of interlinked metropolitan corridors – is sited in a particular experience of living and working in the semi-peripheries of the European Union. This semi-peripheral viewpoint can help one to see things more clearly, not as distantly as if viewed from the global South, but also – hopefully – less prone to ignoring the elephants in the room that roam freely in the global North (such as the privileges of race, gender, class and citizenry that limit access to supposedly horizontal networks of contemporary art). Citizens of countries located in the Central-Eastern Europe are more privileged then most but not as privileged as some. They do not need a visa to get to the West, and do not require a work permit to find a job there. And they migrate often, fleeing from authoritarian tendencies at home, looking for stability, better wages and basic welfare.

Even though the *ABC* focuses on the weird universe of contemporary art, very similar experiences are shared by anyone who works and lives in a project-based world. It's not just in contemporary art that people have to chase intermittent jobs, operate from the home/office, fill in applications and network ceaselessly. Moreover, this book addresses the field of contemporary art in the process of its decomposition. Art is not as exceptional as it used to be, and neither it is as autonomous as it would like to pretend. Behind the glossy facades of large institutions and international events, the cogwheels of artistic machines grind relentlessly. This book is like a field recording that catches the sound of fluid assembly lines, picking up the clatter of networked machineries, echolocating the jingle of logistical chains.

The *ABC* was written across a weird decade and more, which started with the 2008 financial crises, unfolded in the occupations of the early 2010s, and stuttered with the authoritarian onslaught five years later. It concluded with the tumultuous year of 2020, shaken by social movements like Black Lives Matter in the USA and Women's Strike in Poland, and brought to a grinding halt by the COVID-19 pandemic. The final edits of the book were made when nothing was on the move, projects were suspended and networked activities shifted online. I have referenced this disruption throughout the narrative, but the crisis caused by the COVID-19 pandemic is far from the only factor in this analysis of global networks that rely on interconnectedness and speed. In contrast – as discussed in → <u>A is for aftermath</u>, the first entry of the *ABC* – the pandemic only unearthed the underlying tensions of the artistic circulation, such as the seemingly contradictory relationship between individual freedom and the chronic precarity of artistic labour. The frictions mapped by the *ABC* will not go away, and sooner or later they need to be addressed. It can be done by overworked individuals, who seek to understand their own precarity, trying to make sense of their own burn-out. However, individual strategies that privatise responsibility for systemic mishaps only make things worse. The systemic causes of this condition have to be addressed collectively or will remain unchallenged. For this reason, the book ends with → <u>Y is for you are not alone</u>, and proceeds from independence to interdependence. The book focuses on the radically pragmatic approach to the challenges identified, backing it with thorough scrutiny of the conditions of networked labour. This analysis is founded on a basic premise that it is even less possible to establish socialism in one project than it was to enact communism in a single country, as one is unable to fully ameliorate systemic deficits on a microlevel of an artistic project or collective. Thus, the defects of artistic circulation have to be resolved on a grander scale, in the (much) longer run and by political means. Throughout this book I argue that artistic projectarians can only thrive when other precarious workers do just as well, and that it is in their best interest to engage in the struggles for better, more egalitarian, democratic, and inclusive global (art) world order. Where freedom of movement is granted to all and not a tiny few, where opportunities are distributed regardless of gender, race, citizenry or class of origin, where each contributes according to their abilities, and each receives according to their needs.

Acknowledgements

The *ABC* stems from years of doing artistic projects, swapping thousands of emails, chatting endless hours, taking far too many flights and staying too long at numerous parties. This reflective account is based on a pretty long, multithreaded and distributed conversation that involved multitudes of other projectarians: friends, comrades, colleagues, partners in crime. I have tried to reference as many people as only possible in the main body of text. However, quite a few of the conversations that impacted on my writing have not had a formal character. And precisely because these labours of love and works of pollination are not authored, they deserve an acknowledgement.

The place of love and honour is reserved to Natalia, Elżbieta and Cyryl Romik; Jan, Jolanta and Agnieszka Szreder; and to Rafał Żwirek. Not only have they collaborated on some of the projects mentioned here, like the summer camps of the Free/Slow University of Warsaw, that were organised in a family cottage, but also because only with their unwavering support was I able to carry on in the long periods of precarity and doubt. I have been able to finish this book only because Natalia turned our home/office into a joyful, caring and supportive environment. I am forever in their debt.

The *ABC* is a text with some history. Some of the theoretical threads elaborated here originated in the process of writing my PhD thesis at the Loughborough University School of the Arts. They were hammered out in endless, critical discussions with my tutors – Jane Tormey, Mel Jordan and Gillian Whiteley – and sharpened in friendly exchange with my peers – Vlad Morariu, Aria Spinelli, Joe Graham, Michelle Fava, Viviana Checchia and Corina Oprea. I am really grateful to all of them.

I have already devoted an entire entry to the Free/Slow University of Warsaw, but want to yet again emphasise its importance by thanking the entire team of F/SUW for our collective research process, in which this book is embedded: Bogna Świątkowska, Joanna Figiel, Janek Sowa, Michał Kozłowski, Szymon Żydek, Agnieszka Kurant, Krystian Szadkowski, Kasia Chmielewska, Teresa Święćkowska, Tomasz Żukowski and Ela Petruk. Special mention goes to the Bęc Zmiana Foundation, who published the Polish version of the *ABC* in 2016, but also to the dozens of people who contributed to the Free/Slow University's projects over the ten years of its existence.

Another collective that influenced my understanding of self-organisation, and educated me on the importance of generosity, is Critical Practice from London. In this thought-sustaining environment I forged lasting friendships that shaped the ideas presented in this book, and it helped me to work out what interdependent curating might mean in practice. I particularly want to thank Marsha Bradfield and Neil Cummings: the value of their friendship is incalculable, but should be accounted for, as they just keep giving. We have spent hundreds of hours walking and talking with other members of the team, to whom I also owe my sincerest thanks: Ben White, Eileen Simpson, Cinzia Cremona, Metod Blejec, Karem Ibrahim, Amy McDonnell, Michaela Ross, Scott Schwager.

The lessons in interdependence would not have been the same without Kathrin Böhm, with whom I established the Centre for Plausible Economies, and colleagues from the Communities Economies Research Network: Katherine Gibson, Cam Jarvis, Binna Choi, Katharine McKinnon, Bianca Elzenbaumer, Kate Rich.

This book is embedded in the artistic activism of the Citizens Forum for Contemporary Art and the independent trade union Worker's Initiative. I owe my gratitude to friends and comrades: Kasia Górna, who masters the hard art of herding cats, Rafał Jakubowicz, Mikołaj Iwański, Karol Sienkiewicz, Tomek Fudala, Monika Weychert, Waldek Tatarczuk, Zuzanna Janin, Mikołaj Ratajczak, Agata Szydłowska, Paweł Nowożycki, Staszek Ruksza, Sarmen Belgarian, Irmina Rusicka and Kacper Lecnim, Gregor Rozanski and Antek Burzyński. Special credits are reserved for Ewa Majewska, with whom I have spent years in – often tumultuous and yet usually productive – exchange.

The *ABC* is steeped in the most recent wave of post-artistic activism, and thus I wanted to thank my comrades and friends, with whom I organise demonstrations of paintings: Kuba Depczyński, Bogna Stefańska, Sebastian Cichocki, Marianka Dobkowska, Aleksy Wójtowicz, Michał Frydrych, Marta Czyż, Anka Siekiera, Małgorzata Gurowska, Diana Lelonek, Adam Kozicki, Michał Szota, Kolektyw Łaski (Julia Golachowska, Jagoda Kwiatkowska, Anna Shimomura), Olga Dziubak, Arek Pasożyt, Zuzanna Hertzberg, Grzegorz Prujszczyk, Adelina Cimochowicz, Mateusz Kowalczyk, Weronika Zalewska, Daniel Rycharski, Kasia Kalinowska, Cecylia Malik and many, many others. Special thanks go to Stephen Wright and Teresa Drace Francis for their role as shadow curators and backers, supporting some of our endeavours.

I owe my gratitude to the participants of the post-artistic block at the anti-fascist street party *For Your and Our Freedom*, organised by the Antifascist Coalition on the 11th of November 2019 in Warsaw. The cut-outs from the images documenting this action are featured on the cover of the *ABC*. I would like to thank the designers of the flags: Krzysztof Bielecki, Magdalena Frankowska, Małgorzata Gurowska i Anna

Siekiera, Jakub Jezierski, Zofia Kofta, Kaja Kusztra, Miłosz Lindner, Krzysztof Pyda, the choreographer Bożna Wydrowska and all the flag bearers who creatively and collectively resist growing fascism.

I would like to thank my colleagues from the Department of Visual Cultures at the Academy of Fine Art in Warsaw, for creating an excellent work environment, open to generating new ideas and shaping old ones. My personal thanks go to Kasia Kasia, Wojciech Włodarczyk, Waldemar Baraniewski, Marika Kuźmicz, Paweł Ignaczak, Agnieszka Nalewajka, Agnieszka Jakusz-Gostomska, Piotrek Plucienniczak, Karolina Thel, Luiza Nader, Łukasz Ronduda, Łukasz Izert, Kuba Mazurkie-wicz, Kuba Banasiak, Kuba Dąbrowski, Andrzej Leśniak, Ewa Kociszewska.

Most of the best ideas appear somewhere in a fluid in-betweenness of conference breaks, party chats, email swaps, summer camps, walks and talks. They unfold in both long-term exchanges and in transitory moments. Thus, I would ideally like to thank multitudes of people, the discussions with whom shaped my ideas on living and working in (and beyond) the project. It is impossible to name them all, but even a short and inadequate list is better than none: Michał Muraw-ski, Angela Dimitrakaki, Jesús Carrillo, Rena Raedle, Vladan Jeremić, Corina Apostol, W.A.G.E., Maya and

Lutka Gordon, Stéphanie Noach, Piotr and Karolina Jakoweńko, Maciek Czeredys, Krzysztof Grzybacz, Małgosia Bocheńska, Christopher Page, Celementine and Florence Keith-Roach, Paweł Wodziński, Bartek Frąckowiak, and Marta Michalak from the Warsaw Biennale, Aneta Szyłak, Marysia Lewandowska, Jonas Staal, iLiana Fokianaki, Georgios Papadopolous, Jenny Marketou, Gregory Sholette, Noah Fischer, Hans Abbing, Stevphen Shukaitis, Marco Baravalle and the entire team of S.a.L.E. Docs, Emanuele Braga and Mao Mollona from the Institute for Radical Imagination, Brian Holmes, Gigi Argyropoulou, Matthias Tarasewicz and Andy Newman, and Sophie-Caroline Wagner from the Journal for Research Cultures, Dmitry Vilensky and David Riff from Chto Delat?, Florian Malzacher, Joanna Warsza, Jesper Alvaer, Isabela Grosseova, Pavel Sterec, Peg Rawes, Simon Sheikh, Andrea Phillips, Suhail Malik, Michaela Crimmin (together with Nelson, Hex and Hector), Tomek Rakowski, Alicja Rogalska, Raluca Voinea, Natalia Sielewicz, Alistair Hudson, John Byrne, Gemma Medina, Alessandra Saviotti, Charles Esche, Nick Aikens, Zdenka Badovinac, Ida Hirsenfelder, Mabel Tapia, Steven ten Thije, WHW, Onur Yildiz, Sara Buraya, Tomislav Medak, Valeria Graziano, Rosalie Schweiker, Precarious Workers Brigade, Keep it Complex, John Roberts and Karen van den Berg, and the team of FEINART.

Special thanks are owed to the Foundation for Arts Initiatives, who supported my work on the English version of the *ABC*, and to the amazing team of the FfAI whose emphatic understanding helped me to pull it out: Merve Elveren, Antoine Schweitzer and Vasif Kortun. Last but not least, I wanted to thank Vicky Carr from the TEXTBOOK STUDIO, who designed this book with wit, patience and creative skill, Caroline McPherson who copy-edited it, and the excellent editors of this book, Emma Brennan and Poppy Bowers, whose invaluable comments, insights and suggestions shaped the *ABC* into its final form.

A   is for...

A

is for aftermath (COVID-19 as a forced suspension)

In the following entries I address social engines that are usually based on the ultra-fast turnover of projects in the moment of their forced suspension. The disruption caused by the global pandemic unearths the underlying tensions of the global → circulation of contemporary art, revealing its self-contradictory, exploitative and inherently unstable character. When this business runs as usual, the accelerated multiplication of → projects glosses over the structural conflicts between → art workers, and people or institutions who amass cultural capital (→ O is for one percent). In this book, I sketch out a critique of the political economy of contemporary art from the wormhole perspective of the artistic → projectariat, considering COVID-19 as a catalyst that only revealed the prevailing fragility of their cherished autonomy and – supposedly – unbridled mobility. Pandemic or not, independence always stems from → interdependence and relies heavily on accessing infrastructures and technologies that sustain the seamless flow of projects. These infra-structures and technologies are maintained by the invisible, frequently underpaid and overtly feminised → labour of love, and yet the crisis had particularly dire consequences for → precarious workers worldwide, including many art workers. The latter were deemed as 'non-essential' by authorities worldwide, adding insult to the injury caused by lockdowns. This most recent crisis is only one of many disruptions proving that new – more just, egalitarian and accessible – arrangements of artistic networks are necessary. Expressing this hope, I agree with Zarina Muhammad from the White Pube, a critical duo specialising in debunking the 'male, pale, and stale art world':

> The art world is close to the brink of collapse. We have got to radically restructure the way we do things; no one wants to return to normal, because normal was bad. We have got the capacity to make a mad little industry that's sustainable, accessible, genuinely diverse, fundamentally joyful, and I think we should do that. Right now (White Pube 2020).

In the following entries, the vast majority of which were written before the COVID-19 crisis struck, I attempt to analyse what is wrong with artistic circulation, especially when it runs at its highest speed, whilst trying to sketch out some alternatives. In the materialist tradition, I focus on the conflicts between a precarious workforce, which maintains artistic networks, and the beneficiaries of global artistic circulation, who amass social, cultural and economic → capital. Just as the capitalist economy relies on the exploitation of labour, the global circulation of contemporary art is underwritten by the precarious labour and dispersed creativity of artistic → dark matter, which, as activist and author Gregory Sholette argues, is not recognised and valued for the substantial role it plays (Sholette 2011). Typically, the majority of artistic production runs on the fumes of → enthusiasm, as the artistic → projectariat expects a return on its current → precarity and counts on delayed rewards, notoriously accepting tokens of merely symbolic recognition. And most projectarians do not have any other choice if they want to stay tuned to the networks of art. The COVID-19 crisis has revealed just how risky these artistic 'investments' are, but even at the best of times, one cannot eat symbolic capital nor be fed by mere aspirations. For everyone but the most privileged, freelancing is not a promising prospect of unrestrained mobility and youthful creativity, but rather a vulnerable and precarious existence. This fundamental truth is typically glossed over by the empty promises of future careers, hidden behind the glittery surface of exhibition openings and hushed in the competitive rush of hectic mobility, where everything and everyone moves so fast that nothing can ever change.

I doubt that we will be faced with a shortage of artistic labour in the future – there will be enough people of privilege to fill in the shrinking ranks – but we will likely witness the collapse of the ideology that used to justify the exploitation of artistic → dark matter. In the best possible scenario, it may prompt a realignment of class consciousness amongst → art workers. Quite a few artistic freelancers, especially from middle-class backgrounds and with citizenship in the global North-West, have nurtured an ideological illusion of a classless society and meritocracy. They aspired to be the one percent, or at least to become like the one percent (→ O is for one percent). Even if they were not as rich as the ultra-rich, and travelled with budget airlines rather than private jets, they still roamed the globe in search of new opportunities, following the patterns of the ultra-rapid flows of international capital (→ F is for footprint). Freelancers far too often imagined themselves as independent producers, as rootless as the capitalist class they copied, and relied on a privileged access to infrastructure, goods and technologies, produced and maintained by the even more precarious labour of others. The global pandemic of 2020 shattered this illusion – and may yet continue to do so. Due to the disruption of their global supply chains, some things and services, relied upon in the global North-West as basic to existing, might become much more expensive: luxuries that not everyone will be able to afford, and definitely beyond the reach of a badly paid artistic projectarian. Before anyone starts to mourn the status quo ante virus, it is important to remind ourselves that the 'old normal' was devastating for the vast majority of humans living on this planet. Just as Achille Mbembe wrote in his essay 'Universal Right to Breathe', one of the most insightful accounts of the early months of the pandemic:

> In Africa especially, but in many places in the Global South, energy-intensive extraction, agricultural expansion, predatory sales of land and destruction of forests will continue unabated. The powering and cooling of computer chips and supercomputers depends on it. The purveying and supplying of the resources and energy necessary for the global computing infrastructure will require further restrictions on human mobility. Keeping the world at a distance will become the norm so as to keep risks of all kinds on the outside. But because it does not address our ecological precariousness, this catabolic vision of the world, inspired by theories of immunization and contagion, does little to break out of the planetary impasse in which we find ourselves (Mbembe 2020).

The artistic networks of peak globalisation were based on the same expansionistic philosophy, debunked here by Mbembe, even if the reality of the coronavirus pandemic pales in comparison to the threat of the climate catastrophe.

Facing the urgencies we have to deal with, it seems plausible that the current architecture of the global art world is part of the problem and not a solution, as it is based on the fast turnover of artistic and intellectual fashions, in contrast to (and leaving little time to engage with) the structural and persistent character of the problems encountered.

The pandemic has been a major event, further destabilising an already unstable (and extremely unjust) global economy. Its aftermath holds an urgency that should provoke renewed efforts at enacting better, more equal and sustainable alter-globalisation. Marxist sociologist Immanuel Wallerstein termed this possibility 'utopistics' (Wallerstein 1998). He argued that in a moment of systemic bifurcation – and COVID-19 disruption definitely contributes to the systemic crisis of late capitalism – usually stable systems become chaotic. In such volatile situations, even modest actions may have a great effect. So here is our opportunity: while the post-COVID-19 world order is in its nascent stage, pointed interventions might make the difference between socialism and barbarism.

Organising yet another project won't resolve anything, but diverting the flow of artistic and curatorial projects towards the political project of democratic socialism and climate justice might contribute to this systemic change – at least a little. This (grand) project requires compatible institutional forms, collectives, movements, museums and non-governmental organisations that are artistically charged, theoretically aware, socially useful, democratically accountable and politically placed. The blueprints for all this are already in development, and have been discussed many times worldwide (Aikens et al. 2016; Byrne et al. 2018; Casco, Office for Art, Design and Theory 2018; Raunig and Ray 2009a; Steeds, O'Neill, and Wilson 2017). In order to combat the joined forces of neoliberalism and recurrent authoritarianisms, these endeavours have to root locally and connect internationally, rewiring artistic circulation for the sake of political and social struggles (→ I is for instituting the commons).

A   is for Anti-fascist Year

To firmly ground the following entries in the social and political urgencies of our period, let me briefly discuss the Anti-fascist Year, a fine example of the politics of radicalised art workers and proof of their capacities for self-organisation. The Anti-fascist Year was organised in Poland between 1 September 2019 (the eightieth anniversary of the outbreak of the Second World War) and 8 May 2020 (the seventy-fifth anniversary of the end of the Second World War in Europe). The goal of the Year, as stated in its manifesto, was to:

> commemorate all anti-fascist activists, men and women, who actively resisted fascism in the past, and to oppose the reoccurrence in the public domain of neo-fascist and neo-Nazi movements as well as of any and all parties endorsing and idolizing fascist ideas, discourse and practices. The Anti-Fascist Year is a collective expression of protest against the glorification of war, the cult of violence, authoritarianism, nationalism, intolerance, misogyny, homophobia and racism which wreaks havoc on human conscience and destroys our community and natural environment. The coalition is guided by the ethos of equality, freedom and solidarity of all human beings and deep care and concern for non-human beings (The Anti-Fascist Year 2019).

The Anti-fascist Year is an umbrella name for a wide array of anti-war and anti-fascist cultural and social projects conveyed by the independent, countrywide grassroots coalition of Polish cultural institutions, NGOs, social movements, art collectives, individual artists and activists. It involved exhibitions, summits, conferences, theatre pieces, site specific interventions and artistic blocks at various anti-fascist demonstrations throughout the year (→ D is for demonstration of paintings). In the end, at least 179 events were organised by 117 partnering organisations in 20 cities and towns all around Poland (Wójtowicz 2020), which is not a small achievement for an alliance that operated on a shoestring. The budget was scraped together by a couple of friendly institutions who each pitched in a bit of money, whilst trying not to label the Year as 'their own' project. Driven by the ethos of → interdependence, these institutions did not want to → capture this effort by claiming ownership, but rather supported it, whilst giving space for the coalition to emerge organically. The semi-secret structure of the Year, with an anonymous steering collective, was the iteration of → radical pragmatism: not only efficient, but also avoiding any potential backlash from the authorities, wanting to ensure that cultural producers toe the official party line.

The Year managed to achieve such scope by tapping into the social energies and resources of hundreds of people and institutions all over Poland, mobilised by a shared urgency. They embedded their projects in a much wider → struggle against recurring fascism, → repurposing the → apparatuses that regulate networked production. Obviously, as pointed out by Ewa Majewska, this mobilisation could be considered a 'bitter victory' (Majewska 2019) as, despite its scale, it has not managed to turn the tide of authoritarian politics. Disappointment aside, it makes sense to remember the scale of the challenge. None of the organisers of the Anti-fascist Year ever claimed that the authoritarian surge could be turned by 179 cultural projects. All in all, the historical victory over fascism, the 75th anniversary of which the Year commemorated, was achieved only as a result of enormous military effort and at the horrendous cost of millions of human lives. However, even this analogy is slightly unjustified, as contemporary authoritarianisms pale in comparison to historical fascism, especially in terms of brutality and their 'achievements'. For this reason, Enzo Traverso, a historian of fascism, introduced such terms as 'post-fascism' that he applies to contemporary forms of authoritarianism (Traverso 2019). Taking these differences into account, the organisers of the Anti-Fascist Year decided to define fascism along the theoretical lines developed by Umberto Eco (Kozłowski 2019), who twenty-five years ago, decades before Kaczyński, Orban, Erdogan, Putin, Salvini or Trump, diagnosed 'Ur-fascism' or 'eternal fascism' as an unremitting threat to democratic societies (Eco 1995). Ur-fascism, according to Eco, is a recurrent tendency shared between historical and existing fascisms, which are linked by a family resemblance rather than any logical coherency of their programmes. Ur-fascism is a bundle of values, a kind of attitude or even a sentiment that cannot easily be defined due to the eclectic and incoherent nature of actually existing fascisms, but still, according to Eco, can and must be analysed. The amalgam of fascist traits includes: the cult of tradition; the rejection of modernism; the cult of action for action's sake; labelling disagreement as treason; fear of difference; appeal to social frustration; obsession with plot; painting the enemy as both strong and weak; reverence of violence, machismo, cheap heroics; selective populism based on newspeak; contempt for truth, reason and artistic freedoms. The essentialist definition of Ur-fascism is even more important nowadays, when in countries like Poland or the USA fascism has started to be used by right-wing propagandists as a general moniker for political enemies. For example, pro-choice activists are smeared as 'feminist-fascists', and advocates of social democracy as 'leftist-fascists', testifying to Ur-fascist skill in spinning half-truths, not-truths and post-truths. Leaving the peculiarities of Polish public debate aside, the theory of Ur-fascism comes in handy precisely because it lists concrete traits around which fascist assemblages tend to coagulate.

The anti-fascism of the Anti-fascist Year should be understood in this context. This definition also informs the reading of slogans such as 'Resistance Against Fascism is the Best Art' that in February 2017 was brought to a picket in the lobby of MoMA in New York by a group of artists and activists who demanded the removal of one of the members of its board due to his connections with the Trump administration (Vartanian 2017). Both the protest in New York and the Anti-fascist Year were part of the same cycle of struggles organised globally in response to the wave of authoritarian politics that unfolded in the second half of the 2010s, documented in the special issue of the *Field* journal from 2018 (Sholette 2018).

Even though the Year has already concluded, the trust and connections that emerged in its course have not simply dissipated, but rather cast firm foundations for → art workers' involvement in other struggles, such as the current pro-choice protests of the Women Strike in Poland, in which many of the core organisers and supporters of the Anti-fascist Year actively partake. The anti-fascist impulse that motivated MoMA protesters in 2017 was carried over into the actions of Decolonize This Place, People's Cultural Plan (more in → C is for curatorial mode of production / revolution). Interestingly, the image with the banner 'Resistance Against Fascism is the Best Art' was used by the editors of *Hyperallergic* to illustrate the most recent protest in MoMA, whose organisers declared in early February 2021, after the inauguration of Joe Biden as the president of USA:

> (...) we must think seriously about a collective exit from art's imbrication in toxic philanthropy and structures of oppression, so that we don't have to have the same conversations over and over, one board member at a time (...) This thinking can only catalyze action once we state plainly: We do not need this money. Museums and other arts institutions must pursue alternative models, cooperative structures, Land Back initiatives, reparations, and additional ideas that constitute an abolitionist approach toward the arts and arts patronage, so that they align with the egalitarian principles that drew us to art in the first place (quoted after: Bishara 2021).

Even though it would be an overstatement to identify 'toxic philanthropy' with Ur-fascism, it is not surprising that the radicalised → art workers are inclined to protest both, rightfully identifying them as blatant manifestations of the will to power, in either authoritarian or neoliberal guise.

A   is for application

The COVID-19 pandemic has had no effect on one thing: the fact that projectarians apply. Even when the regular flow of projects is partially suspended, projectarians have to apply for stipends and other forms of support made available by governments. In the second week of the first UK lockdown, a friend of mine in London, who was about to apply to the Arts Council England using an online form, received a message: 'owing to the impact of COVID-19 on our funded organisations and individuals, we have had to take the difficult decision to suspend this fund. This will allow us to redirect the funding to the COVID-19 Emergency Response Package. To find out more, click here. (...)' and written below, in bold letters: 'GET STARTED'. Get started with what? Obviously, with yet another application. It was understandably infuriating, not only that people have to spend precious hours on filling in yet another form, but also that they are forced to compete with other art workers when everyone should be in it together. This disgrace was called out by many art activist groups, such as Citizens Forum for Contemporary Art in Poland (Citizens' Forum for Contemporary Art 2020), the artist-run self-help platform State of the Arts (SOTA) in Belgium (State of the Arts 2020) or the Keep it Complex collective in the UK. The latter proposed to establish a Solidarity Syndicate that would serve as a kind of platform for mutualising the risks incurred by competitive systems of applications by equally sharing the awarded grants (Keep it Complex 2020).

On the other hand, the need to apply for everything can serve as a calming signal that business as usual continues, if taken with a hefty pinch of salt. Global pandemic or not, millions of freelancers around the world waste endless hours on applying. Networked labourers spend sleepless nights on their laptops, browsing databases in search of new opportunities (→ O is for opportunism), writing applications, filling in forms, waiting for results. A projectarian applies for everything. For relief funds. For residencies (if there are any left). For grants. For commissions.

For participation in conferences, online or offline, both. For scholarships. For research visits. For a job. Paraphrasing a popular joke:

- How many freelancers does it take to change a lightbulb?
- Five hundred. Everybody applies, but only one gets the job.

Hundreds of competitions are announced every month, and projectarians respond, willingly or not. The most prestigious positions can attract thousands of applicants per post, in competition so fierce that often friends or colleagues are set against each other. During COVID-19, this competition did not abate, but actually was even fiercer, as → opportunities became scarcer. In the typical state of affairs, conversations, Zooms or Skypes are ruptured by an awkward silence when it turns out that everybody has applied for the same grant or position. Sometimes projectarians even compete with themselves, because one person can apply for a given opportunity partaking in various project teams, trying to diversify the risk, but in fact just outbidding oneself and everybody else, multiplying the time needed by everyone to fill all those forms. In order to maintain friendly relations (→ C is for co-opetition), it is better not to talk about one's current applications at all. It is more elegant to utter a general complaint about life in quarantine, grumble about yet another stupid application, whine about looming → deadlines, while being grateful that there are still any projects left that one can apply for. In such cases, everybody sympathises, as they are very well aware how utterly nonsensical most of these applications actually are. In moments of self-doubt, projectarians often say: no more applications! I am done with this shit! But as the circulation never relents, such decisions prove to be as binding as New Year's resolutions. The reasons why applications are so prevalent in contemporary society are the same as the ones justifying the proliferation of bullshit jobs. As analysed by David Graeber, the routines of bureaucratic capitalism simply require an array of silly and unfulfilling jobs that keep people in check whilst adding a veneer of respectability to these otherwise nonsensical roles (Graeber 2018).

And yet, despite this critical awareness, the projectariat applies, as every application is the → apparatus that mediates between the projectariat and the institutions controlling access to opportunities (→ G is for grant art). Usually, only if an application is successful are applicants able to complete their projects, get a job, receive a scholarship or go to a residence. It is of no surprise that applicants so nervously expect a confirmatory email or letter, starting with magic words 'we are pleased to inform you that your application has been selected'. More often than not, people receive letters or emails with a generic formula of rejection. The application system is a Kafkaesque castle refurbished for the age of distributed networks, where juries of anonymous experts decide the fates of the projectariat, determining their futures.

Applications bind time into schedules that petrify the future and colonise the present (→ T is for time machines). At first glance, there is nothing wrong with planning your project. Schedules and milestones might support an efficient organisation of activities. However, such schedules – when turned into bureaucratic mantras – reproduce the illusion that people are capable of the impossible task of controlling the unpredictable. Eventually though, applications prevent experimentation and prohibit unplanned developments, eradicating risks that are otherwise considered as indispensable tenets of artistic creation. This paradox has been analysed by Boris Groys in his short, ironic and pointed criticism of an art system that runs on projects and applications (Groys 2008). Comparing project-based bureaucracies with the grand projects of artistic and political avant-gardes, Groys emphasises that the very process of applying requires a certain degree of formalisation of a project before it unfolds, i.e. while writing an application people need to conceptualise a project before they are able to embark on its realisation, thwarting its potential to challenge social or aesthetical conventions (Groys 2008: 3).

Unfortunately, instead of vouching for non-conformist visions of artistic avant-gardes, the projectariat applies. The application is a device of distributed → control, a genetic derivative of grant systems (→ G is for grant art), turning ideas into sequences of numbers and calculations (→ N is for numbers and measures). Applications are not just a harmless form of projectarian fiction, consisting of empty promises. They are kernels of new futures, tools for shaping reality in accordance with the expecta-tions of people who control access to opportunities. Applications not only conjure realities, but also constitute applicants as supplicants who petition the cultural bureaucracies to fulfil dreams and desires – often not of their own making. In the process of applying, applicants are screened by a number of committees and experts. Applicants must create an attractive image of themselves to get selected. But it is not a mere crying game, though application systems are ridden with hypocrisy. Because projects turn visions into reality, applicants' personalities and work routines are transformed in accord with their applications. This is the risk of → grant art.

But the problems with applications run even deeper. When masses of people are forced to apply, and such was the fate of many recipients of social welfare or COVID-19 rescue grants, the very system of distribution reliant on applications is naturalised as the most reasonable way of distributing limited resources amongst the growing number of applicants. However, this mode of governance is both a side effect and a tool in the process of dismantling the welfare state (especially where it still exists). In fact, this system is embedded in → neoliberalism, because certain rights (such as the right to participate in culture, the right to creative self-realisation, the right to make decisions upon a shape of society, not to go hungry or to survive a pandemic etc.) are overwritten by a Darwinist principle of fierce competition. In the society of bullshit jobs everyone has only one right: to apply. In this manner applications are embedded in an ethical and political project of neoliberalism, aimed at promoting competition as the main mode of organising the bottom layers of society (while the → one percent has a right to do whatever they want), validated by references to economic rationality. When citizens are pitched against each other as applicants, they are less willing to defend systems based on social solidarity or redistribution against the pressure of capital. Instead, applicants are fiercely competing with each other for what seems like a shrinking pool of resources, which diminishes in effect the same socio-economic dynamic that promotes applying as the main mode of ensuring access to social welfare. Applications are aimed at manufacturing consent, evacuating risks and thwarting resistance, turning applicants into docile grant recipients.

On the other hand, the accountable and transparent systems of applying for public funding are preferable to private patronage, entirely dependent on the whims of rich donors. And, obviously, the right to apply cannot be taken for granted, as it remains a 'privilege' of the citizenry of the Global North-West. Even though the private foundations, government agencies and international bodies that operate in the global South and East follow the same project logic, the resources available are much smaller. In any case, the formalisation of the process of gaining access (to goods, positions, possibilities, etc.) secures a partial transparency and accountability. Therefore, systems of distribution based on applications, despite their pathologies, might be considered as a positive alternative to nepotism or the arbitrary whims of the people in charge. The applications can be compared to 'tests of strength', defined by Luc Boltanski and Eve Chiapello in the following words:

> The test is always a test of strength. That is to say, it is an event during which beings, in pitting themselves against one another (think of an arm-wrestling match between two people, or the confrontation between a fisherman and the trout that seeks to elude him), reveal what they are capable of and, more profoundly, what they are made of. But when the situation is subject to justificatory constraints, and when the protagonists judge that these constraints are being genuinely respected, the test of strength will be regarded as legitimate (Boltanski and Chiapello 2005: 31–32).

Because applications formalise the tests inherent to the world of networks, the competition for prestige and resources attains a veneer of moral justification. In this context, the application is naturalised as a fair way to organise the distribution of insufficient resources. However, the process of legitimisation engenders yet another vicious cycle. Projectarians apply because they are forced to compete for resources. With the growing numbers of competitors, and thus failed applicants, applications become even more formalised because this is a cheap way of securing legitimacy. At the same time, projectarians are kept occupied with their applications, too busy to → struggle for the truly democratic redistribution of social resources.

A   is for Artyzol

'Artyzol' is a Polish neologism, invented by the → Free/Slow
University of Warsaw to describe the affectionate relationship between
art workers and art work (Kozłowski, Sowa and Szreder 2015). We generated this term to denaturalise the same love of art that the art world
mythologises. Artyzol is a linguistic hybrid of 'art' (in Polish, part of the
word *artysta*, i.e. artist) and 'Muchozol', a bug spray produced during the
good, old, communist times. This etymology is pretty fitting, as Artyzol
might be fairly intoxicating in overdoses. But in small quantities, Artyzol
is somewhat stimulating, as it is sprayed to infuse the atmosphere – of
events or institutions – with artistic allure. Artyzol in its gaseous form
is characterised with an elusive and yet pervasive scent, with smoky
undertones, hovering over larger art events like the smell of vegan sausages
grilled at a hipsters' barbecue.

But on a more serious note, thinking about Artyzol was not
only a flight of theoretical fancy, but rather a tongue-in-cheek way of
dealing with a pretty serious problem, because the artistic projectariat
most of the time runs on fumes, unpaid or underpaid for their art work,
crammed into small apartments in zone four of metropolitan centres,
flocking to major shows and biennales via budget airlines (when they
actually take off, which is far less certain than it used to be before
the age of COVID-19). Even if Artyzol is a theoretical hypothesis, the
artistic projectariat makes actual sacrifices to pursue their love for
art. Artyzol is the opiate of creativity, which emerges in the process
of artistic circulation. The affectionate relation to art causes artists,
curators or assistants to pursue their artistic ambitions – even if it
means that their other needs have to be curtailed. Despite living on
the threshold of poverty (as accounted by the standards of the global
North, → P is for poor), the artistic projectariat is stimulated by an
obsessive interest in their own artistic projects. Some projectarians
have the natural ability to release Artyzol and infect others with their
→ enthusiasm.

The potency of Artyzol should be accounted for in every discussion about the power of art and artistic autonomy. In itself, affection for art can be considered harmless. After all, there is nothing wrong with people doing what they believe in and devoting themselves to their endeavours. However, overdosing on Artyzol leads to precarisation (→ P is for precarity), → burn-outs and depression, which are endemic conditions of the → projectariat. The side effects of Artyzol are all the more dangerous because the substance is sprayed cynically by artistic institutions that abuse enthusiasm to exploit → art workers, as if doses of symbolic recognition could replace proper fees and social security. It is based on a presumption, naturalised by artistic institutions, that the artistic projectariat works for the love of their projects, artistic or otherwise, not because they are paid. Even worse, the abuse of Artyzol can cause the atrophy of critical sense and an aversion to political mobilisation. As noted by Gigi Roggero, an Italian co-researcher of workers' movements at a conference organised by the Free/Slow University of Warsaw in 2011, artists, unlike workers, do not want to abandon their galleries and projects, as if only by staying in artistic → circulation they were able to ensure a continuous supply of the desired substance.

The notion of Artyzol is theoretically aligned with the feminist critique of the 'affective remuneration' of the → labour of love that is frequently overexploited in the service sector, in domestic labour or in the arts. In the words of artist and curator Jenny Richards:

> If the term 'a labour of love' was coined in 1975 to call out the mechanism for the exploitation of social reproduction, today we could add the term 'affective remuneration', which denotes the mass incorporation of this process beyond the realm of social reproduction, in which affect becomes a form of payback (Jenny Richards in: Child, Reckitt, and Richards 2017: 150).

But it has to be noted that when the notion of Artyzol was officially introduced in the *Art Factory*, a critical report of Free/Slow University of Warsaw on the conditions of artistic labour in Poland (Kozłowski, Sowa, and Szreder 2015), it prompted a mixed response. Some fellow art workers welcomed this as a tongue-in-cheek take on their daily struggles. After all, who has not felt intoxicated in the rush of running from one project to another, or become slightly tipsy from making art? On the other, Artyzol has been taken at face value – as if it was an academic term that reifies complex social relations as some sort of material substance. The lovers of art hated it just as much, rightly identifying it as a poke at artistic autonomy, with all its romantic underpinnings and fixations. At the end of the day, it is a humorous metaphor coined to denote a serious issue. But it is not a spray. Nobody sane would start running around the Giardini in Venice to test the air for mysterious perfumes enticing unconditional love of art, unless it would be framed as a re-enactment of one of Robert Barry's conceptual art pieces, made for the very fun of doing it. However, a high concentration of Artyzol would explain why all those people run around Venice as if they were a flock of headless chickens – and suffer withdrawal symptoms when their biennales are suspended.

A   is for assemblage or
                    apparatus

For obvious reasons, people who work on artistic projects are often compared to nomads, even when they are temporarily grounded in a world split by quarantine and lockdown regimes. In the good old days, Lena Relyea started his excellent analysis of the 'everyday art world' with a scene from the Grand Tour of 2007, when the art crowd roamed between the Venice Biennale, art fairs in Basel and Skulptur Projekte in Munster (Relyea 2017). In a world dominated by projects, even socially engaged artists, whose ambition is to make site specific and community-based works, had to travel from one place to another, as analysed by Miwon Kwon in her seminal study of the new genre of public art (Kwon 2002). Pascal Gielen derided such nomadic agents, the natives of international art circulation, as 'joy riders', who professionalise → opportunism and → cynicism, roaming the globe in search of new opportunities (Gielen 2009). But to analyse and venture beyond the political economy and social ontology of this nomadic condition, a methodological note is in order. Projectarians who move from one project to another, and roam the networks in search of opportunities, have to be understood not as private individuals, but as components of multi-faceted assemblages whose exploits are enabled and regulated by social apparatuses underpinning artistic circulation. Thus, the critique of political economy of the projectariat involves a rigorous analysis of the apparatuses that bring it into being.

In a famous passage from *A Thousand Plateaus*, Gilles Deleuze and Felix Guattari analyse a nomadic war machine, an assemblage composed from the human body of a nomadic warrior, his skills and stamina, a bow, a saddle and the body of a horse, tearing at the imperial borders and rupturing the smoothed space of the state (Deleuze and Guattari 1987). Such an assemblage is more than the mere sum of its parts: it is a nomadic war machine that impacts on a type of warfare waged by nomads, their behavioural codes and their economic and social organisation, all geared against the state. Obviously, the nomadism of roaming artistic agents is far more domesticated and embedded in the cycles of capitalist accumulation than the untamed energies of pre-modern peoples. A mobile phone is a projectarian's bow, an application their arrow, a budget airline their horse, a project team their war party, a commission their tactical aim and a tenured position their dreamed tent-palace. Taken together, they form a collective whole that moulds the qualities of its constituent parts.

The notion of the assemblage was developed further by Manuel DeLanda in his proposition for a realist social ontology, a new theory of society based on the analysis of dynamic processes of assembly (De Landa 2006). He defines the assemblages as 'wholes whose properties emerge from the interactions between parts' (De Landa 2006: 5) that impact on the qualities of parts thus composed, not impairing their capacity to assemble with other elements to compose new wholes. I am less interested in DeLanda's attempts to analyse society as a multilayered overlapping of different assemblages and networks, as it does not support the critique of the political economy of → neoliberalism that underpins the fight and plight of projectariat. I am keen on using his dynamic vision of emergent assemblages as it inspires my understanding of artistic circulation and its impact on the social ontology of art and the division of labour that permeates it. This entire book is composed in accordance with this theoretical intuition, as particular entries map the component parts of the apparatuses that regulate the work and life of projectarians, to compose a larger picture of tensions and struggles. In this attempt, I am more aligned with the materialist tradition of analysing social structures of artistic production. Such tradition understands art worlds as sites of labour characterised by specific division of tasks and unequal distribution of prestige. The most recent and excellent example of this line of thinking is *Working Aesthetics* by Danielle Child, where she analyses the role played by manufacturers and technicians in the creation of the seminal works of minimal art of the 1960s and 1970s or the young British Art of the 1990s and 2000s (Child 2019).

The classic division of artistic labour, specific to what Cynthia and Harrison White described as the dealer-critic system (White and White 1993), was defined by a dominant assemblage composed from a number of spaces, objects, personas, habits and discourses. It was ideologically centred on the mythologised space of the artistic studio, where a romantic genius produced discrete art works, subsequently peddled by art dealers in their galleries to collectors who collected for the love of art, informed by writings of art critics, whose task was to pronounce upon timeless qualities of art works thus revered. As analysed by Luc Boltanski, under the pressure of financial capitalism this domestic mode of circulation transformed into the capitalist mode of speculation (Boltanski 2014). The studio was replaced by a project or an expanded manufacture, a paintbrush by a personal computer, a gallery by an auction house, artists by entrepreneurs who manage their careers in a rapid flow of sales, commissions and opportunities, flying from one exhibition or art fair to another, commented upon by critics whose task is more that of a columnist than that of a pronouncer of eternal truths. This mutation changes the social ontology of artists and art works, impacting on the ideological notion of artistic autonomy. Hito Steyerl provides one of the most thorough critiques of the artistic condition intrinsic to this state of artistic assemblage, populated by overextended people who are always spread-too-thin, producing art works that circulate in a shadow network of artistic storages located in duty-free airports, mega-museums and transitory events:

> (…) the contemporary economy of art relies more on presence than on more traditional ideas of labor power tied to the production of objects. Presence as in physical presence, as in attendance or being-there in person. Why would presence be so desirable? The idea of presence invokes the promise of unmediated communication, the glow of uninhibited existence, a seemingly unalienated experience and authentic encounter between humans. It implies that not only the artist but everyone else is present too, whatever that means and whatever it is good for. Presence stands for allegedly real discussion, exchange, communication, the happening, the event, liveness, the real thing (…) The artist has to be present, as in Marina Abramović's eponymous performance (Steyerl 2017).

Following with the premises of Steyerl's analysis of the presence-economy, the critique of both the political economy and social ontology of artistic → circulation cannot stop at the description of an artistic universe in ever-changing flux. Regardless of its temporary suspension by the injection of coronavirus into the global system of artistic flows, the question remains: why, despite its apparent dynamism, is this social world so hierarchical – and why do such a lot of seemingly free agents reproduce systemic conditions of their own → poverty and → precarity?

My understanding of these patterns is founded on the work of two great theorists – Walter Benjamin and Michel Foucault. Benjamin, in his seminal essay 'The Author as Producer' (1934), shifted the focus of his contemporary debate from the author and his oeuvre to the social totality of the apparatus of symbolic production. On the one hand, Benjamin recognises that the apparatus facilitates the production, dissemination and consumption of literature. On the other hand, he argues that the apparatus is not a neutral infrastructure which simply enables an artistic creation. The main thrust of his argument is that the apparatus is always embedded in the class struggle. In effect, the apparatus does not simply transmit an artistic message, but rather utilises it for the sake of the class who controls it. This embeddedness in class relations is addressed by authorial technique which, in contrast to authorial tendency, partakes in the revolutionary struggle of the proletariat to reclaim the apparatus from the hands of the bourgeoisie (Benjamin 1970: 7). Famously, Benjamin describes the apparatus as the 'intellectual means of production' (Benjamin 1970: 8), which could be socialised in a manner similar to other means of production, such as factories, by a group of revolutionary 'authors as producers' (→ A is for art workers). As Hal Foster pointed out sixty years later, this analysis should be updated to cover the colonial and patriarchal modes of constituting and exploiting racially defined Others (Foster 1995). One such attempt is a system of reverse gentrification, mapped by the Institute of Human Activities and the Congolese Plantation Workers Art League (Roelandt, Barois de Caevel, and Cercle d'art des travailleurs de plantation congolaise (CATPC) 2017). In a diagram of the global art system, co-designed by the Metahaven, they describe how the major art institutions and metropolitan artists are not only directly sponsored by the companies that exploit workers on palm-oil plantations in Congo, but also benefit directly from the images of poverty created in such manner. Their solution is to reclaim the means of artistic production by creating and selling images of their own plight – as their motto says: moral problem – economic solution, a pointed intervention in a complex system of relations that links together such remote places as Lusanga in Congo and Turbine Hall in Tate Modern in London.

In line with their argument, the apparatuses of artistic circulation do not resemble a Fordist factory, or a typical assembly line. It is a distributed factory of creativity, rupturing strict temporal and spatial divisions between work and life, friends and co-workers, self-driven enthusiasm and exploitation. In light of its distributed character, the apparatus should be understood as an assemblage-of-assemblages, composed of diverse components, such as subjects, things, practices, discourses, institutions and resources. Such an apparatus operates according to an 'organisational grammar' that manages the relationships between its various elements in a way that replicates power formations – like neoliberal capitalism with colonial, racist and patriarchal undertones. In other words, the apparatus is both a systemic codification of the social relations and their tangible materialisation in the form of particular projects, institutions, subjectivities and networks. Such a definition of the apparatus refers to the concepts of Michel Foucault, who describes social apparatuses ('dispositif' in French) as 'systems of relations' or 'heterogeneous ensembles' that link together such elements as:

> discourses, institutions, architectural forms, regulatory decisions, laws, administrative measures, scientific statements, philosophical, moral and philanthropic propositions – (...) the said as much as the unsaid (Foucault 1980: 194).

As Foucault suggests, the elements of social apparatuses are both implicit and explicit (i.e. 'the said as much as the unsaid'). Some of them, as he says, 'can figure at one time as the programme of an institution, and at another it can function as a means of justifying or masking a practice which itself remains silent' (Foucault 1980: 195). Applying this to the world of the artistic → projectariat, the apparatuses regulating artistic networks are composed from both very tangible and explicit mechanisms such as public grant systems, explicitly codified in legal formulas or → applications. On the other hand, they include tacit knowledge and aspirations that define the sense of selfhood of independent artists and curators or the organisational formats of project management.

The apparatus is not only a means of production, but is also in itself productive, producing and reproducing social relations. According to Foucault, power relations do not only discipline or prohibit; rather they have a 'directly productive role, wherever they come into play' (Foucault 1990: 94). Power relations prompt the emergence of social forms, while subduing them in the 'interplay of non-egalitarian and mobile relations' (Foucault 1990: 94). Power flows through all our social relations, fluctuating in time, shaping social forms and moulding the links between people and things in ways specific to the kind of power in question.

The apparatuses of networked production regulate the daily lives of → art workers – their practices, habits, patterns of working and means of securing survival – whilst shaping the overarching architecture of the artistic → circulation. Grasping the interconnectedness of micro practices and grand structures is one of the main tasks of the Centre for Plausible Economy, a → patainstitutional research cluster affiliated with Company Drinks, an artistic enterprise located at the eastern edge of Greater London. I established CPE together with an artist, activist and organiser Kathrin Böhm in 2018 to analyse and reimagine the everyday economies – in the contemporary art and in society at large (Szreder and Böhm 2020). Borrowing a well-known technique from Frederic Jameson, we embarked on cognitive mapping (1991) of artistic economies, with the ambition of reclaiming them. In 2018 and 2019 we collaborated on a research project *Re:drawing the Economies*, co-organised with the Communities Economies Research Network, a feminist think-tank devoted to the promotion of community economies (→ I is for interdependence). As part of this exercise, we organised a series of workshops during which we worked together with a group of art workers to create diagrams illustrating their own daily economies. Unsurprisingly, their diagrams resembled complex spider webs. In order to make ends meet, they linked together non-artistic jobs, part-time teaching assignments, occasional sales, commissions or projects, and a bit of family and community support. When we collectively tried to imagine artistic economies at large, we picked up the visual metaphor of an iceberg, used by J.K. Gibson-Graham to analyse the patterns of (in)visibility characterising the capitalist economy (Gibson-Graham and Dombroski 2020). A small peak of financially trackable economies – monetary transactions, wage labour and capitalist enterprises – hovers above a hidden mass of financially unremunerated and thus economically invisible labour (such as the feminised → labour of love), non-monetary exchanges and social self-organisation. Together with CPE, we used this notion to cognitively map the – symbolic and monetary – economies specific to the global circulation of contemporary art. Our findings were published in a short visual essay, *Icebergian Economies of Contemporary Art* (2020), in which we pictured the artistic economy defined by the sharp hierarchies between the small yet extremely visible sector of prominent institutions, and a hidden mass of → artistic dark matter. The → apparatuses of artistic production shape the daily spider webs of informal artistic economies and the patterns of flows that regulate global → circulation, whilst policing the relations between them by enforcing the rules of the cruel economy of art (→ W is for winner takes it all) where (in)visibility comes hand in glove with exploitation.

In other terms, every apparatus is strategically embedded in the general relations of production and power formations. According to Foucault, although apparatuses do not constitute a coherent form of social organisation, every apparatus is defined by its 'dominant strategic function' (Foucault 1980: 196). In this respect, every apparatus is 'a rational and concrete intervention in the relations of forces, either so as to develop them in a particular direction, or to block them, to stabilize them, and to utilize them' (Foucault 1980: 196). However, this strategic function and power formation is never totalised, nor all-permeating. Michael Hardt and Antonio Negri argue in *Assembly* that power is not a primary mover of social relations but rather coalesces in response to bottom-up resistance of unruly multitudes (Hardt and Negri 2017: 76). Similarly, the nomadism of artistic 'joy riders' is not so easily subdued, governed or industrialised according to Angela McRobbie's studies of young creatives, quite a significant section of whom – instead of following on the path of self-marketisation – are engaged in various forms of resistant self-organisation (McRobbie 2015). Even though artistic circulation domesticates critical impulses and nomadic desires, it is also a crucible of resistance, of → art strikes, → productive withdrawals, → interdependent networks and radical → patainstitutions, also on an international scale, as exemplified by the CATCP's practice of reverse gentrification. One has to read Walter Benjamin's call for socialising the means of artistic production in this light. Even though it would be naive to think that it is possible to simply recuperate social apparatuses, or that it would be enough to change their tack by installing more socially conscientious cadres, the apparatuses could be rearranged as a result of social → struggles and collective mobilisations of the artistic projectariat (→ P is for productive withdrawals), which could use shocks such as the one caused by COVID-19 to challenge the exploitative economies and structures of inequality.

A   is for art strikes
                        (lessons to be taken)

In circulation, FOMO (fear of missing out) is not only a natural state of mind, it is a mechanism of self-preservation. Taking a break might mean that → opportunities will be seized by competitors, and a person not present will be → excluded from further ventures. This is one of the main reasons that women, or other people, who care for kids or other dependents find it so hard to make it in the art world. Even the pandemic – when seemingly nobody can move anyway – proves the fundamental character of this inequality as women, who disproportionately have to care for others when public services are locked down, do not have much time left for artistic or intellectual production. More urgently than ever, the specific tenets of this partial suspension should drive radical critique of the scrambled life–work conundrum of a flexible work force.

And among the legacies that are often rekindled in such context by contemporary theoreticians of post-Fordist resistance is the one of art strikes, the refusal of labour and radical laziness (Dimitrakaki 2013; Kunst 2015; Lazzarato 2014; Raunig 2013; Shukaitis 2014). The history of art strikes dates back to the time of the first avant-gardes, riffing on the legacy of refusal of labour and unorthodox Marxism of Paul Lafargue and his *Right to be Lazy* (Lafargue 1883), a pamphlet originally published in 1883, in which Lafargue argued against social-democratic demands for full employment and, instead, for the right to be idle or differently-productive, following the programmatic lines drafted by the young Karl Marx. This trope resurfaces all along the debates about the status of artistic labour under capitalism. Commenting on this topic, Bruno Gulli advocates for creative labour to be considered as an expression of a living labour, a human force uncoupled from capital (Gullì 2005). Such labour is neither productive nor unproductive for capital, as its ontology is unbound from the constraints of capitalist accumulation. Creative labour is an expression of this general capacity of living labour, even though, in order to become truly unbound, artists have to question the constraints and ossifications of the institution of art, especially when, as Kerstin Stakemeier and Marina Vishmidt argue, contemporary art is embedded in the cycles of exploitation characteristic to late capitalism (Stakemeier and Vishmidt 2016). Furthermore, if and when artists want to overcome systems of their own alienation, they have to go on art strike.

The art strikes about which Bojana Kunst, Maurizio Lazzarato, Gerald Raunig and Stevphen Shukaitis write challenged the institution of art in the name of unbridled creativity, which artistic institutions were supposed to endorse but did not – at least according to the artists who decided to strike. Artists like Gustav Metzger, Marcel Duchamp, Lee Lozano, Mladen Stillinović or Goran Dordjević withdrew or contested the field of art because it did not stand up to the values of bohemian living, of imagination embodied in daily existence. Thus, they resisted an institutional system that contained artistic imagination within the constraints of the class society and capitalist economy, thereby corrupting it. Classic art strikes addressed the dialectic of resistance and corruption, of promises given and failed, challenging the trappings of the art system in which artists participate reproducing conditions of their own → co-optation.

For the theoreticians of contemporary forms of strike, what previously used to be perceived as an exceptionalism of artistic labour became a widespread condition of flexible labour under post-Fordism. Stevphen Shukaitis justifies his interest in art strikes by pointing towards changes in the class composition of contemporary capitalism, analysing the fundamental similarities between artists and flexible labourers in terms of the individualisation, creativity, communicative character and diffused organisational patterns of the new forms of creative labour (Shukaitis 2014: 387–91). Bojana Kunst is more interested in the conditions of artistic labour, looking for models of resisting frenzied rhythms of artistic production in the radical laziness of Mladen Stillinović (Kunst 2015). Already in the early 1990s he pictured himself slacking on the coach, giving this self-portrait an ironic title 'artist at work', a satiric jibe aimed at the productivity of Western artists, who even in the beginning of the 1990s, at the early stages of global artistic circulation, busied themselves with countless projects, exhibitions and sales. Stillinović, in response, praised artistic laziness as a conceptual strategy of refusal. Following a similar route Maurizio Lazzarato analyses Duchamp as a proponent of radical laziness, who withdrew not only from art, but from all forms of social production, undermining systemic fixations of personal, professional and gender identity:

> Marcel Duchamp remarks somewhere that while 'John Cage boasts of having introduced silence into music, I'm proud of having celebrated laziness in art.' Duchamp's 'great laziness' shook the art world more radically and durably than the profusion of activity of a Picasso with his 50,000 works. Duchamp maintained an obstinate refusal of both artistic and wage-earning work, refusing to submit to the functions, roles, and norms of capitalist society. He did more than challenge the definitions of art and the artist (Lazzarato 2014: 5).

Even if this sounds like a slightly romanticised and bombastic account of the life of bourgeois privilege that Duchamp never really abandoned, Lazzarato's essay is an engaging analysis of the central figure of contemporary art, as in his view, in order to fully realise himself, Duchamp had to refuse art as a career.

Gerald Raunig, on the other hand, focuses not on individual artistic gestures but rather on collective forms that emerge in response to modes of temporality embedded in the contemporary industries of creativity. He asks:

> What does interrupting the time regimes mean, when exactly the same time regimes are based on governing through interruption, through (...) dispersing temporality? (...) What can strike mean for the creative workers and industrialists whose punch-clocks know no on and off but only countless versions of on? (Raunig 2013: 142).

All of them agree that contemporary forms of art strike need to account for the engagement of producers in their own activities. Artists and curators are usually not very eager to abandon studios or galleries, and instead enthusiastically engage in projects, despite being disenfranchised by the systemic shortcomings of their flow (→ A is for Artyzol).

However, it is instructive to look at the legacy of art strikes not only as a positive model of action, but also to acknowledge the structural problems that their organisers encountered as a precaution against over-romanticising this form of action. One of the most interesting of such 'failed' initiatives was a call for an international art strike issued by Yugoslavian artist Goran Djordjević. In 1979,

Djordjević sent a circular to hundreds of artists worldwide urging them to boycott the international art system. Eventually, he received over forty responses, some from prominent artists of the period, but the majority of them were negative and his proposition was never collectively enacted (Wade and Gillick 2002: 23). This is in contrast to the contemporary forms of → productive withdrawal, which always engage multitudes.

Talking from my own experience as an independent curator and researcher engaged in unionising freelancers, I am pretty certain that many critical artists and curators would wholeheartedly agree with the polite yet negative response of Lucy Lippard. To the invitation from Djordjević, she answered: 'rather than strike I spend all my energy on striking back at the art system by working around and outside of it and against it and letting it pay for my attempts to subvert it' (Wade and Gillick 2002: 23). Multitudes of practitioners expend all their energy in striking back at the → apparatus that is, paradoxically, tuned to → co-opt such rebellious impulses. Moreover, due to the competitive nature of artistic circulation and resulting atomisation of the projectariat, an organiser of any art strike has to cope with the influx of potential strike breakers, considering that the picket lines, due to the porous and distributed nature of apparatuses at play, are very easily crossed. In this context, it is interesting to quote another counterargument to Djordjević's initiative, formulated by Hans Haacke:

> Museums and commercial galleries will go on functioning very well without the cooperation of the socially concerned artist, and these of course would be the only ones to possibly join such a strike. Rather than withholding socially critical works from the art-system every trick in the book should be employed to inject such works into the mainstream art world, particularly since they are normally not well received there (Wade and Gillick 2002: 23).

Even though Haacke expressed his concerns in the context of the contemporary art circuit of the 1970s, his remarks remain even more valid in the competitive environment of the global artistic circulation of the early 2020s. However, Haacke's claim that the very presence of critical art works challenges the mainstream art world seems to be rather naive or hollow considering the all-encompassing, and yet so hard-to-challenge, nature of → apparatuses at play. For this reason, as Angela Dimitrakaki argues, a strike can never be understood as an individual undertaking, but rather has to be seen as a collective endeavour. Especially in the context of the feminist struggles for recognition one has to remember that:

> As a political stance, refusal can only be practiced collectively and with a loud bang. If not, it becomes a *Drop Out Piece* (begun c. 1970) by an individual artist – Lee Lozano – more likely to be recuperated and neutralized as an 'original artistic vision' by the institution rather than having an impact on the latter's function; or it dilutes into disparate micro-events of women's withdrawal from the art economy without leaving any trace, affirming the myth of female weakness in the harsh conditions of the 'jungle' outside the home (Dimitrakaki 2018).

This remark is valid not only in the context of feminist strategies, but is also applicable more generally to the → struggles of radical projectarians. There are throngs of → networkers who are eager to turn even the most radical ideas into devices of self-promotion – and institutions happy to serve as outlets of → co-optation. Furthermore, the individual refusals lead simply to individual → exclusion. Such actions must unfold on a collective level, galvanising multitudes of critical practitioners to boycott, occupy and go on strikes, as analysed in the entry on → productive withdrawals.

A   is for art workers

The very concept of an art worker used to be paradoxical, before it became a common sense after a decade of advocacy by unions, collectives and individual researchers who managed to popularise the idea that artistic activities should be remunerated, just as other types of work are. But for people not so familiar with the nuances of this debate, the notion of an art worker still might seem like a contradiction in terms. Either someone is a worker or an artist: someone either fulfils his calling or toils in a factory or a logistic centre. Bohemians and artists, according to romantic mythos – with strong Christian underpinnings – are like 'the fowls of the air: for they sow not, neither do they reap, nor gather into barns' (Matthew 6:26). As a matter of fact, they are not fed by a heavenly father, but rather by inheritance, relatives, side jobs, academic positions or – much more rarely – by commissions or the art market. More often than not they are expected to sustain themselves on the fumes of → Artyzol. The point of using the notion of the art worker is to debunk these assumptions, advocating for social security and wages for the people working in these artistic and academic sectors and to consider them as a subspecies of a larger group of precarious workers (→ P is for poor). Thus, the concept of the art worker is used as a tool for mobilisation and advocacy by artistic trade unions and collectives like the Citizens Forum for Contemporary Art and the Worker's Initiative trade union in Poland, Working Artists in Greater Economy (W.A.G.E.) from the USA, and the Precarious Workers Brigade and Artists' Union from the UK. This notion informs action research on the systemic underpinnings of work in artistic sectors, and its accompanying woes, such as overwork, precarity and lack of social security. Using the notion of the art worker implies that the art world is a kind of social factory with its own specific division of labour, systems of distribution, mechanisms of exploitation and extraction of values, situated in a broader social, economic and political context.

According to Corina Apostol from Art Leaks, a platform unionising radical art workers in the region of South Eastern Europe, the history of using the term art worker harks back to Russian productivists and constructivists, who considered themselves as technicians designing the aesthetic dimension of new, revolutionary societies (Apostol 2015). Actually, very similar sentiments were expressed by Polish artists and writers, who in 1936 organised the Congress of Cultural Workers in Lviv, emphasising their solidarity with working men and women, and ethnic minorities, aligning themselves with the Popular Fronts against Fascism (→ A is for Anti-fascist Year). Also in the 1930s, in the USA the Artists' Union unionised artists as workers employed as part of the federal programmes of public art commissions organised by the Work Progress Administration. One of the best-known groups directly referring to this legacy is the Art Workers Coalition (AWC), which operated in New York in the 1960s and 1970s. AWC understood artists as workers subordinated to gallery owners, curators, museum directors, collectors, just as 'ordinary' workers are dominated by bosses or owners of the means of production. As Julia Bryan Wilson suggests, the AWC has not used the term art workers literally, but rather as a politically charged metaphor to signal their class affiliations with the proletariat, to highlight political radicalism and to direct discussion towards problems related to the economic underpinnings of artistic production (Bryan-Wilson 2010; 2011). Contemporary art activists use this notion in a very similar manner: to unionise people working in the sector of contemporary art.

This political call can be easily misapprehended as a factual analysis of the division of artistic labour, resulting in somewhat academic arguments which reinstate quite obvious observations that artists are not employed by capitalists in order to extract surplus value from their labour (Beech, Jordan and Hewitt 2011; Beech 2019). As a matter of fact, only very few artist activists would even try to argue that artists are wage labourers, as clearly they are not. Even less so that anyone would be eager to subjugate artists to the discipline of an assembly line or office hours. Pointing out that the art worker holds a rather privileged position, enjoyed by an elite minority of cultural producers in the global North-West and legitimised by the traditional belief in artistic exceptionalism, just as Dave Beech does, is definitely sensible (Beech 2019) and should be taken into account in discussing the complex class composition of the artistic projectariat. Beech says:

However, to demand wages from the state or publicly-funded institutions rather than capitalists directly, entails a different kind of
confrontation. If Marx envisioned the struggle between workers and
capitalists over the wage as a necessary but not sufficient element
of revolutionary struggle, this is not necessarily duplicated in the
confrontation with the state and non-profit art organisations. If the
artist's wage is not dependent on the artist being converted into a
productive or unproductive labourer, then the demand for a wage for
artists has to be explained differently. While the artist's wage appears
to affiliate the artist with the worker, it is more accurately understood,
I would argue, as an expression of entitlement and privilege – a
demand for a portion of the common wealth justified by the status
of art – rather than a cancellation of the division between the artist
and the working class. In this context, the argument that the artist
is a worker has acted as the perfect alibi for the amplification of
the real social division between the artist and the wage labourer
insofar as the artist aims to secure an increase in resources and social
esteem. This is why we need to ask whether the demand for income
for artists uses the social esteem of art to redistribute public funds
to artists (Beech 2019: 62).

Even though this argument is useful, it needs to be set in a wider context.
First of all, art does not occupy such an exceptional social status as it
used to. As described by George Yúdice, starting in the 1990s, people who
advocated for public subsidies for the arts typically had to prove their
other uses to justify public investments (Yúdice 2003), a process which
creates problems of its own (i.e. the instrumentalisation of art, see → C
is for curatorial mode of production / revolution). Furthermore, public
subsidies for the arts are miniscule when compared to health, education
or sport. The same goes for the culture of charity and crowdfunding.
Donations flow to many charitable causes, from adopting seals to herit-
age protection (and art typically does not score particularly highly in
crowdfunding campaigns). The same applies to the culture of volunteering.
People invest themselves fully in many other activities, like community
gardening, modding computer games, creating wikis or playing LARPs
(life action role playing games). There are differences between the realm
of contemporary art and the world of 'mundane' activities, no doubt
about it, but I would argue that they are not as stark as they used to

be for many reasons only partially touched upon in this book. Second, the arguments for artists' welfare, if any, are typically justified by the reference to general social welfare, like the need to protect people on zero hours or temporary contracts. Third, the struggles with institutions for paying artistic wages are typically embedded in wider discussions about the social function of artistic institutions – whether they serve as mere exhibitionary salons for the art market and rich collectors, or whether they assume social responsibility for cultural producers, with whom they operate, and whose work they utilise to secure institutional reproduction. Fourth, the unions and collectives of art workers typically engage in strategic alliances with the unions of other → precarious workers, and actively partake in other social → struggles, because the status of art is so low that otherwise nobody would even bother to give art(ists) any special treatment (as COVID-19 proved, art is considered a non-essential occupation by both governments and many of their constituents). In this sense, whilst respecting Beech's position, I would still argue for the transgressive and progressive potential of the notion of the art worker, as an index of a wider political project, and a symptom of the changing status of the art, rather than a futile attempt at preserving its romantic vision.

It is pretty obvious that neither curators working on projects, nor artists working on commissions or for the art market, nor art critics working on their texts are working in the same way as an employee works for the capitalist enterprise. However, paradoxically, in the current state of capitalist gig economy even 'regular' workers are forced to behave as if they were micro-entrepreneurs and are remunerated affectively or with reputational tokens (like the infamous five stars of Uber drivers), which is not as entirely different from the worlds of art as it might seem at first glance. This realisation is supported not only by everyday observations, but also backed up by empirical evidence, such as that provided by the artistic research project *The Complaining Body*, conducted in 2016 by the collective Manual Labour in London. Jenny Richards, one of its initiators, described their findings:

> While we are familiar with freelance roles and precarious contracts in the art field, our research with those working in salaried positions, including staff at a London borough council, shared the same challenging conditions faced by freelancers. It appears that many of the traits of precarious work – including the shift of responsibility onto

the individual so that you effectively become your own boss, flexible work hours, and 'hot desking' – become shared working conditions for all. The common denominator is the breaking down of spaces, both verbal and physical, for collegial relationships and collective workplace complaining. Every colleague is a competitor (...) and the ideology that bad working conditions are ones you should be able to cope with makes it impossible to discuss challenges at work (Jenny Richards in: Child, Reckitt and Richards 2017: 153).

In any case, the labour of people working in artistic sectors is only very rarely directly exploited to create a surplus value. It is rather → captured, siphoned or trawled (→ T is for trawling) by mechanisms geared towards the exploitation of distributed, social labour – the general, systemic consequences of which are analysed by unorthodox Marxists, such as Mikołaj Ratajczak, Krystian Szadkowski, Christian Marazzi, Michael Hardt and Antonio Negri (Hardt and Negri 2009; Marazzi 2010; Ratajczak 2014; Szadkowski 2015). The conundrum of labour outside of wage work can be also much better understood by using the tools of feminist theory. Scholars and activists such as Silvia Federici, Angela Dimitrakaki, Kathie Weeks and J.K. Gibson-Graham have analysed the systemic exploitation of the 'invisible' labour of women, whose practices of social care underpin the capitalist economy (Dimitrakaki 2013; Federici 2012; Gibson-Graham and Cameron 2003; Weeks 2011). Their unremunerated (and in Marxist terms, unproductive) labour sustains the capitalist system that as a result of this invisible labour is able to extract surplus value by the means of wage labour – just as discussed in the entry on → labour of love.

The paradoxical class affiliation, emphasised in the notion of the art worker, is also today used as rallying cry of solidarity amongst different sectors of the workforce. A good example of such usage of the term is a manifesto called 'Why Art Workers Must Demand the Impossible', written by Tai Shani, one of the co-winners of the Turner Prize in 2019. In support of the workers (handlers, facilitators, cleaners, service personnel) striking at the Tate in the early months of the pandemic, in protest at being considered as non-essential and thus redundant, she stated that:

The demands of the striking workers at Tate, Southbank and the National Theatre are straightforward: they are asking that their jobs be saved and that creative solutions be deployed, if necessary, to do so. They are asking for their survival to be prioritised, and for their work – so long essential to the basic functioning of the institution – to be recognised as such. Their demands are also much more than that: it is a demand to side with us, to side with the politics that you unthinkingly exploit. If not, you are not just saying yes to a financial model that will make 1000 of the lowest paid arts workers – which may disproportionately impact Black and minority ethnic staffers – redundant in the pandemic's brutal financial reality. You are also complicit in acquiescing to the agenda of the right: you are siding with a politics that also says YES to austerity, YES to privatisation, YES to the normalisation of racism, sexism, homophobia, nationalism, ableism, the refutation of trans rights, and all the other reprehensible 'values' that 'the right' stand for. How can the possible be demanded when what is deemed 'possible' is not even remotely adequate to address the catastrophic world we are creating? We should not be worrying about biting the hand that feeds us. It is our money. We should eat the hand, for it is a delight – much, much tastier than the boot (Shani 2020).

Such manifestos are not examples of mere virtue signalling, especially when they are backed by actual organisational engagement, unionising, expressing public support for striking workers (which takes courage in the art world that lives by the commandment: you shall not bite the hand that feeds you) or participating in picket lines. Within this context, the term 'art worker' should be understood as both a theoretical position and a call for action.

B is for...

B   is for belt-tightening

Growing up in the post-communist part of Europe, I remember the 1990s as a period of belt-tightening. Not only because as a young adult I was rather skinny, but primarily because belt-tightening was a key term of the neoliberal shock therapy applied to Poland and other countries of the region. As I learned much later, it was part and parcel of what Naomi Klein defined as the shock doctrine of neoliberalism (Klein 2007) that instrumentalises social and political shocks to readjust economies in accordance with the neoliberal credo. It was first tested in Chile after the military putsch of 1973, and later applied in USA after the oil crisis, in Eastern Europe after the fall of the Iron Curtain, in Ireland, UK, Greece and Spain in the aftermath of the financial crisis of 2008, and in countries of the global South all the time. The shock doctrines everywhere implicated cuts in public spending, the destruction of organised labour (trade unions, workers associations), a downward spiral of lowering wages, growing costs of living, towering debts and rising inequality. In the aftershock of the global pandemic, this very doctrine has been reapplied worldwide to impose what Klein calls 'coronavirus capitalism': a toxic combination of austerity imposed on workers, huge bailouts for capitalists and authoritarian decomposition of civil rights (Klein 2020).

In any case, belt-tightening has a profound effect on the life and work of the artistic projectariat. Under austerity policies, the public budgets of artistic institutions, programmes and projects suffer severe cuts that reduce the number of opportunities and resources available to artists, curators and other freelancers. On top of this, as a result of belt-tightening the standards of general social welfare are lowered, thus making it much harder for all the working people, including people working in the arts, to make ends meet. Rising rents push art workers out of larger cities where opportunities are more plentiful. It is much harder to patch your income with odd jobs to sustain your artistic undertakings when all of them are badly paid and you need to work long hours just to make a living. It is very hard to find a position in the arts or academia if all institutions lay off permanent staff and new employment is part-time or on zero hours only. If one does not have access to social security or the costs of medical aid are skyrocketing, even a minor accident might lead to personal trauma and permanent → exclusion from circulation, and a major upheaval, such as the one caused by coronavirus, might be literally lethal. When everybody is busy, juggling three or four jobs, it is extremely hard to self-organise (→ P is for patainstitutions). The spaces used by the projectariat are made artificially scarce by forced evictions and real estate speculation, generating money for those at the top of the economic ladder while impoverishing the multitudes at the bottom (the decline in the market for short-term rentals may yet turn out to be one of very few positive outcomes of the COVID-19 pandemic). For most projectarians, austerity implies fiercer competition for scarcer → opportunities, higher rates of → precarity, and exposure to social → control. On the other hand, for the privileged few who come from more affluent backgrounds (→ O is for one percent), the results of austerity are only beneficial. They are the ones who are able to handle long suspensions of activity and can work on projects for which they are not getting paid. Austerity for many means more disposable income for the few, that can be also spent on 'joy riding' in the circuits of contemporary art. Moreover, financial burdens undercut competition, as equally talented but less privileged projectarians need to spend time on matters of survival, instead of competing for more prestigious opportunities. All in all, austerity is one of the most effective forms of neoliberal governance (→ N is for neoliberalism).

The crisis imposed by austerity is so severe that politicised artists and activists, like the Madrid-based collective subtramas, started to use the word 'austericide' to denounce post-2008 austerity-induced social trauma (subtramas et al. 2018: 197). They use it to describe the situation in the Museum Reina Sofía in Madrid with which they worked – on a freelance basis – during the exhibition *Really Useful Knowledge* (2014–15). The ambition of subtramas was to negotiate between the activist knowledges of social movements generated in the anti-austerity struggles, and the institutional structures of the museum, which at this time was hit by budget cuts and attacked by conservative politicians and lobbies of Catholic fundamentalists. The paradox is that on the one hand, the austericide was a condition of the possibility to forge links of solidarity between the institution and extra-institutional projectarians. On the other hand, the resulting scarcity and precarity made it very hard to establish lasting links between them due to the chronic understaffing of the museum and overwork of engaged freelancers. This situation, as unfavourable as it is, might either end up in conflict and erosion of trust, or in establishing the 'ethics of coordination', as proposed by Sara Buraya Boned, Paula Moliner and Manuela Pedro Nicolau, coordinators working with the *Really Useful Knowledge*, based on the feminist ethics of mutualisation and care (Buraya, Moliner and Pedron 2018). Such political acts can find opportunities in the aftermath of economic shocks, when barriers between institutions and workers are at their lowest, to institute the common (→ <u>I is for instituting the commons</u>).

B   is for (no) borders

The early decades of the twenty-first century will pass into history not as an age of unrestrained mobility but rather as an era of restrictions, borders, walls and anti-migration policies. At the point when 'cheap' airlines were shipping throngs of jet-setting cultural producers to various mega-events here and there (→ F is for footprint), those less privileged were being shipped, stopped and deported. Walls were being erected everywhere – both physical, political and social – on the borders of Fortress Europe, in the social networks structured by hate speech, and in public spheres divided by right-wing propaganda, shamelessly spinning authoritarian nationalism in countries like Hungary, Poland, the USA and the UK.

It was not an anomaly, a temporary backlash, or a random glitch in the frictionless world. The borders, according to Sandro Mezzadra and Brett Neilson, are not reminiscences of the past era of national states, but rather basic instruments of globalisation, as the new forms of accumulation profit from the unhindered movement of capital and the more regulated movement of workers and bodies (Mezzadra and Neilson 2013).

The promises of unhindered mobility, on which – seemingly flat – networks thrive, are nothing but an ideological illusion in a world where most people are not able to enjoy even basic freedom of movement. Just as Katalin Erdődi from the Precarity Office Vienna stated in the midst of the so called 'refugee crisis' in Europe:

> I see EUropean migration politics not only as a regulatory system that determines who to include and who to exclude, who can become mobile and who must remain immobile (…), but also as a politics that translates our vision of EUropean society into pragmatic, legal, and bureaucratic measures. In this sense, I would like to connect the question of migration to that of citizenship, of rights and privileges determined by the nation-state we are members of (Erdődi 2016).

What is true on a general level of 'European' policies is even truer in the artistic circulation. → <u>Networkers</u> can circulate freely only due to their privileged position. They typically have 'good passports' issued by one of the countries of the global North-West. They are fast-tracked, rather than stopped, detained or deported, because of the colour of their skin. They can count on the support of their states of origin or the right to work in their countries of choice (or usually both). They have access to a well-functioning infrastructure, running water, electricity, roads, health care and education, can count on regular incomes and basic safety. In the world of glaring inequalities, these 'basic' rights cannot be taken for granted by anyone but a minority.

People who want to get to Fortress Europe, but are stopped, detained, searched and deported, are stripped of their right to move. Instead, they are moved or shipped, as if they were objects, in a stark reminder of the roots of modern logistics in the transatlantic slave trade:

> Modern logistics is founded with the first great movement of commodities, the ones that could speak. It was founded in the Atlantic slave trade, founded against the Atlantic slave. Breaking from the plundering accumulation of armies to the primitive accumulation of capital, modern logistics was marked, branded, seared with the transportation of the commodity labor that was not, and ever after would not be, no matter who was in that hold or containerized in that ship. From the motley crew who followed in the red wakes of these slave ships, to the prisoners shipped to the settler colonies, to the mass migrations of industrialisation in the Americas, to the indentured slaves from India, China, and Java, to the trucks and boats leading north across the Mediterranean or the Rio Grande, to one-way tickets from the Philippines to the Gulf States or Bangladesh to Singapore, logistics was always the transport of slavery, not 'free' labor (Harney and Moten 2013: 92).

And yet, as Harney and Moten propose, this logisticality has an unintended side effect, as it engenders new forms of sociality and solidarity of the shipped and dispossessed; as they say: 'the hold's terrible gift was to gather dispossessed feelings in common, to create a new feel in the undercommons' (Harney and Moten 2013: 97).

This kind of solidarity motivates activists and artists who vouch for the real freedom of movement by supporting refugees and asylum seekers, such as the already mentioned Precarity Office in Vienna, or the CAMP (Centre for Art on Migration Policies) in Copenhagen that was co-established in 2015 by the curatorial duo Kuratorisk Aktion to 'provide refugees, asylum seekers, and ethnic minority Danes in Denmark with a place of support, community, and purpose' (CAMP 2020). Instead of just enjoying individualised access to circulation, they demand freedom of movement for all, thus rewiring the basic tenets of the → curatorial mode of production. By embedding their actions in the → interdependent ethos of undercommons, they testify to a possibility of other, inclusive, truly cosmopolitan and actually trans-border forms of nomadism. As Rosi Braidotti points out, such nomadism could support a theoretical and political project of reimagining EUrope as a federation of nomadic nations, in which people will not be bound by citizenry, but will rather be free to exercise their human right to move freely (Braidotti 2015).

B

is for burn-outs (and other pathologies of responsibility)

It is no wonder that after running on the fumes of → Artyzol and → enthusiasm the project-driven engines stutter and projectarians start to suffer from burn-outs, which often develop into chronic depression. Both are to be expected in the artistic circulation, which blurs distinctions between passion and production putting, as Franco 'Bifo' Berardi quipped, people's very souls to work (Berardi 2009). Burn-out is a natural reaction to networked overproduction, when everyone is expected to spit out one project after another and dozens at the same time. Such rapid turnover might be fine at first. After a while it becomes a nuisance. In the long run, it is simply unbearable. Completing major projects is exhausting, but instead of taking a break, projectarians have to chase new → applications and catch up with other projects that they run simultaneously. To make a living, individual freelancers have to be always on the lookout for new → opportunities – and even more so during the crisis. When opportunities get scarcer, the time in between projects is filled in with hectic attempts to secure them, with energy wasted on → applications and other futile attempts. Institutions, NGOs and collectives capitulate to the same maddening rhythms of production, the only constant result of which is overwork. Not surprising, then, that projectarians are hollowed out, mindlessly floating on the surfaces of mobile screens or hooking on emails, with no spark of energy left, but still keeping up appearances of being always-on, enthusiastic and available (→ E is for enthusiasm), fearing for their own tenuous jobs or precious projects, afraid of competition, → precarity and → exclusion.

Many in this world of industrialised psyche suffer from depression, a widespread epidemic of which was diagnosed as endemic to 'capitalist realism' by the tragically deceased Mark Fisher. As he argued:

> Instead of treating it as incumbent on individuals to resolve their own psychological distress, instead, that is, of accepting the vast *privatization of stress* that has taken place over the last thirty years, we need to ask: how has it become acceptable that so many people,

and especially so many young people, are ill? The 'mental health plague' in capitalist societies would suggest that, instead of being the only social system that works, capitalism is inherently dysfunctional, and that the cost of it appearing to work is very high (Fisher 2009: 19).

Writing along the same lines, Berardi diagnoses depression as a contemporary 'pathology of responsibility' (Berardi 2009: 99). When analysing the psychological consequences of the networked modes of production in creative industries, Berardi diagnoses depression as a mental affliction typical for precarious professions, quoting Alain Ehrenberg who states that 'depression manifests itself as a pathology of responsibility, dominated by the feeling of inadequateness. The depressed individuals are not up to the task, they are tired of having to become themselves' (Berardi 2009: 99). In a similar vein, Angela McRobbie, when dissecting precarious conditions of labour in the British creative sectors, diagnoses depression as the professional illness of creative workers and other artistic professions – a real 'pathology of precariousness' (McRobbie 2011: 32). She talks about exhaustion, insecurity, the impossibility of establishing a family and other social ills intrinsic to the precarious condition. Berardi, on the other hand, focuses on the tension between the ideology of personal success and the competitive pressures of → neoliberalism, which structurally hampers the possibilities of fulfilling the same ambitions that it encourages. According to Berardi, this problem is fundamental, as

> the social norms do not acknowledge the possibility of failure (...) There is no competition without failure and defeat, but the social norm cannot acknowledge the norm of failure without questioning its own ideological fundaments, and even its own economic efficiency (Berardi 2009: 99).

In the artistic networks, where hundreds of projectarians compete for every position, project or other opportunities, there are only few winners, while many fail (→ W is for winner takes it all). As failing is presented as result of personal and not systemic deficiency, it is not surprising that so many independent artists, curators and writers are depressed. As analysed in other entries (→ O is for one percent), the chances of winning in this competitive race are not distributed equally. Eventually, people who win are often predestined to succeed by virtue of their birth. The unprivileged many end up feeling inadequate to the task at hand, blaming themselves for structural inequalities, a consequence of the ideology of merit that shamelessly naturalises inherited privilege.

Many of the tactics presented here, which aim at creating inter-dependent support structures to mutualise risks and facilitate the processes of social cooperation, follow with the political line proposed by Fisher, who poses that: 'the task of repoliticizing mental illness is an urgent one if the left wants to challenge capitalist realism' (Fisher 2009: 7). After his untimely death, his mantle was picked up by the British collective Plan C, who in their workshops on Acid Communism employ militant versions of consciousness-raising to create a field of shared experience and collective joy, unpicking the psychopathologies of individualised responsibility (Plan C 2018). In the early stages of COVID-19, the same collective formulated a clear set of demands, informed by the values of Acid Communism, including the strengthening of public health services, suspension of rents and universal basic income (Plan C 2020). To politicise psychological wellbeing means to target the structural causes of mental suffering. Berardi proposes to combine political action with therapeutic acts in order to deconstruct and reconstruct desires (for freedom, autonomy, etc.) on a collective basis, so that 'new investments of desire become possible, which will be autonomous from competition, acquisition, possession, and accumulation' (Berardi 2009: 140). For this reason, it is of the utmost importance to nourish systems of collective care and support. It is much less plausible to accept individual responsibility for systemic failures, when a group of fellow projectarians establish → patainstitutions, go on strike, share opportunities and conduct their projects interdependently. Such actions are driven by the shared instincts for self-preservation, as unrestrained competition is deadly for many, and beneficial only for privileged few.

C   is for...

C   is for capital (economic, social and symbolic)

When analysing the everyday economies of artistic → <u>circulation</u>, one needs to take into account their multifaceted nature. Independent curators, artists and other people who work on projects compete not only for a narrowly understood economic gain (i.e. money), but also for reputation (i.e. prestige and fame) and social connections (i.e. position in the network).

To analyse these complexities, I refer to a sociological notion of social and cultural capital inspired by the theory of Pierre Bourdieu, who adopts Marx's notion of capital – as objectified human labour – to analyse reputations and social connections that underpin social hierarchies. In capitalism, labour is harnessed in capitalist value form and ultimately transformed into capital, which enables its owner to claim a share of future social production. Bourdieu's sociological amendment to this notion sees him focusing not on economic capital, but rather using it as a model to understand the social reproduction, class distinctions and hierarchies structuring such social fields as art or scholarship and the strategies of actors operating within them (Bourdieu 1996).

Both social and symbolic forms of capital are objectified human labour that determine the success of strategies aimed at the future acquisition of a position, job, or reputation. Even though they are not directly expressed in monetary form, they are potentially convertible to financial gains. As Hans van Maanen suggests, social and symbolic capital operate on three different levels: first, on that of embodied knowledge and social skills; second, on that of field-specific reputations and social contacts; and third, on that of the institutionalised knowledge and social density to be found within the structured fields themselves (Maanen 2009: 55–60). It is precisely this latter aspect of objectified social labour – of all the accumulated past and present efforts of people operating in social fields – that is akin to the general intellect, a term used often by the post-Marxist theorists to explain modes of production based on knowledge and communication dominating within advanced capitalism.

On a structural level, artistic networks operate as generators of social and symbolic capital, expanding connections by means of projects which can, but do not have to, be subsequently turned for profit. They can be monetised when a market niche is found; for example, by tourist industries or owners of real estate who operate in cities such as Venice or Barcelona, capitalising on the atmosphere forged by past and present generations – as analysed by David Harvey in his excellent essay on the art of rent (Harvey 2006). But these forms of capital can be harnessed – by corporations, capitalists, states or municipalities – in their symbolic form without being converted into monetary equivalents in order to acquire prestige or enhance soft power.

The weakening of artistic autonomy does not mean that the fields in question are directly incorporated in the capitalist circuits of production, but rather that they are formatted to enhance the generation of such forms of capital. A key instance of this tendency is corporate sponsorship of art. For example, the Tate group in the UK established a partnership with British Petroleum where the gallery was granted sponsorship, and the company gained a fragrantly artistic cultural flavour – a deal that was criticised as a form of 'art washing' by activist and theorist Mel Evans (Evans 2015). This business arrangement was protested by an activist campaign Liberate Tate, which organised multiple high-profile art-activist actions between 2010 and 2016. In 2016 the sponsorship deal was ended by BP, whose stated reason was 'challenging business conditions' (Khomami 2016).

When such arrangements are made, general social labour, condensed within artistic circulation, is turned into reputational and social capital controlled by more powerful players who direct it for their own benefit, thus enhancing brands, attracting visitors and legitimising corporate agendas by providing them with the aura of benevolent patrons of the arts.

Another example is provided by the non-profit industrial sector – named as such by the activist group INCITE! from the USA (INCITE! Women of Color Against Violence 2009), who criticised the depoliticisation of social movements which came about as they became complacent recipients of grants provided by private benefactors (→ G is for grant art). Both non-governmental foundations and state agencies encourage the endless circulation through their project-related modes of cultural funding, which stimulate the continuous flow of cultural projects, thus causing the overproduction of artistic events with quantifiable outcomes while stupefying political and social engagement. As a result, social and political campaigns are expressed in a networked value form that is easily capitalised by the funders themselves and used in their own pursuit of legitimisation. For example, a government agency can rely on a set of quantifiable data (numbers of projects, participants, visitors, media coverage) to support reproduction of their own institutional structures (→ N is for numbers and measures).

On the most general level, the collective and frequently underpaid or even unpaid labour of the multitude of artists, who still sacrifice themselves for the sake of art, maintains the aura of art as something exceptional and worthy of sacrifice. Hans Abbing suggests that this aura is capitalised by the elites of the sector who cynically benefit from the sacrifices made by others (Abbing 2014). It is important to note that while the bottom of the artistic pyramid might be a quite diverse space, with a strong presence of women and people of colour, the top is predominantly male and mostly white (ten out of ten of the richest living artists are male, and seven out of ten are white, with the net worth of the richest artist estimated to be one billion dollars (Design Museum 2020)). Diedrich Diederichsen, and Mikołaj Ratajczak after him, propose to consider this generalised aura of art as anchoring the prices of particular artworks (Diederichsen 2008; Ratajczak 2014). This is still a matter of discussion though, as other theorists like Luc Boltanski and Olaf Velthuis reject the relationship between socially generated values and market prices, which can reach levels that compete with entire institutional budgets: *Untitled* by Jean-Michel Basquiat, for example, was sold for 110.5 million dollars at auction in 2017. To explain these staggering evaluations, they focus on the arbitrary decisions of the bigger market players who operate as if they were totally independent in their judgements (Boltanski 2014; Velthuis 2007). I think this latter argument holds, but only if one limits the analysis to the prices of individual artworks. If one considers the art market as a social universe, it is hardly conceivable – at least in its current state – that it could work as well as it does without the general aura of art as something precious and worthwhile. The values produced and maintained by throngs of art producers and lovers, being mostly symbolic in nature (captured in the notion of symbolic capital), play their role as anchors of a general, positive evaluation of art, thus enabling speculation on the prices of particular artworks.

Even though the → projectariat's endless → circulation through the bureaucratic structures in which they rotate is founded upon the intensification of multilateral exchanges, the access to opportunities depends on one's position in a reputational economy and social networks (→ C is for capital). Every cultural producer needs to be recognised and is ranked according to their own individual reputations. By ascribing ideas to themselves, and capturing effects of creative processes, individuals are able to secure future remuneration and professional progress. The process of attribution can be understood as an apparatus of extraction, as it constitutes and reproduces a structural inconsistency between demands for extended cooperation alongside individualised competition for access. Moreover, it is underpinned by symbolic violence enacted upon the unrecognised, and thus exploited, cultural producers by celebrated winners of this networked competition.

This mechanism is comparable to the extraction of value specific to financial capitalism, in that it does not preclude any kind of contractual arrangements between exploited and exploiting. This specific feature of financial capitalism is analysed by Christian Marazzi, Antonio Negri, Michael Hardt and other post-Marxist theoreticians. Marazzi discusses the violence of financial capitalism that operates through apparatuses of extraction, aimed at capturing surplus values by, as he argues:

> (...) the compression of the direct and indirect wage (retirement, social security cushions, earnings from individual and collective savings), on the reduction of socially necessary labor with flexible network company systems (precarization, intermittent employment), and on the creation of vaster pool of free labor (the 'free labor' in the sphere of consumption, circulation, and reproduction, with a more intensified cognitive labor). The quantity of surplus-value, i.e., of unpaid labor, is at the root of the increase in the profits not reinvested in the production sphere, profits whose increase does not,

a consequence, generate the growth of stable employment, let alone wage (Marazzi 2010: 52).

A similar argument was spearheaded by Negri and Hardt, who analysed how abstract finance captures the common – that is understood as both natural resources and social goods that belong to all of us together (cultural idioms and habits, urban space, practices of care) (Hardt and Negri 2009). They argue that the accumulation typical to financial capitalism does not necessitate any direct investment in processes of production, and instead it captures its results by the means of debt-fuelled consumption, extraction, rent and intellectual property. By copyrighting cultural idioms, an owner of intellectual property is able to extract rents from consumers and users, who often contribute to the development of a given platform in the first place, as in the case of Facebook or Google.

The same principle can be applied when we think about artistic circulation and the means of privatising social and symbolic → capital. Mikołaj Ratajczak (Ratajczak 2014; 2015) argues that the prices of artworks are underpinned by the surplus value created not only in the artistic studio, but rather through the totality of creative processes and social interactions that unfold in the field of art. Janek Sowa, one of the members of the → Free/Slow University of Warsaw, uses post-Marxist theory to unpick the pursuits of celebrity artists who build their own → capital by presenting ideas as if they were their own, while in fact they are always collectively created (Sowa 2014).

As I have argued in my own analysis of the 'cruel economy of authorship', these privatisations are underpinned by the social conventions of authorial attribution, where an idea, a project or even elusive idioms (such as 'social turn' or 'relational aesthetics') can somehow become attributed to a given artist, curator or writer (Szreder 2013). Nobody even needs to copyright anything: it is enough that an idea becomes attached to an individual by the reputational economies specific to artistic circulation. What matters most is the fundamental act of individual appropriation, in effect of authorial attribution. As Luc Boltanski argues, the act of attribution is a key element in the process of transforming mere objects into works of art which are perceived as illuminated by authorial intention and read in the context of artistic oeuvres and tra-jectories (Boltanski 2014). In contrast to post-Marxist theoreticians, Boltanski does not identify collective processes as generators of value.

He is interested in the social transmutation of objects to oeuvres, to which attribution is indispensable, entrenched in worldviews, habits and values specific to the worlds of art, rather than in legal formulas.

A critical reframing of authorial attribution as a mechanism of capture is vital for the analysis of artistic circulation, where the creative process unfolds in expanded networks of projects and outlets rather than in the relative seclusion of artistic studios. I do not suggest that artistic creativity used to be less socialised in the studio-based system, as artists were always connected with their peers, groups, movements, dealers, collectors, critics and audiences. But it was socialised differently, ideologically obfuscated by what Pierre Bourdieu called an 'illusio' of the autonomous field of art, a central tenet of which was a romantic notion of individual genius and his autonomy (Bourdieu 1996). In artistic circulation the arbitrary and potentially exploitative character of authorial attribution is revealed due to the interconnected character of networked creativity. The critique of the political economy of authorship was spearheaded by Stephen Wright, who not only denounced authorship as one of the conceptual edifices on which the modernist idea of art rested, but also proposed to surmount it with a new political subjectivity of collective usership that displaces individual authors (Wright 2013). Similarly, projectarians – instead of competing for authorship of ideas or projects – should embrace their own interconnectedness and engage in the processes of cooperative creativity for the benefit of everyone involved (→ I is for interdependence).

C   is for circulation

Circulation is not a thing. Neither is it a place. It moves, as fast as it can. When its current is ruptured, like during the COVID-19 crisis, everybody expects the circulation to abate. But it does not, as the world of projects and events just shifts its form, and moves online, with a flurry of activity seeping from the screens of mobile devices – even if they are now used at home. Even more importantly, the crisis only strengthens the hierarchies that underpin the – apparently flat – world of these fluid flows, which overshadow its own murky foundations, set on the rigid inequalities of class, gender, citizenry and race. The global circulation is an ocean of opportunities for the rich – and perilous waters for the less affluent, who are greeted by visa checkpoints, or even gunboats, and not red carpets. Circulation might seem chaotic as it is in continuous transformation, expanding through the proliferation of connections (→ E for Expansion), its networked apparatuses spinning without respite. But this relentless movement only serves to mask some pretty solid structures of privilege.

To the casual observer, this circulation might seem like a perpetual social machine, a flow that moves due to its own innate dynamic. In this sense, artistic circulation is a mirror image of the global circulation of finances, which envisages itself as removed from the mundane world of goods and labour. In reality, however, this fantasy is underpinned by the realm of invisible and often unrewarded human labour (→ L is for labour of love and → P is for pollination) and is pumped up by the extraction of natural and social resources. This ideology of the ungrounded, self-perpetuating mobility of the creative class is exposed at moments of structural crisis, such as global pandemics, economic or ecological collapses, as they unearth the interdependence of the seemingly independent producers and their reliance on easily accessible infrastructures.

Over the last three decades, the global network of contemporary art has grown exponentially in terms of its geographic scope, its social volume and density of relations. As Hans Belting has argued, the late twentieth and early twenty-first century witnessed an emergence of the truly globalised art world, or rather an artistic universe composed from many differing, and yet interconnected, regional and national art worlds (Belting, Buddensieg and Weibel 2013). This global circulation is an interconnected mesh generated by millions of people who circulate within it, composed of the thousands of art institutions and art schools, hundreds of biennales, myriads of foundations, associations, collectives and galleries, dozens of art fairs, art-dedicated banking branches, art consultancies, specialised agencies and public departments for art, all around the globe.

This is a large and vibrant network, which has evolved out of the modern institution of art, which itself was – as criticised by the German critic Peter Bürger – a contained exception of bourgeois society, the exceptionalism of which the aesthetic and political avant-gardes wanted to overcome (Bürger 1984). The circulation traverses these traditional boundaries, linking the field of art with other sectors, twisting claims for artistic autonomy by combining the institutions and concepts inherent to autonomous art with other elements, creating new networked → assemblages. This process of hybridisation transforms the notion of artistic autonomy as it was originally developed in nineteenth-century Europe. According to Pierre Bourdieu, the autonomous field of artistic production emerged initially as a social space where art could be practised for art's sake, relatively sheltered from external influences and value judgements. In this sense, the autonomous field of art was a laboratory of bohemian living directed by the ideals of art, poetry, intensity, creativity and love, in contrast to the dull routines of the bourgeoisie (Bourdieu 1996). This field had at least partial autonomy, driven by its own anti-economy, in which money was despised, art celebrated and artists revered. Obviously, it had its economic underpinnings and dependencies on the field of power, but this was a shameful secret that art discourse openly rejected.

With the recent expansion of artistic circulation, the autonomy of this field has weakened, while it has been partially incorporated into the markets, policies and mechanisms of social reproduction specific to global capitalist society (Graw 2009; Kozłowski et al. 2014; Lind and Minichbauer 2005; Malik 2013; Phillips and Malik 2012; Sholette 2017; Stallabrass 2006). Yet, the art universe is still, relatively speaking, less incorporated into cycles of accumulation than other creative industries, to say nothing about traditional branches of industry. For example, global museums – which are large employers – are usually listed as non-profit enterprises, and this non-profitability remains an integral part of their corporate policies, business models and their expansion as globally recognised brands. Another example is bohemian ideology, which is cherished on the art market as a sales point, while motivating thousands of students to become indebted in order to study fine arts – supporting what Greg Sholette calls the 'bare art world' (Sholette 2017: 54).

On the other hand, artistic circulation shares similar traits to other social fields in cognitive capitalism, on which capital does not directly accumulate by the means of organising production and the direct employment of labour power (Vercellone 2007), but on which values are indirectly → captured in service of accumulation, such as in higher education (Szadkowski 2015). The best and most frequently discussed example of such capture is the process of gentrification, which David Harvey analyses in his essay on the 'art of rent' (Harvey 2006) and Sharon Zukin labels an 'artistic mode of production' (Zukin 1989: 176–92), in the framework of which artists contribute indirectly to the real estate value which rentiers and capitalists then proceed to siphon off, leaving artists with naught (→ C is for capture).

In terms of organising work, highly individualistic models of studio artists are mixed and matched with more recently introduced trajectories of freelancers and the self-employed (independent curators, artists working beyond the studio, art writers, intermittent art teachers), the institutionalised employment of technicians, accountants or curators, academic positions in higher education, a plethora of temporary jobs in NGOs and projects, all underpinned by the underpaid or unpaid labour of assistants and volunteers. Despite this diversity, flexible and project-related systems of organisation are dominant in this sector, where even larger institutions organise their content-related operations (educational programmes, exhibitions, etc.) as projects, activating both their employers, freelancers and volunteers to maximise efficiency. And it is precisely this over-reliance on precarious labour that put so many freelancers at risk during the coronavirus pandemic when, as a result of lockdown, all their projects, jobs and events were suspended and so many projectarians lost their sources of income overnight.

The systems of value adopted in artistic circulation reflect the fundamental paradox of this network, which is caught between nostalgia for artistic autonomy and its incorporation into the social and economic systems of global capitalism. People of art are still partially invested in the traditional bohemian beliefs in the value of art, but rearticulate them as demands for personal freedom, creativity and self-directedness that are specific to the new spirit of capitalism as mapped by Free/Slow University of Warsaw in its research on the Polish field of visual art (Kozłowski, Sowa and Szreder 2015). The typical exceptionalism of art, namely the belief in its special status, which legitimises personal sacrifices and which Hans Abbing criticises as one of the reasons for artists' poverty (Abbing 2014), is reformulated as a more down-to-earth assessment of networked reality wherein it is not only artistic talent that matters, but also social skills, reputations and networked → visibility. Cultural producers only seldom subscribe to a romantic ethos, and so they are not as enticed to sacrifice themselves for the sake of art as their bohemian forerunners used to be. Instead, they test their chances for establishing a professional trajectory that would enable them to do both – to make art and make a living. In this way, the topsy-turvy economy of art is recalibrated by people working in circulation, who consider their present sacrifices as investments – in prestige, connections, skills – the conscious aim of which is to generate portfolio of social and symbolic → capital used to enhance their professional prospects. However, the COVID-19 disruption revealed that most of those investments were based on false hopes: in times of crisis, their independence reveals itself as a self-deception, obfuscating the fundamental → precariousness of the projectariat.

C   is for control

The project is not a prison, a hospital, nor a school. It is not a disciplinary device, but rather the → apparatus of control that operates by employing more subtle means. Freelancers are not forced to deal with a particular topic, to apply for a grant, assemble with any particular team of people, work during specific hours or follow strict rules. In artistic circulation, people like to imagine themselves as free floating individuals, who work without supervisors, sergeants, teachers or bosses. And yet, everybody chases one project after another and is chronically overworked. They do so because they are subjected to distributed, networked and internalised forms of social control, which affect people's behaviour without the need for direct supervision. It is power without a centre, flowing through the capillary routes of → applications and fashionable → turns. A must-be event is literally an event that everybody who wants to be anybody in the artistic networks must attend, just as a must-have gadget is a badge of honour for any self-respecting fashionista.

After all, projectarians are very efficient at controlling themselves and each other, covering the costs of manufacturing their own consent. The distributed character of networked control is accurately explained by Gilles Deleuze in his seminal essay 'Postscript on Societies of Control' (Deleuze 1992), where he argues that in contrast to disciplinary societies – which enclose time, space and bodies in the limited framework of factories, hospitals or prisons – contemporary 'societies of control' create 'ultrarapid forms of free-floating control that replace the old disciplines operating in the time frame of a closed system' (Deleuze 1992: 3). Even though networks traverse institutional boundaries, freeing people from confinement in institutionalised frameworks, societies of control replace those frameworks and implement diffused, ultrarapid and free-floating systems which penetrate every aspect of life. In Deleuze's own words:

> (...) the different control mechanisms are inseparable variations, forming a system of variable geometry the language of which is

numerical (which doesn't necessarily mean binary). Enclosures are molds, distinct castings, but controls are a modulation, like a self-deforming cast that will continuously change from one moment to the other, or like a sieve whose mesh will transmute from point to point (Deleuze 1992).

In the spaces of enclosure that were characteristic of industrial societies, time was regulated by a rhythm of assembly lines: monotonous, with clear intervals. The societies of control, on the other hand, are subject to constant change, and time is both coagulated and ruptured in the uneven flow of simultaneous projects and processes. The seemingly chaotic arrangement of time and space does not mean, however, that a freelancer is not being managed, but that the governance is often inter-nalised, penetrating social networks by a mesh of milestones, deadlines, applications, reports, more often than not engaging the projectarian's own desires and enthusiasm.

These forms of controlling the self and each other, which are the daily bread of the artistic projectariat, were at first perfected by the new management, and analysed by Boltanski and Chiappelo in the *New Spirit of Capitalism* (2005). They emphasise the central paradox of the new network-based forms of management, explaining that managers operating in the unstable environment of the just-on-time modes of production specific to post-Fordism had to control the uncontrolla-ble. Their ambition was to manage 'self-organized teams working in a network that is not unified in time or space' (Boltanski and Chiapello 2005: 80). New management responded to this challenge by letting 'people control themselves, which involves transferring constraints from external organizational mechanisms to people's internal dispositions' (Boltanski and Chiapello 2005: 80). In addition, networked enterprises replaced the traditional, hierarchical discipline with market-related control. According to Boltanski and Chiapello, 'creating competition has replaced control of work by the directors of these units, who in return can rely on customer demand to exercise control that seems to issue no longer from them, but from the market' (Boltanski and Chiapello 2005: 82).

Even though the networks of contemporary art and academia differ significantly from the networked enterprises analysed by Boltanski and Chiapello, both are permeated by very similar systems of distributed governance. The early stages of this realignment were analysed by Brian Holmes in his essay on 'Flexible Personality':

> The computer and its attendant devices are at once industrial and cultural tools, embodying a compromise between control and creativity that has temporarily resolved the cultural crisis unleashed by artistic critique. Freedom of movement, which can be idealized in the figures of nomadism and roving desire, is one of the central features of this compromise. The laptop computer frees the skilled intellectual worker or the nomadic manager for forms of mobility both physical and fantasmatic, while at the same time serving as a portable instrument of control over the casualized laborer and the fragmented production process; it successfully miniaturizes one's access to the remaining bureaucratic functions, while also opening a private channel into the realms of virtual or "fictitious" capital, the financial markets where surplus value is produced as if by magic, despite the accumulating signs of environmental decay (Holmes 2002).

Currently, this state of affairs is totally normalised, and the mobile technologies of access and control so normalised that we can hardly imagine life without them – and they became even more so in the peak digitisation of COVID-19. And as the hardware of control became popularised, so were social technologies of project-related control. External management is replaced by the pressure of peer groups, overwritten by the simulation of market competition by the competitive systems of distributing opportunities and prestige (like peer-reviewed publishing). In artistic circulation, the system of governance employs projectarians' own enthusiasm, which is amplified by a general informality of relations. When freelancers work on their projects with teams of friends, they will hardly refuse to take on yet another task to be completed over a weekend. If they do not write yet another application or go to yet another event, conference, biennale, they are afraid that they will simply not secure access to → opportunities. On the other hand, the lack of direct supervision is still a privilege in the world where most of humanity is subdued by the discipline of work and sometimes literally enslaved. At the very least, your own internal boss will not shout 'you are fired!' or crack a whip. Instead, the response to the self-supervision is → burn-out, anxiety and other psychopathologies of responsibility. On the brighter side, it should be easier to subvert internal control than to overcome brutal management and armed police, though history proves that even the latter was possible. Just as proletarians had nothing to lose but their chains, the projectarians have nothing to miss but their → deadlines.

C

Co-opetition, or cooperative competition, is a managerial neologism invented to denote the situation when enterprises need to cooperate in order to create a pool of resources, but also compete to acquire the best share of them (Brandenburger and Nalebuff 1997). In co-opetition, the incentive for getting involved in cooperative processes derives from the potential rewards for individuals or enterprises. This term is well suited to describe the paradoxes of artistic circulation, as the ability to link seemingly contradictory strategies of cooperation and competition constitutes the backbone of any successful career in a world infused with the new spirit of capitalism.

The general rule of thumb of artistic circulation is that every project is a result of collective cooperation, but atomised projectarians compete for limited → opportunities. The cooperative teams dissolve, and only competitive individuals circulate. Even though concepts are created collectively, eventually they have to be attributed to individuals (→ C is for capture), to build their competitive advantage. This conundrum of cooperative competition resembles the situation in sectors of information technology (IT). Tiziana Terranova refers to enterprises specialising in advanced programming who engage in replenishing intellectual commons to underwrite their commercial operations (Terranova 2000). They participate in open coding platforms to secure access to common pools of knowledge. Their profits are made through providing highly sophisticated programming services. They lower their research and development expenditures by pooling knowledge with the open source programming community. Moreover, through working for the common benefit, those enterprises establish their reputations, which later attract commercial clients. Thus, individuals flourish because they secure access to the → common, to which they contribute by their own activities.

Such co-opetitive strategies differ from the business models based on intellectual property. The most commonly recognised form of profiteering in cultural industries is based on the aggressive copyrighting and safeguarding of intellectual property through rigid licensing. This practice is founded on a fundamental contradiction. The innovation and creation of symbolic content derives from an unhampered flow of ideas. But if they are to generate profit, the ideas have to become, by definition, scarcities, and are transformed into commodities through copyright. However, in a world where every symbol has an owner, the creation of new content simply becomes too expensive. For this reason, intellectual property owners have to exploit the 'tragedy of the commons' for their own advantage. They need to appropriate and exploit the non-copyrighted reservoirs of symbolic imagination that can be sourced at small cost.

Artistic circulation is more nuanced than this, but still the competitive strategies prevail over cooperative undercurrents. The hegemonic ideology of neoliberalism naturalises the unequal distribution of reputations and social connections by presenting this inequality as a justified outcome of individual merit rather than as a consequence of the competitive acquisition of the fruits of social cooperation. This competition is entrenched in a highly individualised and acquisitive psyche, reconstructed by Dawn Foster, a feminist social journalist:

> Every colleague is competition. As a result you're constantly on edge, aware that the tiniest slip of the tongue or careless mistake could mean a fall from grace and attendant loss of income. In such circumstances, it's almost impossible to organise collectively. No one employed so precariously dare step out of line first, knowing the inevitable consequences. Such workplaces rarely recognise unions and actively discourage workers from joining or trying to form unions (Foster 2016: 39–40).

In this way, the ideology of competitive individualism masks the importance of social cooperation. Despite this ideological mystification, even the → winner-takes-it-all economy depends on the maintenance of cooperative systems. Artistic circulation cannot constitute itself as a solely competitive environment because social cooperation facilitates the emergence and organisation of projects and mediates the flow of opportunities, connections and ideas. Co-opetition is an insufficient means of resolving this paradox, as the incentives for cooperative processes are miniscule in comparison to the rewards provided by egoistic pursuits. This not only results in growing inequalities, but also undermines the very basis of circulation. As Boltanski and Chiapello insist, the overtly competitive strategies result in the decay of networks, because they eradicate the trust necessary for the networks to function. As they write:

> It is likely that in a network world (...) opportunistic behaviour, even if it were adopted only by a few people to start off with, would tend to spread rapidly. We may define opportunism as consisting in not acknowledging debts contracted with other persons, either individual or collective (Boltanski and Chiapello 2005: 378).

In this sense, competitive → opportunism results in the erosion of the cooperative ties that enable the maintenance and functioning of the circulation. The structural response to this conundrum has to be inherently anti-neoliberal, and involve collective strategies aimed at securing the → common and sharing the fruits of social labour.

The capacity of the organisational grammar of projects and networks to incorporate and placate radical forces, even the ones openly hostile to capitalism, is its inherent trait (→ C is for curatorial mode of production). The new spirit of capitalism evolved in response to the radical spirit of countercultural dissent, in particular the workers' and students' upheavals of the 1960s and 1970s, which new management tried to placate, incorporate and, eventually, disarm. This capacity for co-optation is transmitted to other project-based social apparatuses, such as those regulating artistic circulation. Project-based co-optation amplifies the – often decried – ability of artistic institutions to incorporate their own critique by changing it into 'mere art', utilised to expand the boundaries of the artistic universe (Fraser 2006; Wright 2013). For example, a poster created to support social movements, such as Black Lives Matter, in the space of three months could be turned into an exhibitable object by a museum that – instead of printing and distributing it widely, making it accessible – wants to put it into a vitrine, thus changing an art-activist tool into a token of institutional appreciation (Liscia and Bishara 2020). The forms of network-related co-optation are equally insidious if not more pervasive. As Lane Relyea argued in his insightful analysis of the 'everyday art world' based on platforms, networks and projects:

> (…) the cultural left's continued parroting of a formerly radical battle cry about defending open over closed form, the temporal over the static, the flexible and transient over the stable, the communicational and performative over the representational, doesn't just ignore but indeed risks glamorizing the harsh realities of today's more networked status quo (Relyea 2017: 11).

The networked modes of production utilise even radical desires – of autonomy and self-realisation – to forge the ideological credo of both the creative industries and artistic circulation, which peddle promises of creativity, independence and freedom to attract young creatives, freelance artists and independent curators, whose influx reproduces and expands the very systems that are geared towards their exploitation.

Boltanski and Chiapello provide evidence on how new managerialism historically co-opted the 'artistic critique of capitalism' which specifically promotes such bohemian values as personal freedom, self-realisation and creativity (Boltanski and Chiapello 2005: 97). Their understanding of co-optation is often misread as direct subjugation. Actually, they argue that the critique of capitalism prompted its evolution towards new organisational mechanisms and value systems centred around the notions of projects and networks, that – while keeping intact the principle of accumulation – catered partially to the social demands of more fulfilling, flexible and creative workplaces (Boltanski and Chiapello 2005: 4–41). However, as their study is based on the analysis of new management literature, they downplay the agency of ground-up social movements, arguing for the rift between bohemian critique – somewhat more agreeable to capitalism in its individualism and thus easily co-opted – and the more egalitarian forms of critique spearheaded by trade unions that were eventually destroyed or seriously weakened.

By contrast, post-Marxists like Maurizio Lazzarato focus on social movements of immaterial labourers and precarious workers, identified as agents of anti-capitalist transformation that fight for a combination of creative freedom, self-fulfilment, equality and security (Lazzarato 2009; 2011). Discussing the example of Coordination des Intermittents et Précaires, a French activist group gathering precarious creative workers, Lazzarato pointed out that the demands for freedom and self-governance are complementary to and not opposed to egalitarian forms of critique (Lazzarato 2011: 43). Analogically, artistic trade unions and collectives of art-activists in Poland, the UK, Germany or the USA fight for both creative freedom and social welfare. What seems to be mutually exclusive in the context of new management, is reconciled in the practice of anti-capitalist activism. Furthermore, global ruptures such as the one caused by the COVID-19 crisis provide yet another case in point, as they reveal that sustainably autonomous and creative lives have to be grounded in equalitarian access to social welfare.

C

is for curatorial mode of production / revolution

Analysing the first wave of artist-induced gentrification in New York of the 1970s and 1980s, urban sociologist Sharon Zukin identified what she termed as the artistic mode of production. As a result of the activities of artists, who lived and worked in lofts and opened new bars and galleries, various previously derelict, post-industrial districts, such as SOHO, became fashionable zones of real estate development and speculation (Zukin 1989). By identifying the artistic mode of production, Zukin did not imply that all artists should be held to account for the actions of developers or financiers. In contrast, most artists were later evicted from the same districts they had involuntarily helped to gentrify. She rather highlighted the relationship between the seemingly harmless activities of artists and real estate speculation, which went on to have a negative impact on the urban environment, resulting as it did in gentrification and social cleansing.

What the artistic mode of production did to the urban environment, the curatorial mode of production does to the ecosystem of radical ideas and critical art. It moulds them into a networked form of short-term projects and transitory events, uprooted and generic formulas for equally formulaic catalogue activism. In the curatorial mode of production, everything moves so that nothing can change. Projects roll over, one after another, some of them with a leftist twist, following yet another fashionable turn in post-modern, post-colonial, post-Marxist, post-feminist, post-human discourse. Independent networkers, → entrepreneurs of the self in everything but name, privatise radical ideas as their own → capital. This situation is favourable for artistic institutions, who can create a semblance of criticality through entirely tokenistic action. Angela Dimitrakaki talks about this in the context of feminist art, where institutions include works by feminists in order to avoid pressures to feminise their own operations. As she writes: 'In many cases, the art institution is found to perform a dubious ideological trade-off: the exclusion or discrediting of feminist politics and struggles is compensated by the inclusion of women artists' work' (Dimitrakaki 2018). Similar mechanisms were identified and contested in the context of anti-racist social movements such as Black Lives Matter from 2020, when activists and art workers called out institutions that were eager to voice their support, but whose own boards, internal hierarchies, exhibition programmes and collections had been founded on white privilege that remains unchallenged on the structural level (Shaw and Carrigan 2020).

The curatorial mode of production is sustained by the charms of networked life, driven by promises of individual freedom and circulated agency. From this vantage point, an international art event represents a peak of productivity and an opportunity not to be missed. For people who continuously circulate, circulation is an end in itself. They are not wrong insofar as international artistic circulation secures global visibility, resources and audiences, and provides access to power otherwise unattainable to individuals with a middle-class upbringing. Partaking in artistic circulation offers a semblance of agency and encourages a political illusion that one can transform society by making one project after another. However, as Luc Boltanski and Eve Chiapello stress, the world constituted by networks and flows 'can win over forces hostile to capitalism by proposing a grammar that transcends it'. In this networked world 'anything can attain the status of a project, including ventures hostile to capitalism', creating a situation in which 'capitalism and anti-capitalist critique alike are masked' (Boltanski and Chiapello 2005: 111). A biennale can offer a platform for uttering critical slogans precisely because the organisational grammar of global circulation neutralises their meaning. Paraphrasing Walter Benjamin, one can say that these organisational → apparatuses can be fed with anything, because only circulation matters and not the content that is circulated through it. The pseudo-radical rhetoric of functionaries who operate these apparatuses is a sentimental expression of the self-contradictory consciousness of *bourgeoisie boheme*, a testimony to politics compromised by individual egoism and class privilege.

In this vein, sociologist Pascal Gielen criticises 'catalogue activists', curators whose politically correct views do not suffice, despite all their good intentions, to recompose apparatuses at play (Gielen 2010). By decrying catalogue activists, Gielen emphasises the lack of reflectivity characteristic of contemporary star curators, who curate projects thematically critical of global capitalism while organising those projects in a manner complicit with neoliberalism (Gielen 2010: 14). The interesting point in Gielen's analysis is not his denunciation of curatorial hypocrisy, but rather that he contextualises the divergence between (neoliberal) social form and the (declaratively progressive) content of curatorial activities in project-related modes of production. Gielen criticises 'catalogue activism' because 'independent' curators fail, or are unwilling, to critically address their own position as opportunistic project developers (Gielen 2010: 19).

The curatorial mode of production detaches the circulation of ideas and art from social and political movements, supporting uprooted trajectories of ultra-mobile celebrity curators and artists and all those who aspire to become just like them. According to John Roberts, in order to unmake this mode of production, curators should become 'out of sync' with the demands of artistic circulation, institutions and the art market alike, by activating artistic 'powers of negation' and 'infinite ideation'. He postulates that:

> curators need to become artists if the artist as producer is to retain its meaningfulness. Those curators who have no interests in being artists should step back and reclaim a subsidiary – in no less engaged – role: that of organizer, adviser, agitator, negotiator (Roberts 2010b: 57).

In discussing his proposals for curators as producers, Roberts refers to his concept of the 'power of negation', fundamental to his theories about the progressive character of the artistic avant-garde. As Roberts says in another text: 'the determining framework of art is of necessity that of negation' (Roberts 2010a: 87). He develops the genealogy of such artistic negation in relation to the tradition of the artistic avant-garde, especially in its anti-productivist iterations (Roberts 2009). By 'negation' Roberts means the negation of artistic tradition, of artistic skill, of the hierarchy of representation, but also more generally the negation of art's institutional frameworks and even of the realm of capitalistic production at large. Roberts' propositions for freelancers are motivated by his theoretical belief in the specific position of artists in the art world, determined by the artist's possession of 'sovereign access to powers of negation that leave him or her "out of sync" with the prevailing institutional, bureaucratic, and academic frameworks' (Roberts 2010b: 57). Roberts postulates that the critical powers of artists 'set out from a place very different from non-aesthetic reason; namely (...) the realm of negation, non-identity, and destabilization' (Roberts 2010b: 53).

Consequently, when Roberts urges curators to become more like artists, he suggests that they should become 'out of sync' and negate their own instrumental function in the → apparatuses that regulate artistic circulation: in other words, they should destabilise the curatorial mode of production.

What interests me here are the practical implications of his programme for → interdependent curating. On the one hand, Roberts underlines that it is not his intention to romanticise 'the non-reconcilable pathos of art, as opposed to the dark machinations of art's mediators' (Roberts 2010b: 57) and acknowledges that 'artists are no less bound to institutions than art's curators' (Roberts 2010b: 57). On the other, he downplays the importance of the division of artistic labour. When Roberts suggests that curators who are not interested in being 'out of sync' should simply 'reclaim a subsidiary role', he unconsciously affirms the internal hierarchies of art-related labour that devalues all forms of non-artistic and non-authorial labour.

Any power that artists have is not extra- or anti-institutional, but rather structurally embedded in the structures of the art world. To paraphrase Andrea Fraser, artists are embedded in the institution of art and should not be considered as romantic outsiders, unspoiled by the artistic business (Fraser 2006). Just as Howard Becker, Pierre Bourdieu and other sociologists of art assert (Becker 1984; Bourdieu 1996), artists are able to indulge in infinite ideation because they are partially sheltered from the administrative pressures or other organisational necessities by people occupying the 'subsidiary positions of organizers, advisers, negotiators'. In other words, the autonomy of artists derives from the → labour of love of multitudes of technicians, assistants, curators, etc., who administer, produce, distribute and organise artistic production.

To go even further, in the tradition of institutional critique, artists could be understood not as unbound spirits, but rather as role models that epitomise the values of the Western, bourgeois institution of art, thanks to which they thrive. To quote Rasheed Araeen, who scrutinised the track records of ultra-mobile cultural operators in early 2000s, documenting the development of a globalised art world:

As for the ruling classes of the Third World, most of them have capitulated to the power of global capitalism and what they now all want is to share some of its spoils – even when they know full well that this is causing unbearable misery for most people. The ambition of most artists, critics, historians and curators from the Third World is no different from the aspirations of these classes. Although many of these intellectuals are now part of the global art scene, performing as functionaries of the system in pursuit of their careers (in the West), it would be unfair to target only them with special criticism. With globalisation, and the collapse of the idea of the Third World offering an ideological opposition to (Western) imperialism, what remains is just hollow rhetoric of the Westernised middle classes whose objective is only to embarrass the liberal conscience of the big bosses in order to extract some more benefits from them for their own vulgarly selfish life. However, it is important to point out that self-interest and opportunism are not the prerogatives of Third Word intellectuals only, but are universally endemic as part of the intellectual life of the globalised world today (Araeen 2010: 63–64).

Just as Araeen deliberately inflated his rhetoric to debunk tendencies that he despised, I have used the term 'curatorial mode of production' to address the industrialisation of → opportunism in artistic circulation, even if risking theoretical oversimplification. There are multitudes of independent curators and artists who go against the flow, embedding their projects in → struggles for social justice. Just as the term 'artistic mode of production' is a theoretical tool tuned to support critical analysis of the economic effects of artistic practice, nevertheless of the politics of particular artists who partook in it, the term 'curatorial mode of production' ironically challenges the lofty rhetoric of curatorial celebrities, with the aim of contributing to the critical reflection on the politics of curating.

Just as Martha Rosler proposed to think about 'artistic modes of revolution', emphasising the radical turn in politics of artistic multitudes who occupied squares and parks worldwide in early 2010s (Rosler 2014), one can think about 'curatorial modes of revolution' that politicise the flows of curatorial and artistic projects by affiliating (in)directly with social and political → struggles, sustaining → patainstitutions, working for the → common and engaging in the political formations that aim at establishing democratic socialism. Only by creating lasting affiliations are we able to collectively amplify the political messages of projects at play. In other words, to validate claims for criticality so popular within artistic circulation, one has to rebuild its basic tenets. This must involve a change in institutional ecosystems, because institutions, events and NGOs will have to be decolonised and 'liberated', detached from their associations with the wealthy and powerful. Collectives such as MTL, Decolonise This Place, and Occupy Museums, have advocated for this change, mainly in the context of the New York art world (MTL Collective 2018). Their aims are described by an independent group of art workers, the People's Cultural Plan, in the following words:

> A series of actions spearheaded by Decolonize This Place (DTP) and taking place at the Whitney Museum of Art presents the opportunity to transform how we build and fund our cultural institutions. It suggests the need for a complete system change including a new focus on private money, to a system that justly taxes Wall Street and the wealthy, as well as asking cultural nonprofits to amend the way they create boards and accept charity (The People's Cultural Plan 2019).

To activate the curatorial mode of revolution projectarians have to get out of sync with the circulation in which they are bound to look for new idea(l)s as soon their projects expire, surmount structurally imposed fixations with the entrepreneurial self and develop → interdependent potency, in order to become – to quote yet again Rasheed Araeen and his manifesto of ecoaesthetics – a 'radical force for the twenty first century' (Araeen 2010).

These instances of social and political creativity reinvigorate ways of practising and thinking about art by revamping existing infrastructures and giving shape to new institutional assemblages. This echoes what Antonio Negri described in his collection of letters, *Art and Multitude*:

> To conclude, let us return to the 'republican' definition of the beautiful, which I oppose to its 'angelic' definition. By republican I mean the tradition which sees the collective as the basis of the free production of being. And *by* the 'beautiful' I understand an excedence, an innovation. A freedom which is liberated, a liberty which is ever-increasingly free, ever-increasingly potent. Whereas the angel is the symbol of a deficit, of a relationship which will never be resolved. An

unexpected illustration of the confusion of being, which is opposed to the construction of being and to its collective clarification. What a bad taste the angel has in his mouth. What impotence he expresses. At bottom, the angel remains the demonstration of a power which is disillusioned and malign (Negri 2011).

Currently, this angelic being of art, with its pretence of autonomy, circulates restlessly, chasing interchangeable → opportunities, losing even its capacity to memorise or to imagine beauty. This angelic spirit runs in circles, chasing its own angelic tail. The dominant biennale-fairs nexus – based on the financial subsumption of aura and an accelerated peddling of contents – erases artistic qualities of idioms thus circulated. As Neil Cummings once put it, markets mark the things which are circulated through them (Cummings 2014a). The curatorial mode of production depends on the fast circulation of networked commodities (the faster they move, the more valuable they become). When this form of circulation is ruptured as an effect of → art strikes, and → productive withdrawals, new → patainstitutions and → institutions of the common emerge to sustain not only artistic practices, but also artistic values. Hito Steyerl, looking for a refuge from endless circulation and related subsumption, envisions an alternative system of artistic currency, a current of social and artistic energies redirected from propelling exploitative circulation and directed towards the welfare of art workers, their cooperative networks and gift economies:

> (…) everyone involved also contributes in all sorts of other ways to art's circulation, thus making it stronger as currency. Even artists who live 'off their work' subsidize the market by way of enormous commissions in relation to other industries. But why should one sponsor VIP previews, bespoke museum extensions without any means to fill them, art-fair arms races, institutional franchises built under penal-colony conditions, and other baffling bubbles? This bloated, entitled, fully superfluous, embarrassing, and most of all politically toxic overhead is subsidized by means of free labor and life time, but also by paying attention to blingstraction and circulating its spinoffs, thus creating reach and legitimacy. Even the majority of artists who cannot afford to say no to any offer of income could save time not doing this. Refusing sponsorship of this sort might be the first step towards shaking the unsustainable and mortifying

dependency on speculative operations that indirectly increase authoritarian violence and division. Spend free time assisting colleagues, not working for free for bank foundations (Steyerl 2016).

By refusing to sponsor the 'free' flow of circulation, → art workers form an institutional habitat, where art regains its function as a collective practice of freedom and exercises its powers of negation, infinite ideation and existential playfulness.

C

is for cynicism and cliques

In the *Grammar of the Multitude*, Paolo Virno identifies cynicism, opportunism and fear as the triad of negative sentiments that plague contemporary, post-Fordist societies. According to him, cynics:

> from the outset (...) renounce any search for an inter-subjective foundation for their praxis, as well as any claim to a standard of judgement which shares the nature of a moral evaluation. The fall of the principle of *equivalency* (...) can be seen in the behavior of the cynic, in the impatient abandonment of the appeal for *equality*. Cynics reach the point where they entrust their self-affirmation precisely to the multiplication (and fluidification) of hierarchies and inequalities which the unexpected centrality of production knowledge seems to entail (Virno 2004: 86, italics by author).

A cynic experiences rules as social conventions, which has several implications as to how a cynic approaches 'social games' because, as Virno says: 'one is no longer immersed in a predefined "game," participating therein with true allegiance. Instead, one catches a glimpse of oneself in individual "games" which are destitute of all seriousness and obviousness, having become nothing more than a place for immediate *self affirmation*' (Virno 2004: 87). Such tendencies for self-affirmation run rampant in the networks of contemporary art and academia, as in these social systems ultra-mobile free agents compete for access, unbound by the 'principles of equivalency' and 'appeals for equality'. In case something goes wrong within one cluster or a project, an offender can simply migrate to another. The mobility can provide a relief from the stiff social norms of traditional societies, as non-conformists can move somewhere else, but on the other hand this situation is a hotbed of cynical self-affirmation.

However, cynicism should not be mistaken for the strategy of lone wolves. In fact, most cynics are extremely sociable, but a form of sociality most often adopted by cynics is a clique – a cluster of cynically minded individuals who network together to secure their own advancement or to defend already acquired privileges. In fact, the very word network, before it was adopted by the language of cybernetics, Internet and new management, used to denote criminal networks or networks of shadow operators. This tendency of cynical cliques to emerge in seemingly open networks is often misidentified by the resentment-driven conspiracy theories that condemn the global art world as a conspiracy of leftist-liberal clique. Often, like in the recent cases of Poland or Hungary, this resentment has an ostensible authoritarian thrust. In a typical feat of rightist doublespeak, the cliques of alt-righters fume against hypothetical leftist-liberal conspiracies, while attempting to monopolise access to resources and institutions and presenting their own power grab as if it was aimed at democratising access. The problem is that even though artistic circulation is populated by cynical cliques, cliques of right-wingers just want to extend and solidify their own reach in exactly the same way. It is a cynical self-affirmation at its finest. In contrast, the → interdependent response to the problem of cliques is to open networks by preventing cynical self-acquisitions, easing competition, facilitating social cooperation and distributing its outcomes equally.

D is for...

D   is for dark matter

The relationship between exploitation and invisibility is one of the definitive features of the global artistic circulation, as it reinforces the causal link between poverty and lack of recognition, which has traditionally haunted artistic careers. Just as capital shines with the stolen light of exploited labour, so the upper echelons of artistic circulation glimmer with social energies not of their own making. This is the fundamental proposition of Gregory Sholette, a New York based artist, activist and academic. In his book *Dark Matter: Art and Politics in the Age of Enterprise Culture*, Sholette uses the metaphor of dark matter, the physical phenomenon that pulls the universe together despite its own invisibility, to discuss the political economy of artistic visibility (Sholette 2011). According to him, artistic dark matter 'includes [...] all work made and circulated in the shadows of the formal art world, some of which might be said to emulate cultural dark matter by rejecting art world demands of visibility, and much of which has no choice but to be invisible' (Sholette 2011: 1). Dark matter is based on a 'structural invisibility of most professionally trained artists whose very under-development is essential to normal art. Without this obscure mass of "failed" artists the small cadre of successful artists would find it difficult, if not impossible, to sustain the global art world as it appears today' (Sholette 2011: 2). Furthermore, as Sholette points out, 'while astrophysicists are eager to know what dark matter is, the denizens of the art world largely ignore the unseen accretion of creativity they nevertheless remain dependent upon' (Sholette 2011: 1). In other words, Sholette not only reports inequality, but also traces the relations of exploitation between the official art world and dark matter. He seeks to demonstrate that the high status of the artistic mainstream is a result of the unremunerated and unrecognised efforts of dark matter. As he says: 'the art industry must ghettoize the majority of its qualified participants in order to generate artistic value' (Sholette 2011: 120).

To understand the forms of exploitation inherent to the artistic universe, Sholette applies the Marxist vocabulary, identifying artistic dark matter as a reserve army of artistic labour: i.e. all those people who are not currently employed but create a supply of cheap labour that enables the exploitation of everyone. The labour of artists is so cheap because there are always hundreds of artists competing for a given commission or a position within the marketplace. This way of thinking explains some of the structural causes of circulated poverty (→ P is for poor (artists)), as there are always many more → applicants than → opportunities that lower the price of networked labour.

However, Sholette's argument can be furthered by the reference to feminist economies, like that developed by a pair of feminist economist geographers writing as J.K. Gibson-Graham. They posit that the capitalist economy is underwritten by the realm of hidden, often feminine labour, non-monetised exchanges and informal modes of organisation (Gibson-Graham 2006). Just as this un-monetised and economically unaccountable realm of informal economic activity sustains the capitalist economy, artistic dark matter, located at the bottom of the art pyramid, sustains it. Artistic dark matter maintains the gravity of the art world by attending art colleges, buying supplies, spreading reputations, flocking to exhibitions, maintaining infrastructures and creating and communicating artistic idioms. These activities are not exploited by means of wage labour, but the values thus produced are → captured or → trawled as individualised capital by those who have enough power to claim the results of social cooperation as if they were of their own making.

D   is for deadline

The projectariat bends under the yoke of overlapping deadlines. Literally, a deadline is a line that should not be crossed, a death strip of time. And the deadlines refuse to die. To take a large-scale example, even though the coronavirus pandemic suspended some deadlines, they quickly started to proliferate again. In any case the forced suspension of circulation is definitely not as liberating as, let's say, the general abolishment of deadlines would have been under democratic socialism. Anyway, the everyday life of the projectariat is structured by looming deadlines. Technically speaking, a deadline is defined as a date of sending an application, delivering a text, preparing a concept for future projects – or a report from the already completed ones. Deadlines shred time into tiny packets, ground to dust by → applications and other → apparatuses. An endless rush of deadlines overshadows any long-term horizon of action. After all, the projects flow one after another, dissolving into an eerie stream of emails, places, people and events.

Because of deadlines, the projectariat can never rest. On a more optimistic note, projectarians do not succumb to the monotony of routinely performed chores: they are able to pursue many projects simultaneously. Each project creates its own spatiotemporal pocket: it starts with an application, ends with a report – and its passing is marked by deadlines. As every project lasts only for a moment, and an average projectarian has to perform several projects simultaneously, deadlines tend to accumulate. At the same time, people report on one project, plan the next one, write a text or apply for a scholarship, distributed between past, present and future, between here and elsewhere.

There are people who have mastered to perfection the art of managing deadlines. They simultaneously answer emails, talk on the phone, conduct strategic meetings and eat lunch. They combine ADHD with the focus of a Zen master. Such awareness accelerates under the pressure of looming deadlines. Running ahead, they leap into the future. Pearls of consciousness grow on the particles of projects, woven on the threads of their succession, flickering from one task to another. Decisions have to be taken; problems have to be solved. In this race against time, not only is the past blurred, but the very horizon of action dissolves. An influx of simultaneous deadlines engenders an excess of tactical efficiency. The adrenaline-pumped responsiveness hardwires a short attention span that precludes reflection and removes all capacity for strategic planning. After all, who has time to think about the next five years, make preparations for a major upheaval, or a pandemic? There are too many things to be finished by tomorrow.

D

is for demonstration of paintings

In March 2019, a group of → art workers in Warsaw joined the annual anti-fascist march carrying placards with copies of historical anti-war and anti-fascist posters and paintings, including the fragments of Guernica (in the grand tradition of → repurposing this painting for the sake of street performances and demonstrations) and anti-fascist collages of John Heartfield. This protest-exhibition was → interdependently self-curated on the basis of the Atlas of the → Anti-fascist Year, a database of historical and contemporary examples of anti-fascist art (The Anti-Fascist Year 2019). The 2019 demonstration of paintings was inspired by 'Demonstration of paintings', a 1934 artwork by communist artist Henryk Streng. The image depicts a group of painters carrying their paintings as if they were banners, expressing the artistic and political ambitions of the Popular Front against fascism. Streng was active in the circle of artists and writers who in 1936 organised the Congress of Cultural Workers in Lviv (→ A is for art workers). In March 2019, Streng's image became a blueprint for actual demonstration, fulfilling its previously unrealised potential. An ad-hoc artistic and curatorial bloc – who took the reproduction of 'Demonstration of paintings' to the actual demonstration of paintings – put conceptualist tautologies to better use, endowing an otherwise obscure painting with new energies. The demonstration was an iteration of expanding artistic methodologies (→ E is for expanded field), embedding artistic and curatorial → projects in the overarching → struggles against emergent authoritarianism (→ A is for Anti-fascist Year).

The action was organised by the Consortium for Postartistic Practices, a → patainstitutional alliance of art workers who seek to activate their competences beyond the narrow confines of the market-oriented art world, chronicled – amongst many others – by Sebastian Cichocki (Cichocki 2019). The CPP (whose acronym echoes the Communist Party of Poland, the memory of which is currently being erased by the right-wing urge to rewrite history) uses as a motto the passage from Jerzy Ludwiński's essay 'Art in the Postartistic Age', written in 1971: 'Perhaps, even today, we do not deal with art. We might have overlooked the moment when it transformed itself into something else, something which we cannot yet name. It is certain, however, that what we deal with offers greater possibilities' (Ludwiński 2007: 26).

The sigil animal of the CPP is a duck-rabbit, known from the optical illusion frequenting philosophical debates on language and perception, and coincidently an object of fascination for anti-fascist writer and journalist Natasha Lennard (Lennard 2019). In the case of the CPP, a duck-rabbit signifies what Stephen Wright calls the 'double ontology' (Wright 2013: 22) of practices and objects which have both form and function, conceptual potential and practical use, with possibilities much greater than 'just' art. The key intuition, practised by the CPP, is that artistic competences unfold in various modulations, under surprising circumstances, more often than not in response to social and political urgencies. In other terms, the Consortium uses the connectionist capacities of networks and projects to link what was previously unlinked and move contemporary art beyond the limitations of its own field and institutions, thus practising the → curatorial mode of revolution.

E   is for...

E   is for enthusiasm

Any meaningful evaluation of the function of enthusiasm in the world propelled by projects must take into account the paradoxes of freelancers' capacity for self-directed and self-fulfilling action. On the one hand, uncorrupted forms of enthusiasm are expressions of collective power, what Italian post-Marxists call *potenza*, a collective capacity for radically democratic self-organisation. On the other, it is undeniable that in artistic → circulation, enthusiasm is utilised as a resource, the main function of which is to facilitate the overproduction of projects, reproduction of institutions and expansion of the network.

At a first glance, enthusiasm is something very positive. A number of bottom-up initiatives are driven by voluntary commitment. This could mean a grass-roots university, an artistic cooperative, a neighbourhood garden, an artistic NGO, an independent publishing house or an artists' trade union. People engage not because they expect high earnings, but because they are motivated and invested. Enthusiasts set their own goals and achieve them, not waiting for the intervention of higher powers. Critical Practice, a research cluster from London, even devises the 'index of enthusiasm' as a tool for self-management. It operates in a very simple manner. Members of the collective declare the level of their enthusiasm for various ideas on the cluster's wiki. Based on this declaration, collective decisions are taken, and the organisation follows the flow of collective desire.

In itself such an attitude is not to be condemned. On the contrary, if it wasn't for enthusiasm and collective commitment, a number of crucial initiatives, social movements, → support structures and → patainstitutions would have never materialised. The problem emerges when institutions, larger events or other gate keepers use people's willingness to engage as a justification for not paying them. This tendency is endemic among networks and more predatory institutions. Enthusiasm drives artistic circulation, just as → Artyzol saturates the art worlds. The artistic projectariat is expected to accept underpayment and precarity due to its supposed love of art and enthusiastic pursuit of its own projects. This situation is very similar to other social → <u>apparatuses</u> that industrialise creativity by → <u>controlling</u> the seemingly uncontrollable cohorts of freelancers and flexible project teams. While analysing the rise and fall of the creative industries in the UK, Angela McRobbie sketches an uncomfortably accurate picture of aspiring creatives: 'The cheerful, upbeat, passionate, entrepreneurial person who is constantly vigilant in regard to opportunities for projects or contracts must display a persona that mobilizes the need to be at all times one's own press and publicity agent' (McRobbie 2015). Like Richard Sennett, she diagnoses this 'ideal worker' as responsible for the corrosion of character, i.e. an atrophy of people's capacity for maintaining personality, interests, skills and craft over their lifespans, in spite of changing circumstances (Sennett 1999).

In project-driven circulation, this corrosion of character is a side effect of → <u>apparatuses</u> that generate and capture enthusiasm. This paradoxical mode of governance works by interrupting the spatiotemporal continuum in which projectarians circulate (→ <u>D is for deadline</u> and → <u>S is for sprint</u>). Short-term projects allow a peculiar form of freedom, as everybody is free to circulate as they wish, roaming the networks in search of new → <u>opportunities</u>. Curators and artists are believed to be 'independent' because they are 'free' to choose between different projects, while not being bound to any particular institution or workplace. And this kind of freedom can be exhilarating, as – at least in theory – they are able to enthusiastically engage in whatever project they want. This disposition is intrinsic to the new spirit of capitalism at large, as Boltanski and Chiapello write about the psychic disposition of people working on projects:

> When they engage in a project, everyone concerned knows that the undertaking to which they are about to contribute is destined to last for a limited period of time – that it not only can, but must, come to an end. The prospect of an inevitable, desirable endpoint thus accompanies *engagement* without affecting enthusiasm. This is why engagement is conceived as voluntary (Boltanski and Chiapello 2005: 110, italics by authors).

According to Pascal Gielen, this kind of enthusiastic engagement contributes to establishing a 'work ethic in which work is always enjoyable

– or should be, in which dynamism is boosted unconditionally by young talent, in which commitment outstrips money' (Gielen 2009: 53). These approaches to work result in the willingness of projectarians to remain committed despite compromised financial conditions (→ P is for poor (artists)) and structurally imposed → precarity. However, even if one is free to choose between transitory projects, one is doomed to chase one project after another and many projects at the same time.

E   is for entrepreneurs of
                           the self

In the world of projects and networks success is individualised. Even though people make their projects together, they move between them as atomised individuals. In order to access the flow of opportunities, they need to take risks, rationally plan their activities and invest in future projects. In the → winner-takes-it-all economy, independent curators or artists need to become competitive, often despite their own attitudes or values, in → fear for their own survival. They are gamed into competitive behaviour, → controlled by apparatuses similar to those implemented in other sectors of the gig economy, where atomised workers compete for often symbolic rewards and statuses, enhancing productivity captured by the owners of platforms such as Uber or Mechanical Turk. The beginnings of this tendency date back to the neoliberal reforms of the labour markets in the 1980s and 1990s, and the rise of digital economies and social networks. Boltanski and Chiapello observe how, in this context, artists adopted the peculiar model of 'mini-firms'. They describe this social process by referring to the research of Pierre-Michele Menger (1999) on creative industries in France:

> (…) artists respond to a very changeable and uncertain professional world by spreading the risks and equipping themselves with 'portfolios of activities and resources containing different risks', which confers on 'the individual organization of artistic work certain properties of a mini-firm'. For them, irregular work represents the most widespread form of employment, with a succession of short periods in work and more or less prolonged periods out of work. A career consists not in filling 'vacancies', but in engaging in a multitude of often very heterogeneous projects (Boltanski and Chiapello 2005: 312).

This shift from cultural producer to entrepreneur became so naturalised over the course of time that neoliberal ideologues frequently present artists as role models of entrepreneurialism in a flexible labour market, just as described by Gerald Raunig in the context of industries of creativity (Raunig 2013: 105).

The model of the 'mini-firm' is not ideologically neutral, as artists and curators have to become entrepreneurs of the self in accord with the premises of → neoliberalism. Michel Foucault created the concept of the 'entrepreneur of himself' to discuss this tendency towards individuation, describing this state as 'being for himself his own capital, being for himself his own producer, being for himself the source of [his] earnings' (Foucault 2010: 226). The entrepreneur of himself is not only individually responsible for his own success, competing on an open market with other entrepreneurial individuals. Even more importantly, he has to consider his own knowledge, skills, emotional capacities and social networks as a form of → capital to be invested in order to secure opportunities and future gains. As a result, the entrepreneur of himself establishes a profoundly instrumental, capitalist relationship to his inner and social self, which prevents more value-oriented stances or politicised action.

In this wicked manner, labour power is ideologically presented as if it was capital, which is simultaneously true and not true. It is not true because, just like in the typical labour market, the networked labourers are in a drastically disadvantaged position, and enhancement of their labour power mainly serves the people who purchase it – the capitalists themselves. On the other hand – and here artistic circulation proves an interesting case in point – people who → capitalise on themselves (and others) are able to find better opportunities (→ W is for winner takes it all). This access is mediated by the → capital at their disposal, because in the process of acquiring social and symbolic capital, entrepreneurial individuals not only capitalise on their own labour, but also – or even especially – on the labour of others.

The trajectories of successful entrepreneurs of the self are rarely directly related to the exploitation of any individual projectarian by the means of wage labour. Their careers are underpinned by the general social labour of artistic → dark matter. The social and symbolic capital is of a contextual nature; it cannot be quantified nor monetised directly (though it can be moulded into forms that are prone to → capture). When I say that such capital is invested, I do not mean it literally, like in investing money as capital in the pursuit of surplus value. Rather, I have in mind people who invest – their reputations, knowledge, social contacts – in their undertakings. A small minority of such 'investors' are far more successful than others, not only in terms of recuperating their own investments but also a disproportionate portion of the accumulated social labour of others. In such situations, the distinction between labour and capital is not predefined as it is in other sectors of the economy. Instead, it is processual and defined only retrospectively. For example, people may engage in a project as freelancers, and nobody actually employs anyone. Each person invests themselves in collective undertakings, but only a few of them will thrive by accumulating enough kudos to secure access to future opportunities. Others will end up with naught. Only in retrospect can they be identified as labour-givers and not as accumulators of capital. Another complication is that this accumulation happens not only (and not even predominantly) around projects, but within the vast, chaotic nexus of networks and transient relations. For entrepreneurs of the self typically thrive on the general social labour accumulated in circulation and not on the small bits acquired from individual projects.

E   is for exclusion

Exclusion is the dead end of circulation; it is one of the mechanisms reproducing artistic → dark matter, and the main sanction enacted on disobedient projectarians. Exclusion is privatised, though there are whole cohorts of disprivileged (due to their gender, nationality, class, impaired mental or bodily abilities, or colour of their skin) people who are much more likely to be excluded. In addition, projectarians are getting excluded as individuals, as if it was solely their own fault and responsibility. Such ruptures as the one caused by COVID-19 will accelerate systemic tendencies that exclude those who won't be able to afford to stay in → circulation. Excluded are the wretched of the circulation: some withdraw willingly, looking for greener pastures, but most are marginalised against their will, suffering from the slow burn of inequality, exclusion looming at the horizon of rejected → applications, missed → opportunities, → projects that remained invisible for anyone but their makers. Getting demoted is a process: it is like a slow-motion train wreck, as a result of which slowly but inevitably projectarians fall behind their more successful friends and colleagues, who spin around, circulating ever faster.

Exclusion is defined by the lack of → projects, connections, → opportunities and → visibility. As one artist succinctly responded to the Free/Slow University of Warsaw's query: to be present you have to circulate; when you stop moving, you cease to exist. You are side-lined, voiceless and invisible. This exclusion, as Boltanski and Chiapello argue, is both a form of deprivation and a mode of exploitation embedded within a networked society (Boltanski and Chiapello 2005: 346–55). They describe the excluded as:

> those who have seen the ties that bound them to others severed, and have thus been relegated to the fringes of the network, where beings lose all visibility, all rationale, and virtually all existence (Boltanski and Chiapello 2005: 348).

In other words, the excluded do not have access to circulation and are downgraded to the status of an anonymous resource; they are mobilised only for projects initiated by others and from which others benefit most. Boltanski and Chiapello do not only diagnose exclusion, but also analyse its systemic functions. They attempt to illustrate that the success of people who are well connected in the network derives from the exclusion of the ones who are less so (Boltanski and Chiapello 2005: 371). Some businesses or individuals are able to exploit others because they are better networked and more mobile. In this context, Boltanski and Chiapello analyse links between visibility, connectivity, exclusion and deficits of justice. Because those who are excluded are not any longer connected, they cease to be visible in the network, which results in eradicating common ground where the inequalities between connected and disconnected people can be publicly discussed. Their analysis highlights precisely this aspect of the networked society which is at the basis of inequalities specific to artistic circulation, where differentials of mobility are multiplied by the disparities in artistic → visibility. The circulation excludes losers of the → winner-takes-it-all economy. Adding insult to this injury, the excluded are deprived of access to the only platforms that would enable them to voice their concerns publicly and denounce the injustice suffered.

These insights are corroborated by the → Free/Slow University's research into the division of labour and distribution of capital in the Polish field of visual art (Kozłowski, Sowa and Szreder 2015). We were surprised by the general complicity of our respondents with the structures of the field. Even if people voiced more specific concerns about their economic conditions, precarity or other burdens of networking, they generally tended to agree with how the field is organised. When we assessed these outcomes, we concluded that the results were possibly skewed by the fact that we researched people who are still active in circulation, i.e. present and visible, and managing to acquire enough capital to keep circulating by accessing new projects, frequently at the cost of their own unpaid labour or other sacrifices.

Such reputational hierarchies reproduce themselves, as social status and reputation regulates access to → opportunities, which reciprocally magnifies chances to acquire social or symbolic → capital. When projectarians manage to secure a good project, their social status is enhanced, bettering their chances of securing further opportunities. If they fail to access the flow of opportunities, they gradually lose their capacity to enter new projects, the process leading eventually to marginalisation and disappearance from the network.

Since in the world of networks there is no income without projects, exclusion leads to deterioration of the material basis of existence. Additionally, exclusion is associated with → burn-outs and depression, understood as pathologies of responsibility, as every projectarian is expected to take personal responsibility for remaining visible and employable. Lack of success in this respect is framed as an individual and not a systemic failure. In a world where the scope of success is so narrow, and attention flickers, most projectarians will experience exclusion, invisibility and failure. The → fear of falling out of → circulation is so prevailing because every projectarian is always at the verge of exclusion. A short absence can easily turn into a longer pause and this can develop into a complete disappearance.

Due to the perception disorder inherent to the network, artistic → dark matter is invisible, and so people see only those who successfully circulate, appearing in the most visible and best-connected nodes of the network – prestigious institutions, international biennials or art fairs.

The twisted horizons of social visibility maintain the illusion of artistic circulation as a world of opportunities, roamed by joy riders. This disorder affects particularly young projectarians, who fall for perceptual aberration, unrealistically assessing their own chances of winning in the race for visibility. They take an individual risk, hoping that 'I will be the one to make it', instead of striving to rewrite the rules of the game that doom so many to exclusion, amendable only through collective action.

E   is for exodus

Such tactics as → <u>productive withdrawals</u> or establishing → <u>patainstitutions</u> are examples of what Paulo Virno theorises under the term 'exodus', usually held to mean a kind of mass departure. In contrast to idle escapism, exodus is a productive act of contestation, which destroys the existing structures in order to free up social energy. For Virno such exodus is:

> the polar opposite of the desperate cry 'there is nothing to lose but one's own chains': on the contrary, exit hinges on a latent kind of wealth, on an exuberance of possibilities (...) Defection allows for a dramatic, autonomous, and affirmative expression of this surplus; and in this way it impedes the 'transfer' of this surplus into the power of state administration, impedes its configuration as productive resource of the capitalistic enterprise (Virno 2004: 70).

In this sense, exodus is an expression of constituent power, a form of collective potency fundamental for establishing new institutional forms. This concept was picked up by a group of thinkers assembled around the European Institute of Progressive Cultural Policies (EIPCP) from Vienna, to reflect upon and encourage alternative forms of social self-organisation. They were working with Antonio Negri's concept of constituent power (Negri 2003; Raunig 2009b) – a power expressed through collective action to find and offer systemic alternatives to the status quo, and to establish a new mode of social organisation that would be responsive to the shifting desires of the people who constitute it. For EIPCP exodus leads to the productive realisation of social surplus by, for example, establishing social centres in the squatted buildings, constituting alternatives while avoiding capture by the hostile forces of the state or the capitalistic economy. It is clear that exodus is not a movement in space, but rather a systemic rupture in modes of social organisation. Instead of becoming luxurious condos, available only for people who can afford them, squatted buildings are turned into centres of cultural and social activity, accessible to all. In this sense, exodus is a direct opposition of exclusion, it is an emancipatory withdrawal rather than forced evacuation. It is not atomised punishment, but a form of collective expression. Writing in a similar vein, Stephen Wright, a theoretician of usership, formulates the pataphysical concept of escapology, a theory and practice aimed at perfecting techniques of avoiding → capture. He understands capture in ontological terms (naming something as 'just' art to capture it in the mechanisms of the art market), but also as an economically performative category, just as it is used here (→ C is for capture). Escapologists have to master modes of thriving beyond the radar and are not interested in circulation at all costs. Not for them are fairs or biennales: they avoid the vicious cycle of opportunism. They politicise escapism, just as striking artists radicalise laziness, as a mode of refusal. Thus, exodus remains one of the modes of action fundamental for the → struggles of the projectariat.

E

is for expanded field
(of art)

When projects were introduced in the world of business and corporations, the aim of new management was to cross stiff boundaries between departments, fields of expertise and varied corporate bodies. The idea was that projects could join what was previously separated, stimulating creativity and encouraging innovation. Projects as a way of conceiving and supporting artistic activities emerged in the 1960s and 1970s to support the expansion of artistic practices beyond the narrow confines of the artistic studio and the white cubes of galleries and museums, so called 'gallery-exhibition nexus' (van den Berg 2013: 66–69). Currently, projects are the dominant form of organising artistic production in the expanded field of art, as Lane Relyea describes:

> With the increasing adoption by artists of itinerant and post-studio approaches, and by museums of commissions and residencies, this shift from production to project now characterizes the art world—and many other areas of social and cultural life as well (Relyea 2017: 10).

Similarly to Relyea, other scholars such as Karen van den Berg, Ursula Pasero and Claire Bishop locate the first utterances of the term 'projects' in descriptions of artistic and curatorial practices of the 1970s (Bishop 2012; van den Berg and Pasero 2013). The term 'expanded field of art' was first coined in the 1970s by Rosalind Krauss, who introduced this notion to discuss the formal evolution of site-specific art, land art, durational interventions and minimal art (Krauss 1979). All these genres or methodologies were not easily accommodated by the modernist canon, which is structured by the divisions between nature and culture and between function and autonomy. By proposing the concept of the expanded field of art, Krauss proposed that these binaries were false, thus providing a theoretical framework to host expanded artistic practices. Krauss was one of many contemporaries (Buchloh 1990; Lippard 1973) who responded to the developments of conceptual, minimal, land, site-specific and new genres of public art. Nor was she the last: similar theoretical frameworks, criticising the limitations of modernist art theory, have emerged and been developed since in the context of site specificity (Kwon 2002), ethnographically oriented art (Foster 1995), the expediency of culture (Yúdice 2003), dialogic practices (Kester 2004; 2011), neo-avant-gardes (Léger 2012; Roberts 2015), collectivism (Stimson and Sholette 2007; WHW 2005), new genres of public art (Lacy 1995), relational aesthetics and participatory art (Bishop 2006; 2012; Bourriaud 2002), political art-activism (Malzacher 2014; Thompson 2012), durational practices (O'Neill and Doherty 2010), etc.

All those genres operate on the expanded field of art, where projects are the main modes of facilitating artistic production, both conceptually, organisationally and financially. Just as white cube and studio are constitutive parts of → assemblages inherent to the field of art in its modernist form, projects, processes and platforms are indispensable to its expanded state.

The expanded field of artistic practices cannot be conflated with the most visible sectors of artistic circulation, which are organised around the core of metropolitan institutions, dominant galleries, global biennials and art fairs. Importantly, the artistic mainstream reassembles and absorbs both traditional elements (like studios and galleries) and ultra-rapid and networked devices (like newsletters, rankings, art banks and vaults, etc.). But the expanded field is larger than that, as it encompasses also artistic → dark matter, and is constituted by the plethora of what Stephen Wright and Basekamp (an art collective from the USA) call 'plausible art worlds' (Basekamp Group & Friends 2013), a variety of artistic universes transversal to the mainstream art world.

The expanded field should not be conceived of as a distinct social space but rather a modus operandi of practices that transgress the traditional boundaries of artistic autonomy, such as → demonstrations of paintings. These activities frequently constitute themselves as an alternative to both traditional art institutions and the commercial art market, by establishing various → support structures and → patainstitutions. In the expanded field, projects play an important role in sustaining 'independent' production. Importantly, projects should not be conflated with grants, as the latter are already bureaucratically formalised manifestations of project-related apparatuses. Projects are and can be much more universal, as they provide convenient organisational forms for sustaining ephemeral and temporary endeavours, enabling people coming from a variety of backgrounds to efficiently pursue their goals.

F   is for...

F   is for fear

Mobile projectarians resemble mice in flight, frenetically looking for new opportunities to survive: just keep going for another day, month, year or two. This apt metaphor was proposed by Massimo De Carolis, an Italian scholar of post-Fordism, who commenting on Virno's notion of → opportunism, wrote:

> The first theorists of opportunism, the Sophists of ancient Greece, were usually exiles deprived of every right of citizenship, hobos of knowledge hunted by the law and institutions. Diogenes, the founder of ancient cynicism, personally knew both exile and slavery. It is said, in fact, that Diogenes conceived his doctrine while observing the course of a mouse, admiring the animal's blind ability to take advantage of every opportunity for salvation—an illuminating comparison that demonstrates how the dominant sentiment in this second type of opportunism is none other than fear, the anxiety of an animal in flight (De Carolis 1996, 41).

By recalling the story of Diogenes and a mouse, De Carolis tries to illuminate the ambivalent condition of post-Fordism, where nomadic subjects, as homeless as ancient cynics, have to behave as if they were animals in flight. Their opportunism is dictated by a survival instinct, as they are personally and professionally dependent on the flow of fleeting opportunities. It is of no surprise that De Carolis, following Virno, identifies fear as a primordial sentiment of post-Fordism, linked to → cynicism and → opportunism. In the age of COVID-19 this fear is only magnified, not only by health hazards, as scary as they are, but also by the scarcity of opportunities, both indicating deterioration of the chances of survival.

Anxiety is not distributed equally. Some have many more reasons to fear than others. The privileged few are well sheltered from the risks of → precarious existence, enjoying the spoils of the global art world. Most people do not enjoy the levels of security that the North-Western middle classes take for granted when they move freely, with a good passport in hand. And yet → <u>fear</u> is one of the dominant emotions of the projectariat, as it usually takes only a couple of rejected applications, a few months of bad luck, an accident or a virus to strip even a middle-class person of their privileges, which are not truly guaranteed for anyone but the → <u>one percent</u>. In any case, projectarians are in constant flight, because you either make projects or you perish.

To counter this privatisation of fear, Gerald Raunig invokes such concepts as 'fleeing while searching for the weapon' (Raunig and Ray 2009b: XVII), which reimagines flight as a productive act of withdrawal, an impulse that leads to imagining and enacting alternatives. Instead of being blinded by panic, people can collectively embark upon → <u>productive withdrawals</u>, go on strike, occupy a building or a square, boycott a biennale or organise a → <u>demonstration of paintings</u>. In this way, instead of suffering silently from their own individualised fear, projectarians can sketch out routes of escape that, if taken by many, collectively challenge the same conditions that fill them with dread.

F   is for Free/Slow
                             (University of Warsaw)

My thinking on artistic circulation is so embedded in the collective research of the Free/Slow University of Warsaw (in short F/SUW, and in Polish *Wolny Uniwersytet Warszawy*) that it deserves an entry of its own. The Free/Slow University of Warsaw was established in 2009 by a group of radicalised cultural producers (Michał Kozłowski, Janek Sowa, Bogna Świątkowska, Szymon Żydek, later joined by Joanna Figiel, and others), fed up with the pointless acceleration of artistic networks and projects. All of us were working on too many projects at the same time, always on the move, with no time to consider the sense of all this rush. In Warsaw, back in the day, there were enough opportunities for freelancers to be busy all the time, but never paid adequately. So, independent curators like myself always had to make one project after another and many simultaneously. In the late 2000s, Poland saw yet another attempt at implementing neoliberal cultural policies, with experts in cultural management parroting the global discourses of the creative class and cultural industries, seeking to replicate models of gentrification first tested in New York and Bilbao. Sometimes the results were unintentionally parodistic, like in the case of the so-called 'SOHO Factory' in Warsaw. A bleak post-industrial zone, basically a thicket of weeds and bushes spotted with a couple of abandoned industrial halls and derelict 1970s office buildings, was rechristened after a famous district of New York. Not surprisingly, it was a total flop, and after a few years this 'artistic hub' was developed into 'luxurious' condos. Nevertheless, on the cultural scene in Warsaw, a bit of money available for artistic projects could be accessed through the competitive grant systems, maybe not particularly well managed and rather bureaucratic, but still there to be sourced. A freelance curator's chore was to fill in loads of detailed forms and to write equally tedious reports in case they were lucky enough to get the money and make their projects. In the late 2000s, some funding was there to patch together even ambitious projects: a bit from the city council, a bit from the ministry of culture, a bit from foreign cultural institutes and cultural foundations (thank you Goethe Institute, Pro Helvetia, British Council, Mondrian Fund, European Cultural Foundation, etc. etc.) and a bit from the European Union. By combining all those bits and pieces, it was possible to generate (although not very impressive by Western standards) quite sufficient budgets. Poland seemed to want to implement the (continental) European model of cultural policies, but in a → semi-peripheral version and with a slight neoliberal veneer. The art market was nascent and still is, though in the early 2010s, the new Polish bourgeoisie started to buy art, enjoying the spoils of social inequalities in a manner similar to the metropolitan bourgeoisie they were trying to imitate. Art institutions still played an important role in the local cultural ecosystem, some managing to successfully reposition themselves in the global art world. The non-governmental sector was on the rise too, counterpointed by a cohort of not very numerous but pretty visible informal collectives. In this scene, F/SUW emerged as a platform of radical → art workers who combined resistance to neoliberalism (in culture and elsewhere) with critical reflection on the systems of production of contemporary art. We quickly allied ourselves with other like-minded artistic unions, patainstitutions and radical art workers, on both the local and international levels, forging friendships and alliances that have lasted until the moment of writing.

'Free/slow' is a direct translation of a Polish word game, as the term *wolny* (usually used in Polish to denote free universities) signifies in Polish both 'free' and 'slow'. This double meaning was adopted as the core element of the curatorial concept of F/SUW, which attempted to link two contradictory stances – of slowing down and speeding up – in its struggle for → interdependent autonomy. At later stages, the slogan was slightly upgraded by adding the word *powolny* which means both slow and submissive, coining its motto *wolny bo powolny*, yet another linguistic pun which means 'free/slow because slow/submissive'. The slogan of F/SUW ironically highlighted the position of structural weakness from which the collective operated, as it submitted to the flow of opportunities (applications, deadlines, reports, etc.) while trying to facilitate long-term studies, resisting the pace of artistic circulation in which it was submerged. Despite its inherent limitations, the Free/Slow University managed to persistently continue with its line of thinking for about a decade, generating a repository of books and reports and creating an intangible yet vital network of alliances and friendships.

The title of the introduction to the catalogue of the 2009 edition of F/SUW, '260% of Norm', was an ironic comment on the productive pressures of circulation, but also a subversive programmatic statement. By stating ironically that the Free/Slow University of Warsaw achieved two hundred and sixty percent of its own preconceived programme, we acknowledged its own paradoxical status of the autonomous zone of hyper-activity. We self-identified as shock-workers of cultural networks, just to borrow the term introduced by Chto Delat?, a cluster of radical comrades from Moscow and Saint Petersburg (Vilensky and Chaguidouline 2018). It was tongue-in-cheek accelerationism, enacted on the micro scale of a collective embedded in the nitty-gritty reality of post-communist Warsaw – otherwise a rather relaxed Central European capital city, especially when viewed from a global perspective. None of us was really keen on accelerationism, particularly not in its enthusiastic embrace of capitalist velocity. However, our research programme, oriented on the critique of the political economy of networked capitalism, was in tune with what later was coined as the 'left accelerationism' of Alex Williams, Nick Srnicek and Paul Mason (Mason 2015; Srnicek and Williams 2016), as we discussed and advocated for such concepts as the right to laziness, backed up by the Basic Universal Income. In the Manifesto of the Committee for the Radical Change in Culture in 2009, we wrote:

> For the Polish authorities, culture appears to be just another life-sphere ready to be colonized by neoliberal capitalism. Attempts are being made to persuade us that the 'free' market, productivity and income-oriented activities are the only rational, feasible and universal laws for social development. This is a lie (...) It is not culture that needs 'business exercises' it is the market that needs a cultural revolution (Committee for the Radical Change in Culture 2009: 1).

In its heyday, the Free/Slow University explicitly aligned with the post-Marxist approaches of Virno, Negri, Hardt, Lazzarato and others, modified to acknowledge the specificity of the semi-peripheral condition where the economy is anything but immaterial, where capitalist accumulation proceeds by extracting raw products and exploiting cheap labour that assembles goods invented and designed elsewhere. In tune with post-Marxist argument, the team of the Free/Slow University of Warsaw approached artistic circulation as one of the exemplary fields of contemporary capitalist production, a testing ground for new modes of subjectivity, production and capture of value, a methodological premise that enshrines my current explorations of artistic circulation.

Viewed in this context, the free/slowness of the Free/Slow University had nothing to do with such pastoral concepts as slow art, or other iterations of romantic consumerism, a fashion aimed at unhurried contemplation of artistic masterpieces. In contrast, the aim of our university was to reclaim the accelerated rhythms of cultural production, carving our space of resistant reflection in the midst of its frenetic flow. In doing so, we acted similarly to other art-activist groups of the period, such as Isola Art Centre from Milan who, according to Gerald Raunig, 'interrupted interruptions' induced by networks and projects, engaging in self-managed productivity that he describes in the following words:

> an inventive reappropriation of time, (…) a wild and no longer servile industriousness allowing smooth and striated times to newly emerge (…) An industry that is no longer creative economy, but rather busyness in the vernacular, wild, disobedient, orgic industry (Raunig 2013: 121–22).

The Free/Slow University embedded itself in the legacy of → art strikes, as we aligned with our contemporary → productive withdrawals, the occupations, boycotts and strikes that shook the global artistic circulation in the second decade of the twenty-first century. The slowness of free/slowness was in tune with the idea of radical laziness, a refusal of networked production, using reclaimed time and resources to build a platform for radical co-research on the conditions of artistic labour.

F

is for footprint
(or carbon miles)

'Can the artworld kick its addiction to flying?' asked Kyle Chayka rhetorically in the December 2019 issue of *Frieze* (Chayka 2019). The same question would not have been asked even a few months later, when all international flights were suspended and national borders reinstated. It seems very unlikely that we will look back on the COVID-19 crisis as marking the end of the era of cheap flights, as even in the midst of the pandemic the spaces of e-communication were filled with a flurry of online activities, and many projectarians made long lists of places to visit, people to meet and events to attend in the post-pandemic world. This specific mindset that accompanies frequent flying does not seem likely to abate any time soon and needs to be reconstructed, as it exemplifies a more general reluctance to address the environmental damage caused by the artistic industries.

Just a couple of months before the COVID-19 crisis hit, Chayka's answer to his own question was tentatively pessimistic, written with an aura of self-confessional resignation as mobility was commonly recognised as a professional hazard of artistic globetrotters who roamed the world in search of sensations and opportunities. Most projectarians, freelance writers, curators and artists used to be poverty jetsetters, as described by Andrew Berardini (Berardini 2014). Often too poor to afford anything but the cheapest fares, travelling around the globe with only light luggage, and yet ranked amongst frequent flyers who according to recent research contribute most to the carbon footprint of the industry that counts among the biggest polluters in the world (Kommenda 2019).

Even if some of the projectarians are well aware of the environmental damage caused by mobility, and openly voice their concerns, it is much easier to talk this talk, rather than to walk the walk from Warsaw to London. Obviously, some people take trains, but flying remains a much easier means of transport. The responses to the short survey on greening artistic practices conducted in New York by *DIS* Magazine were not particularly optimistic either. The survey established that private galleries in particular do not care to or do not see how they might be able to change their practices involving the shipping of people and goods globally (DIS and Ecocore 2019). The commercial sector is particularly uninterested in the matter. Kate Brown, who reported in 2019 on Art Basel, one of the major global art fairs, denounces the 'green hush' that engulfs the trade booths:

> The hesitancy is understandable, sort of. The questions around the art-world's carbon footprint are deeply uncomfortable for everyone, this writer included. It brings up questions of our very existence as an industry. (...) When it comes to the art in Basel, the so-called 'visceral and emotional side' of the issue of climate change just isn't moving the conversation. Nearly every gallerist I spoke to said that collectors are just not that interested in climate change as a topic (K. Brown 2019).

As one of the dealers puts it 'Sexuality is more interesting as a topic than breathing, and definitely sells better' (K. Brown 2019). This self-denial is easily explainable, as the dominant players of the art market cater to the → one percent, a capitalist class that benefits directly from the current organisation of disaster capitalism. This new international incarnation of the 'leisure class', the late nineteenth-century version of which was denounced by Thorsten Veblen in his analysis of early capitalism (Veblen 2009), are uber-consumers, whose carbon footprint is inversely proportional to their utter lack of remorse. It seems only appropriate to contrast this insufferable arrogance with the rallying cry of Achille Mbembe, who wrote in his already quoted essay (→ A is for aftermath) 'Universal Right to Breathe':

> If, indeed, Covid-19 is the spectacular expression of the planetary impasse in which humanity finds itself today, then it is a matter of no less than reconstructing a habitable Earth to give all of us the breath of life. We must reclaim the lungs of our world with a view to forging new ground. Humankind and biosphere are one. Alone, humanity has no future. Are we capable of rediscovering that each of us belongs to the same species, that we have an indivisible bond with all life? Perhaps that is the question – the very last – before we draw our last dying breath (Mbembe 2020).

These intersectional inequalities and political differences are mapped into the projectarians. Radicalised sectors of the projectariat are more eager to affiliate themselves with the politics of climate justice, whilst most of the ultra-mobile celebrity class are satisfied with their own privilege, stemming from their close contact with the capitalist oligarchies. Some of the former appear to be pretty effective in exhorting pressure on public institutions to sever ties with extractive industries, as in the case of the London-based campaign Liberate Tate, which loudly advocated for discontinuing the partnership between Tate Group and British Petroleum (Evans 2015), although BP's stated reason for eventually ending the sponsorship was 'challenging business conditions' and not the years of highly visible activism. As argued by Bogna Stefańska and Kuba Depczyński, one of the organisers of the → demonstration of paintings, the ecologically oriented art activism requires new aesthetical formulas and means of organisation, catering to the postartistic practices more closely integrated with social and natural ecosystems (Depczyński and Stefańska 2021).

TJ Demos provides a very interesting insight into the dynamics of this shift in his text on the climate emergency and the politics of emergence, represented by art-activist campaigns such as Decolonise This Place (Demos 2019). This New York based group campaigned for the resignation of Warren Kanders from the board of The Whitney Museum of American Art in 2019, due to the involvement of one of the companies he owns in the production of tear gas used against migrants and protestors worldwide, as indicated in the report published by Hyperallergic in 2018 (Weber 2018). TJ Demos concludes his argument:

> This means a commitment to 'long environmentalism,' the labor of building solidarity and mutual-aid networks over months, years, generations, as probably the only place where a radical politics of emergency can truly emerge – rooted in the broadly shared concern of collective survival – even if that means rethinking the temporal immediacy of emergency itself in times of unprecedented uncertainty. It entails committing to building relations of responsibility and accountability that can lend trust in justice, in thinking climate emergencies relationally, beginning with the history of Anthropocene violence stretching back hundreds of years and continuing with current and near-future threats of ongoing climate chaos. As such, those of us bound in solidarity and committed to creating a collective future beyond climate breakdown – where tear gas reveals its expansive

entanglements – must certainly decolonize this place, and this and that one too, organizing a transnational network of resistance capable of challenging the transnational power of capital. But we must also decolonize our future, rescuing it from the disaster of green capitalist, and worse eco-fascist, 'inevitability' facilitated by an irresponsible emergency politics (Demos 2019).

Very sensibly, TJ Demos stresses collective rather than individual responsibility, which has to be built up gradually and with a focus on long-term action. Otherwise, it defaults to the consumer guilt of middle-class professionals and risks turning into a paradox of individual withdrawal, already signalled by Hans Haacke when he was asked to partake in an art strike in the early 1980s (more in the entry → A is for art strikes). He refused because, as he argued, only politicised artists would partake – and they are already marginalised. The same rule of thumb applies to mobility. The only people who would even consider stopping flying are radical projectarians – who already hover at the verge of → exclusion. In fact, in order to prevent climate catastrophe, people like them should connect even more, because 'organizing a transnational network of resistance capable of challenging the transnational power of capital' will definitely involve a lot of face-to-face meetings, international travelling, emails sent and data streams used, which adds up to a pretty significant carbon footprint. Instead of hurling personalised attacks against the supposed hypocrisy of activists and → art workers, this fight has to be understood in its strategic and political context. A ton of carbon dioxide spent on fighting for climate justice might be offset by millions of tons not released into the atmosphere if this struggle succeeds. And this type of activism is usually undertaken by people who are already overwhelmed by the plight of living and working at the fringes of circulation. They are often too poor to indulge in zero-waste consumerism and do not have enough time to spend days on walking the walk from Madrid to Berlin (and possibly they would feature amongst those very few who would rather take a train or not travel at all). The one-percenters, who should be really held to account for the profits they make by releasing billions of tons of carbon dioxide, are either too busy marketing themselves or too self-satisfied with their own privileges to be bothered with the climate catastrophe, happy to go on with the flying as usual.

G   is for...

G   is for generosity

Despite the everyday competition and neoliberal onslaught, artistic circulation is populated by multitudes of exceptionally generous artists, curators, producers, assistants, writers and other → art workers. Sometimes they inhabit artistic → dark matter, but just as often they circulate with success. In my experience, entire projects, clusters and movements are run on contemporary forms of the gift economy, where a giver does not expect to be gifted back directly but rather partakes in building the → common. Marysia Lewandowska and Laurel Ptak's research suggests that such generosity could be considered as a form of undoing the contemporary fixations with individual property (Lewandowska and Ptak 2013). Neil Cummings evokes the spirit of radical generosity in his manifesto of unconditional giving, where he writes:

> The traditional logic of the gift, presupposes an already constituted subject – the virtuous man – prior to the act of giving. The virtuous man is a sovereign individual in possession of property. By giving or receiving, by deferring debt, he establishes communal, contractual relations with others. Generosity is radically other. It's not a property, and it's not in the eye of the beholder. It's a collective, temporary evaluation, fleeting, explosive, and transformational. Generosity converts specific values – very valuable values, perhaps the most precious values – into a currency. Generosity embodies and distributes these values. And as such, generosity is always emergent, always a creative intersubjective practice. Generosity creates and distributes radical subjectivity (Cummings 2014b: 326).

Just as Cummings links radical generosity to the process of realigning individual subjects in the intersubjective practice, Rasheed Araeen advocates for abolishing the narcissistic ego of artists alongside the structures of bourgeoisie property in order to release the full potential of the artistic imagination. Otherwise, it is trapped within the ownership structures inherent to both the bourgeois institution of art (via the means of individual authorship → C is for capture) and the capitalist economy alike. As he writes in his *Ecoaesthetics: A Manifesto for the 21st Century*:

> The ideas can be and are turned into institutionally manageable objects, thus contained in their temporalities, but ideas as knowledge can never be trapped as the property of an individual or the institution. They can always salvage themselves, give themselves a new context and move forward within the dynamic of new time and space. They can indeed perform a radically new transformative function in dealing with today's situation. But this art must go beyond what prevails as art and integrate itself with the collective struggle of life today to recover its true social function and become a radical force of the twenty-first century (...) It is in fact artistic imagination, not art objects, which once freed from the self- destructive narcissist ego, can enter this life and offer it not only salvation but put it on the path to a better future (Araeen 2010: 158).

Precisely because I agree with their manifestos, and I am wholeheartedly thankful for the generosity I undeservedly received from countless friends, comrades and strangers, I see the clear need to protect such → interdependent structures against hostile takeovers; against → capture, against → trawling, that leads to the privatisation of what otherwise should be kept in the common. As everyone circulates in vast networks, where → cynicism and → opportunism run rampant, projectarians need sometimes to be a little tactical in their generosity, as there are so many → networkers who are willing to abuse it. Instead of giving unconditionally, agreeing to feed narcissistic egos of → entrepreneurs of the self, always interested in milking others, would it not be better to collectively reclaim privatised properties in order to institute the → common and nourish → interdependent networks? In other words, generosity proper should be considered not as a private virtue, but as constitutive part of popular efforts aimed at collectivising infrastructures and resources.

G

is for grant Art
(NGO-isation)

Grant art is art made for grant's sake. The term is intended as an ironic jibe at art motivated primarily by the availability of opportunities (grants, invitations and commissions) rather than any other (political, artistic, intellectual) concerns. This crack was first made by Janek Sowa to ridicule the curatorial and artistic effects of grant systems, in the first publication of the → Free/Slow University of Warsaw (Sowa 2009). He responded to a systemic tendency engrained in both peripheral and metropolitan systems – basically everywhere projectarians → apply. → Independent curators and artists simply cannot be too picky when it comes to selecting opportunities. They often pretend otherwise, as they are expected to → enthusiastically respond to any opportunity provided, but in fact most of their time is spent negotiating between what they would wish for and what is possible. Writing → applications is an art in itself as writers need to balance between a promising vision and the tedious prose of bureaucratic forms. How poetic can one be while describing 'target audiences' or 'expected impact'? Still, the grant artists do what they can with what is given. More often than not they have to cater to the agendas of gate keepers who control access to opportunities. Only the most skilled projectarians convince funders to support visions of their own making but, taken at large, grant art is a quite dull genre. However, it has its own hilarious moments. All those cross-border partner-ships with fancy titles topping the lists of EU grants, often succumbing to cheap metaphors (obviously, Europeans really enjoy building bridges), or rhetorically overusing adjectives like 'European' and/or prefixes such as trans- or inter-. Most of these projects last as long as the financial streams that support them (→ S is for sprint).

Forms of → control that regulate grant art are comparable to benchmarking. Isabelle Bruno analyses benchmarking as the mode of governance that is 'all the more efficient since it is neither coercive, nor legal. Obedience relies on willingness and incentives, rather than on constraint and punishments' (Bruno 2014: 147). Similarly, for an opportunist involved in grant art, obedience is prompted by incentives rather than direct coercion. The only 'punishment' which suffices in inducing changes in behaviour is the denial of access to the flow of opportunities, as the risk of → exclusion triggers basic → fear.

So even if, at a first glance, the term 'grant art' looks like a theoretical pun, it aims at uncovering the systemic underbelly of artistic circulation, which is anything but funny. Sowa discusses grant art as part of the process of 'NGO-isation'. It is a particular form of self-institutionalisation that has far-reaching consequences, frequently criticised by researchers and practitioners commenting on contemporary forms of civic engagement. For example, Agnieszka Rymsza analyses the mechanisms that turned non-governmental initiatives into quasi-governmental organisations, examining the transformation of civic associations from the USA and Poland (Rymsza 2005). According to Rymsza, the financial support of governmental agencies in the USA since the 1970s has become mediated by bureaucratised grant systems, which have imposed audit mechanisms on formerly informal initiatives, readjusting their priorities and transforming their organisational culture. As Rymsza suggests, similar processes were underway in Poland already in early 2000s, prompted additionally by the relative weakness of the social base of NGOs, lack of tradition for volunteering and the frailty of the culture of charity (Rymsza 2005: 42). The effects of this process on grass-roots action and political organising are so profound that activist groups such as the USA coalition INCITE Women of Colour Against Violence denounce non-governmental organisations as a non-profit industrial sector (INCITE! Women of Color Against Violence 2009).

There are numerous examples of NGO-isation in the context of contemporary art. For example, Brian Wallis analysed the transformation of USA-based artist-run spaces in the 1970s and 1980s into quasi-governmental organisations (Wallis 2002). He describes how the formerly alternative initiatives institutionalised themselves in order to access public support (Wallis 2002: 164). They were required to establish administrative structures and hierarchies that significantly changed the way in which they had previously operated, gradually turning them into professionalised quasi-institutions. Writing in a similar vein, but analysing the rather different circumstances of post-war New Yugoslavia, Belgrade-based Prelom Kollektiv discusses how the exposure to application procedures and grant systems transformed self-organised critical initiatives into 'neoliberal institutions of culture', which are administered, controlled and depoliticised (Vesić and Grlja 2007).

All these authors suggest that NGO-isation (and more widely, self-institutionalisation) influences the social form of self-organised initiatives in order to hamper their critical potential. The mechanism of this process includes establishing professional 'project institutions', the survival of which depends on access to opportunities (and projects) regulated by grant systems. The context of → neoliberalism is crucial to understanding the pervasive character of NGO-isation, as it diminishes other ways of supporting self-organised initiatives by imposing general austerity (→ B is for belt-tightening). Even though every self-institutionalised entity is required to maintain the organisational infrastructure necessary for absorption of grants (i.e. accounting, office, board, etc.), the funds provided only rarely cover the costs of infrastructures established to fit this purpose, and they then have to be maintained by exploiting pools of voluntary labour. Thus, the specific organisational form of 'project institutions' emerge, about which Gerald Raunig, together with Gene Ray, writes:

> The very idea of a 'project institution' is glaringly contradictory. For if the concept of 'institution' implies a desire for long-term duration, continuity and security, the concept of 'project' by contrast implies limited duration and the negative effects, such as precarisation and insecurity, associated with it (Raunig and Ray 2009b: 16).

Raunig further developed this basic analysis of 'project institutions' in *Factories of Knowledge Industries of Creativity* (2013), where he defines 'project institutions' as small enterprises and start-ups which operate in the competitive environment of the creative industries, much like cultural NGOs and institutionalised artistic collectives. According to Raunig, 'project institutions' frequently turn into vehicles of exploitation because they merge temporariness with institutional longevity, project-related enthusiasm with organisational discipline, the vocational involvement of producers with the consequential state of precarity (Raunig 2013: 101–6). In other words, the organisational form of 'project institutions' shapes the collective efforts at self-organisation in accord with the structural pressures of → neoliberalism. Project institutions, instead of → instituting the common, rearticulate → opportunism and → precarity at the organisational level.

H is for...

The projectarians are a curious bunch. On the one hand, they are social animals, constantly in touch with other people. On the other, they are lone wolves, in that they are one-person business ventures. These overtly socialised and yet totally atomised types are constantly on the move whenever there are events to attend and cheap flights to take. Sometimes, it is easier for them to go to an international conference on another continent than to attend a neighbourhood meeting. Anyone who has tried to organise a union of art workers, pull off an art strike or maintain a long-term struggle knows very well that these feats are as difficult as herding cats. On the other hand, a black cat is a symbol of wildcat strikes, often adopted by anarchist trade unions and collectives to underline their untamed yet ferocious character. In a similar fashion, when art workers assemble together, they have to learn the tough art of maintaining the → struggle, despite their own tendencies and structural pressures.

The kinds of actions initiated by assemblies of → art workers are as paradoxical as the notion of herding cats itself. They are not easily categorised. Actions called 'art strikes' frequently resemble protests or pickets and do not necessarily involve any direct refusal of labour by the artists involved – a traditional precondition for calling something a 'strike'. One example of such activity is the Polish Day Without Art, organised in 2012 by the Citizen Forum for Contemporary Art, a group of art-activists, and coordinated by artist Katarzyna Górna and art critic Karol Sienkiewicz. The Day Without Art self-identified as an art strike, though technically it was more like a lockout. A few dozen art institutions across Poland closed their premises for a day in solidarity with artists protesting against appalling working conditions. A press conference was held at Zachęta, a central art institution based in Warsaw, but otherwise the day was not particularly assuming, even though it had many repercussions. One was the emergence of a union of art workers who later initiated a new cycle of struggles by organising around the slogan 'We, precariat'.

A detailed account of the events is given by Joanna Figiel in the *Art Leaks Gazette*, a magazine devoted to art workers' struggles (Figiel 2014). At the point when COVID-19 struck, the same union became a hotbed of action as it responded to the lockdown and subsequent suspension of artistic projects by providing support to artistic freelancers and advocating on their behalf. In their public statement, the forum demanded that freelancers and the self-employed should be recognised by the welfare system and covered by workplace protection – otherwise guaranteed for contracted employees only. In Poland, this would involve a social wage or minimum income paid by the state. The Forum further advocated for:

- Paying freelancers for all contracted projects, as if they had proceeded according to plan (usually freelancers are only paid after a project is completed).
- Following up with projects not yet contracted and paying freelancers for initial research and communication (due to the informality of employment relations in the arts, most freelancers do not have a contract signed in advance of production; usually the agreement is based on trust, which should not be exploited, particularly when it is needed most).
- Loosening the bureaucracy regulating public grants for individuals and prioritising wages for the conceptualisation of the work rather than other expenses (usually 20 per cent of the grant goes towards paying artists, while 80 per cent is spent on materials, travel, accommodation, transport; these proportions should now be reversed).
- Organising alternative public commissions to replace projects that have been cancelled.
- An amnesty for rents of studios (in Poland, these spaces are usually provided by municipalities).
- Providing financial support for institutions and enterprises suffering from the crisis.
- Ensuring that all subsidies are redistributed to the workers, even if they are not employed full-time (Citizens' Forum for Contemporary Art 2020).

This response was embedded in the collective process of reflection and action generated amongst art-activist groups operating worldwide, including the radical collective Plan C from the UK, the international network pirate.care and the antifascist feminist collective Keep it Complex, who also issued a series of demands related to this crisis.

These strategic shifts between union, struggle, occupation, protest and strike repeat across a spectrum of other strikes, boycotts and occupations. J21, an art strike organised in the USA in January 2017 against the newly elected president, also involved the closure of institutions, a media campaign, protests and direct actions, forming a hybrid protest situation, which could hardly be categorised as a withdrawal of labour as narrowly understood. Instead, it had more in common with the occupations of 2011.

Art boycotts, such as the boycott of Manifesta in Saint Petersburg (2014), San Paolo Biennale (2014) and the Sydney Biennale (2014), also depart from what is traditionally understood by the term 'boycott'. Instead of being organised by groups of art consumers, they were organised by art producers, who refused to partake in the event being boycotted. Despite identifying as boycotts, they more closely resembled traditional strikes, due to the central role played by the refusal of production. All these boycotts targeted art infrastructures, identified by protesting producers as complicit in the unacceptable political or corporate agendas of their sponsors. The account of major art boycotts, including their timelines and source documents, is featured in the excellent reader edited by Joanna Warsza and the participants of the Salzburg International Summer Academy of Fine Arts (Warsza and Básthy 2017).

Unlike art strikes and art boycotts, art occupations do not radically depart from the received understanding of occupation-actions. Some of those struggles intersect with the field of art, engulfing entire cities or societies, including artists, many of whom are the first and most active among occupiers. Martha Rosler even discussed an 'artistic mode of revolution' (Rosler 2014) inherent in occupations, in direct contrast to the artistic mode of gentrification (→ C is for curatorial mode of production / revolution). In any case, the repercussions of occupations for the art scenes are tremendous, as discussed using the example of Occupy in New York by Yates McKee (McKee 2016). The occupation of existing art spaces or creation of new spaces as part of occupations testifies to the possibility of better institutions, even as it proclaims loudly that the current infrastructure is hopelessly insufficient, compromised or simply dismantled. Sometimes these acts are as controversial as the occupation of the 7th edition of the Berlin Biennale (2011), accused of becoming an activist zoo and a protest staged for cultural consumption (Fischer 2015; Loewe 2015). But even such debatable occupations galvanise and collectivise otherwise atomised art workers. The occupations of the Guggenheim Museum during the opening of the Venice Biennale (2015), Teatro Valle in Rome (2011), S.a.L.E. Docs in Venice (2007) and Embros Theatre in Athens (2011) were drawing attention to the productive tension between artists organising public protests and artists organising where they worked or will work.

In any case, just as cats are not easily herded together, there is a constant risk that the collectives thus engendered will dissipate after a given protest-project concludes. Forging new unions is not an easy affair, as it is not a simple task to rupture existing connections and sustain new ones. The art workers are ravaged by the forces of capitalism, which makes their lives harder, resources scarce and time precarious. The elites of the art sector are able to maintain their domination precisely because they ride on the same global flows of speculative capital which threaten the existence of everybody else. After the movement subsides, the occupation dissipates or a boycott runs its course, there is a tendency to go back to business as usual. From time to time, though, these new social habitats prove quite resilient, as sometimes links established during an occupation, strike or boycott do not dissipate after the occupying multitudes disperse – as in the case of the Citizens' Forum for Contemporary Art, as the links forged during the Art Strike in 2012 were strong enough to survive till the moment of writing. Strikes, boycotts and occupations can be quite potent in reverse engineering connections, even the ones that are essential for the dominant systems to operate, weakening or even unpicking internal ties between their core elements. When activists occupied the municipal Gezi Park in Istanbul in 2013, this not only led to the curatorial implosion of the Istanbul Biennial, but also to a temporary reconfiguration of the local art scene, later to be thwarted by a brutal backlash on the part of the authorities. In early 2020, a couple of the activists linked to the Gezi Uprising were charged with treason and threatened by prosecutors with life imprisonment; the action was fortunately dismissed by a court that finally acquitted the accused (duvaR.english 2020). Experimentation with institutions themselves, like SALT in Istanbul, had emerged before in the wake of the Gezi uprising. Vasif Kortun, then a director of SALT, recollects this moment:

> I consider myself a good institutional person. I know how institutions work and can push them into the next century, probably, but what really woke me up was the intelligence of the outside and the intelligence at Gezi – left to their own devices they were re-making the world. In light of these developments, our role as producers had to be completely rethought. SALT opened in 2011 and I was hoping that by 2016 or 2017 we would be in a position where we could find new effective tools to transform the institution into a commons: a new kind of commons that would take on the running of the institution in a different way (Kortun 2017: 138).

If art strikes aren't exactly strikes, and art boycotts aren't exactly boycotts, but art occupations are definitely occupations, what connects them? They are each an example of what I call → productive withdrawals, and all are exercises in the tricky art of → herding cats. Cats do not recognise shepherding by an external authority, but rather swarm together and act in accordance with their shared interests, testifying to the capacity of 'independent' creatives to wage long-term → struggles. By acting upon their own → interdependence, they turn atomised and fruitless networking (→ N is for networker) into a weapon. Just as they are able to proceed, gradually, from → independence to → interdependence, they might be able to turn mere socialising into a cradle of socialism.

During the lockdowns of the COVID-19 crisis, every middle-class home became an office, adopting the same routines that projectarians have practised for decades. The projectarian will often transform a home into an office, with help of personal computers, mobile devices, spreadsheets, text editors, social media interfaces, email clients and newsletters. These technologies are indispensable components of the → assemblages that sustain ultra-mobile and scattered lifestyles. In March 2020, they formed an essential infrastructure for most of the sectors dealing with administration, communication and education.

For projectarians, though, the home office is not an exception brought about by the pandemic, but rather their daily bread. Their → enthusiastic engagement in projects is amplified by the informal character of circulation, as projects disrupt the boundaries between previously separated areas of life and work, both in spatial and temporal terms. Projects, after all, are there to link what used to be unlinked. They nullify the differences between time at home, time at the office, playtime and working hours. As Boltanski and Chiapello write:

> In a connexionist world, the distinction between private life and professional life tends to diminish (…) It then becomes difficult to make a distinction between the time of private life and the time of professional life, between dinners with friends and business lunches, between affective bonds and useful relationships (Boltanski and Chiapello 2005: 155).

Networked apparatuses enable projectarians to merge formal and informal activities, facilitating their freedom to act independently of the temporal regimes characteristic of more regulated working environments. But there are downsides to this freedom. Working from their home offices, projectarians are always at work, never only professional nor entirely private. Working with friends might seem a blessing at first. One did not have to 'grow up', as growing up in industrial societies was understood as getting adjusted to the great divide – you were 'yourself' at home, and a mere 'functionary' or a 'worker' at your office or at an assembly line. In artistic circulation, these identities are all scrambled up, as everybody is expected not only to be always → enthusiastically engaged, but also to → capitalise on friendships and intimacy. The walls protecting one's inner self dissolve, penetrated by personal computers, mobile phones and social media, not to mention all those parties or semi-formal meetings where artists and curators talk business and plot yet another project with their (current) friends. Friendships, when integrated into the cycles of frenetic production, can be as temporary as the projects they sustain. Not only does one meet throngs of new people every season, most of them really cool and friendly, but one also has to spend a lot of time catering to these transitory relationships while travelling from one project to another. Moreover, friendships when instrumentalised for the sake of executing projects are the perfect tools of distributed → control. It is very hard to object to your friends when they encourage you to work yet another weekend or press on with yet another exciting project. Especially in the world of flows, projects offer a temptingly easy way of maintaining relationships over time, as they are focal points in distributed personal portfolios.

Thankfully, it is possible to take a break, even from the home office. There are moments of respite to be cherished with friends, even if everyone has other projects on their busy agendas. One can have a pint, walk and talk, or just take it easy. With long-term friends one can engage in the most ambitious projects out there, as usually long-term friendships and comradery are the true → support structures that one can rely on in a time of peril (→ H is for herding cats).

I is for...

I   is for independence

Artistic networks have a tendency to sustain an illusion of individual independence, closely connected with the experience of ultra-mobile and flexible agents, such as supposedly independent curators. In the years before the COVID-19 crisis, independent curators used to imagine themselves as unburdened by long-term affiliations, moving freely around the globe, counting on the network to provide. And it comes as no surprise as typically they assemble their projects by pooling together institutions and people, skills, resources and accumulated knowledge. In order to secure access to these networks, independent agents do not have to even own anything except their own reputations (→ C is for capital). This illusion of independent mobility is encapsulated in such concepts as *radicant*, coined by Nicholas Bourriaud to denote art made in today's global context as a reaction against standardisation and commercialism, and named after a plant that can place its roots in many different places at the same time and is able to freely shift between them (Bourriaud 2009). However, a *radicant* is not a figure of altermodernity, as he would wish for, but rather a manifestation of the → curatorial mode of production, as rootless as the flow of financial capital that it emulates. The assumed independence of cultural and intellectual operators had already been demystified by Zygmunt Bauman, when he criticised early globalisation as a movement that uproots people and embeds social hierarchies in differentials of mobility, thereby privileging a class of ultra-mobile operators to the peril of more localised producers (Bauman 1998). The uncritical admiration of independent mobility is even more ungrounded, as most global populations are constrained by walls and uncrossable borders, and unrestrained mobility is a privilege reserved for a tiny few (→ B is for (no) borders), that leave an enormous ecological and social → footprint.

It is not surprising that critical curators, such as Maria Lind, disagreed with this ideology of independent mobility and engaged in creating glocal institutions (such as Tensta Konsthalle, a small institution placed at the outskirts of Stockholm) that mediate between the global networks of contemporary art and the local context. Instead of being everywhere and nowhere, they decided to put down their roots and tend to the growth of institutions that contribute to the development of interconnected ecosystems composed from local and artistic communities (Lind 2018).

The independence of ultra-mobile operators is a socially grounded illusion in two ways. All independents are dependent on the network at large, on all those platforms and databases that, as Lane Relyea argues, are indispensable elements of the networked architecture (Relyea 2017). Biennales, institutions, collectives and → patainstitutions function as platforms, to which independents can easily plug in. Their projects are working as interfaces that temporarily stabilise flows and mobilise people and resources. On a more fundamental level, all the independents are dependent on accessing the flow of interchangeable → opportunities, their seemingly unbridled mobility constrained by the shifting architecture of gates and metropolitan corridors that deny access to all but a privileged few.

Travelling with light luggage is an exhilarating experience of mobility with an artsy clout, a poverty jet-set of late capitalist *flaneurs*. Regardless of its → footprint and long-term risks, independence gives a momentary kick that drags people along, doing for artistic circulation what → Artyzol does for the art world. And for this reason, a constructive critique of artistic circulation needs to unmake fixations with atomised independence, surmounting it with the notion of → interdependent connectivity, grounding individual autonomy within collective → support structures.

I	is for instituting the commons

Looking for the commons, or our collectively shared resources, both cultural and physical, in fluid artistic networks brings to mind the proverb where one cannot see the wood for the trees. The common is lost in the thicket of fleeting projects, scrambled trajectories, competitive institutions, large events and even larger egos. One does not see the commons behind the shifting horizon of most recent fashion trends and consecutive → turns. But none of this would have been possible if not for the common that underpins every single networked activity. Any project, any connection, any trajectory, any art work or any artistic celebrity rests on the common resources that are generated and reproduced by the labour of the hiving multitudes that partake in, maintain, expand and propel circulation (→ L is for labour of love, → P is for pollination). Artistic circulation is a microcosm of the capitalist economy at large, which, as Negri and Hardt argue, extracts the common at a historically unprecedented rate (Hardt and Negri 2009: 175–84). As Sylvia Federici argues, the commons is currently being exploited to fuel capitalist growth:

> Development planners and policymakers have discovered that, under proper conditions, a collective management of natural resources can be more efficient and less prone to conflict than privatization, and that commons can be made to produce very well for the market.(...) Capitalist accumulation is structurally dependent on the free appropriation of immense quantities of labor and resources that must appear as externalities to the market, like the unpaid domestic work that women have provided, upon which employers have relied for the reproduction of the workforce (Federici 2017: 381).

The commons that she refers to is genealogically connected to the medieval commons, a system of collective usership of land embedded in the feudal legal and social structures, and this legacy is directly referenced by other scholars of the commons (Compare: An Architektur, De Angelis and Stavrides 2010; De Angelis 2003; Gibson-Graham 2006;

Hardt and Negri 2009; Sevilla-Buitrago 2012). Just as a side note – Negri and Hardt refer mainly to 'the common', possibly to distinguish it from the medieval social model, other scholars typically use traditional form – 'the commons' – and in this book, I will use both forms interchangeably as I am not particularly invested in this debate.

According to Massimo de Angelis, the commons epitomise new ways of organising radically horizontal and democratic politics in the age of network capitalism (An Architektur, De Angelis, and Stavrides 2010; De Angelis 2003). The commons propose alternative, non-competitive, non-commodified and not-marketed (i.e. direct) means of organising social production. The commons is under constant threat from the external and internal forces that aim at exploiting and enclosing them on a regular basis. The commons are organised around communities of commoners, who operate according to various rules which protect them against enclosures and individual egoism, securing the sustenance of a resource in common, as described by Elinor Ostrom, who was awarded the Nobel prize in economics in 2009 for her research on the commons (Ostrom 1990). According to de Angelis, such communities do not need to be localised and can operate in the trans-local space organised similar to the social movements demanding other, better globalisation. The commons thus understood can instigate continued acts of commoning that involve not only socialising and using shared resources and spaces, but also establishing the modes of democratic self-governance needed to maintain them.

But to understand artistic circulation, one needs another, more general, vision of the common. For Hardt and Negri, the common is not only a concrete resource or a space; they are more interested in identifying the common that underpins capitalist production at large: the riches of the Earth, like air, water, minerals and plants; the pooled knowledge that underwrites technological progress; the networks of human communication that anchors the value of Internet giants; the distributed movements of biopolitical labour, affects and desires that construct any metropolis as a place for living and for business alike; and the care labour that maintains it all. They argue that extracting such forms of the common is indispensable for the advanced capitalist economy in its pursuit of profit (Hardt and Negri 2009: 175–84).

And precisely this relationship between the generalised forms of common and capitalist mechanisms of extraction comes to mind when we analyse a fundamental paradox of the artistic circulation, repeated throughout this book. Even though the globalised system of contemporary art is grounded in social cooperation, its effects are privatised as every producer moves between projects as an atomised individual, whilst larger players → <u>trawl</u> values thus generated for their own benefit. On the one hand, most cultural producers face precarity, exclusion and poverty. On the other, some of them enjoy unprecedented levels of freedom and mobility, while institutions or larger events are able to reproduce and enrich themselves. In other words: even though all of them build the common, only some individuals or institutions are in position to extract it for their own benefit.

My ambition here is to move beyond a merely analytical mode of debunking evils of this world. The argument is that the neoliberal arrangements of artistic circulation can be surmounted through social struggles waged by art workers, who reclaim, instigate and maintain the common owing to → <u>productive withdrawals</u>, positive valorisation of the → <u>labour of love</u> and → <u>pollination</u>, by establishing → <u>patainstitu-tions</u> and → <u>support structures</u>, acting in accordance with their own → <u>interdependence</u>.

The process of creating the common is distinguished by what the common does and not by what it is. I deliberately avoid discussing the institutional forms that can potentially emerge in the process of constitut-ing the common. Instead, I prefer to trace actually existing, progressive responses to the tensions embedded in artistic circulation, tensions that revolve around the fundamental conflict between socialised labour and privatised → <u>capital</u> and that address the internal contradictions of artistic networks, which can either devolve into the toxic pulp of → <u>opportunism</u>, → <u>cynicism</u> and → <u>fear</u>, or be challenged in the process of social coopera-tion and political action.

To identify where, how and if the common can be instituted, following in Marx's footsteps, let's delve into the abode of networked, cultural production to identify the conflicts that erupt at the nexuses where social labour is extracted as privatised capital. The resistance provoked in the extraction process is socially productive, because it can prompt – under the right circumstances – the circulation of art to become a form of the common accessible to the many, rather than the few. Follow the conflict, one might say, and gain a more acute understanding of what looms at the end of it, thus anchoring theory in social praxis.

To understand this process of commoning, another paradoxical figure can be evoked of the entrepreneur of the multitude, described by Negri and Hardt:

> It may well seem incongruous for us to celebrate entrepreneurship when neoliberal ideologues prattle on ceaselessly about its virtues, advocating the creation of an entrepreneurial society, bowing down in awe to the brave capitalist risk takers, and exhorting us all, from kindergarten to retirement, to become entrepreneurs of our own lives. We know such heroic tales of capitalist entrepreneurship are just empty talk, but if you look elsewhere you will see that there is plenty of entrepreneurial activity around today – organizing new social combinations, inventing new forms of social cooperation, generating democratic mechanisms for our access to, use of, and participation in decision-making about the common. It is important to claim the concept of entrepreneurship for our own. Indeed one of the central tasks of political thought is to struggle over concepts, to clarify or transform their meaning. Entrepreneurship serves as the hinge between the forms of the multitude's cooperation in social production and its assembly in political terms (Hardt and Negri 2017: XVIII–XIX).

Negri and Hardt subvert the neoliberal concept of entrepreneurship to talk about the entrepreneurial productivity of the multitude that is at the core of the common. What's interesting here, though, are the possible ways of socialising the means and fruits of networked production (even though it is not a straightforward task, considering the complexity of the → apparatuses at play). The entrepreneurship of the multitude challenges the → entrepreneurs of the self, unpicking the dependency of an individualised producer on the tenuous flow of interchangeable opportunities. An example of how this is done is provided by boycotts, occupations and art strikes. In the course of → productive withdrawals or other → struggles, → art workers enact opportunism of a different sort, that is, the tactical seizing of opportunities for the sake of collective actions, something that Michel de Certeau discusses in the context of social movements and the urban guerrilla in his *Practice of Everyday Life* (Certeau 1984). When independent artists or curators become → interdependent, they not only seize opportunities for themselves, but also create them for others (just like users do in the context of usership, as described by Stephen Wright (Wright 2013)). In this sense, opportunities become socialised and various semi-open structures evolve, securing access on a cooperative and not competitive basis. This notion applies to countless occupied art centres, as well as to artist-run spaces, international networks and cooperatives, too numerous to even be listed (Argyropoulou 2018; Baravalle 2018b; Basekamp Group & Friends 2013; Byrne 2016; Byrne, Medina and Saviotti 2018; Critical Practice 2011; Dobkowska and Łukomski 2020; Isola Art Center 2013; MTL Collective 2018; Sowa 2009; Spinelli 2018). These collectives entrepreneurially collate resources, secure access to a space, generate willingness and enthusiasm in people, and then share these among their friends, comrades and associates, thus socialising access to opportunities.

What is the qualitative difference between this mode of access and the one of individualised → opportunism? Socialising opportunities means that access is not mediated by privatised → capital but rather granted due to a shared engagement in the necessary social labour, which is an open arrangement per definition, one in which every → art worker is invited to take part, and wherein only their willingness to engage in a process of commoning is a factor determining their access to the common. This engagement can take various forms. Sometimes it is about occupying, building and maintaining the space, as evidenced by the study of a group process conducted by the Macao in Milan – 69,300 hours were collectively spent refurbishing the Macao building to turn it into a cultural centre (Cossu 2015; Cossu and d'Ovidio 2017; Spinelli 2018). In other cases, like in Critical Practice, an open research cluster associated with Chelsea College in London, group members have organised collective processes based on shared → enthusiasm, enacting, as Marsha Bradfield argues, hybrid forms of 'para/pata:institutionalism' (Bradfield 2020). They collated their scarce resources to carry out collective projects such as *#Transacting. The Market of Values* organised by the cluster in 2016, after five years of researching the social modes of evaluation (Cummings, Bradfield and McDonnell 2018).

Such institutional forms are open because the more art workers engage, the more efficient they become. The perpetual rhythm of securing, creating and sharing opportunities is crucial for sustaining any nascent institution of the common, described by Gerald Raunig in the case of Teatro Valle (Raunig 2014), a former theatre building in Rome, squatted in 2011 to become an occupied social centre of art. In this context, a group of Italian art-activists formulated a programme of arts as 'belle commune', i.e. the common goods, that should be accessed and shared by all, the status of which should be enshrined in the constitution. As they wrote in the preamble to the Statute of Teatro Valle:

> On June 14th 2011, the day after a referendum victory in Italy, which prevented the privatization of water in favour of it becoming a 'common good', we occupied Teatro Valle – Rome's oldest functioning theatre – returning it to the community. In so doing we have undertaken a process aimed towards the legal recognition of Teatro Valle as a 'Common': i.e. a common 'land' or entity, owned by all. The right to declare something as a 'Common' is enshrined in article 43 of Italy's constitution (Teatro Valle 2012).

Another example, this time from Northern Italy, is the Isola Art Centre. Across its long history, the Centre has evolved from an art centre established in a squatted factory in the centre of Milan, to a community garden, Isola Pepe Verde, and in the interim taking a more fluid form as a dispersed art centre (Isola Art Center 2013). The longevity of this initiative, in spite of its structural precarity, was due, as argued by Aria Spinelli, to the persistent openness of its organisational form. It welcomed new generations of artists-activists, who engaged in the institutional process by utilising opportunities and generating new ones that their successors then took over and continued to develop (Spinelli 2018).

The institutional forms of the common thus engendered are as diverse as the forms of life of the multitude. This diversity is mirrored by the multiplicity of terms used to denote these initiatives, as people talk about monster-, mock-, pata-, conspirational-, exodus- and alter-institutions (→ P is for patainstitutions). It is possible, though, that the institutions in question will not be single institutions at all. Just as wasps and orchids – in the account of Gilles Deleuze and Felix Guattari – form new assemblages, mutualising not only their habits, but also their beings, so, too, can the common be instituted as interconnected assemblies of collectives, initiatives, public institutions, individuals and affinity groups that sustain the common by reversing the expropriations of artistic circulation, mutualising gains and seizing opportunities.

Even if they take diverse forms, these institutions of the common share an enemy. I do not, even for a second, presume that a university-affiliated group of researchers is exactly the same as an activist-run and occupied space. But even if they are not identical, they often share political affinities with the political → struggles of the left, insofar as they find themselves challenged by similar systemic pressures. This is another important advantage of dialectical analysis, which allows us to understand systemic pressures as political opportunities, in that they bring disparate groups together to form otherwise unlikely alliances of resistance. A progressive university cluster is no less exposed to → neoliberal assaults on social welfare than a collective located in the midst of gentrifying city. For this reason more often than not such clusters tend to align themselves in progressive constellations. In this sense, paradoxically, one of the factors holding the greatest potential for different initiatives to come together on an international scale is the global return of fascism (→ A is for Anti-fascist Year) and the rekindling of → neoliberalism as disaster capitalism. In order to effectively struggle against them, the → support structures engendered in the common will need to become organisational platforms for what artist Jonas Staal describes as propaganda art for the twenty-first century (Staal 2019). In this context, it is important to underline that the common is not to be thought of at the micro-scale of a small collective, a cosy activist group, or a passing occupation. The common does not have to be based on principles of immediacy and direct contact, previously seen as its essential characteristics and since decried as 'folk politics' by leftist accelerationists (Srnicek and Williams 2016). In fact, some of the most interesting experiments in commoning unfold at the threshold between social movements and politicised institutions of contemporary art, which try to become common by decolonising themselves, feminising their structures, becoming socially useful, establishing links with their constituents and deviating from institutional norms (Aikens et al. 2016; Bishop and Perjovschi 2014; Byrne et al. 2018; Choi and Kraus 2017; Esche 2010; Hudson 2015; Keil, Stokfiszewski, and Adamiecka - Sitek 2019; Petrešin-Bachelez 2017). Instead of shunning politics, they become political, establish alliances, form coalitions and propagate more equalitarian, democratic and inclusive social order – using a mixture of curatorial, artistic and activist means. In other words, they try to build the common, instead of exploiting it. It is obviously a very long march. Success is far from being guaranteed, and definitely requires political intervention on a grand scale, to which radical projectarians can contribute with the modest means at their disposal by forming progressive coalitions with other likeminded social agents.

I   is for interdependence

Just as the early decades of the twenty-first century were an era of independent curators and artists, they will be followed by a period when interdependent curatorial and artistic practices will emerge, solidify and thrive. This might sound like an expression of unfounded hope, in dark times marked by a pandemic, economic crisis and political obscurantism. Nevertheless, we must hope that interdependence is not a whimsical delusion, but rather a firm foundation for a coherent theoretical and practical programme. I follow here in the footsteps of Temporary Services, a → patainstitution from Chicago, who almost a decade ago advocated for a move from independence to interdependence, their arguments based upon practical experience of building a shared, collective space instead of running a typical, 'independent' artistic studio (Temporary Services 2012). In the context of pandemic crisis, the shift to interdependent cultural practices was advocated by Zdenka Badovinac, for whom interdependence is embedded in the ethics of unconditional care and in the tradition of cross-national solidarity (Badovinac 2020).

The very notion of interdependence is certainly nothing new, discussed by such feminist scholars as Judith Butler and Isabel Lorey, who shared a view of interdependence as an amelioration of the volatility of precariousness (Butler 2015; Lorey 2015). In feminist economics, the concept of interdependence was developed almost two decades ago by J.K. Gibson-Graham as a foundational idea of their community economies, a programme of 'imagining and enacting alternatives for noncapitalist economies' (Gibson-Graham and Cameron 2003: 152). Gibson-Graham emphasise that the fundamental interdependence of economic subsystems, agents or practices needs to be recognised and acted upon in order to constitute more egalitarian, mutually beneficial economic systems, based on solidarity and cooperation (Gibson-Graham 2006: 79–86). Thus, interdependence is an instance of → radical pragmatism, a way to re-approach the double bind of → circulation, where ideologically framed independence conceals either privilege (→ O is for one percent) or → precarity.

Reflecting upon the viability of interdependent theory and practice, I cannot stop thinking about June 2019, a moment from a seemingly different era, when interdependence was floated as a unifying concept for an international network of feminist economists, cooperativists and artists who rallied for a summit in Northern Italy. The workshop was organised by the Community Economies Research Network and was hosted by a cooperative of radical social designers, La Foresta, in a small cottage in the Italian Alps. Over a sunny weekend, a group of feral traders, community gardeners, feminist economists, social geographers, drink producers, social designers and architects gathered to discuss ways of reclaiming the economy to nourish their communities. Out of collective brainstorming, a concept emerged: we decided to formalise this shared affinity in the form of an international network known as The Interdependence. With the aim of subverting the capitalist formats of enterprise, like a limited liability company (Ltd) or a corporation (Inc.), we came up with a new organisational form of the interdependent (Idt.), with its own charter and ethos, catering to an ongoing process of institutional experimentation with diverse economies, leaning on the legacy of cooperatives (Coop.). An early version of that definition of the interdependent was written in the summer of 2019 by feminist economists Katharine McKinnon and Katherine Gibson:

> The Interdependence is envisioned as a way to bring to the surface the ubiquity of community economy activities by inviting affiliated organisations to add a mock business identity to their organisations name: to use 'Idt.' (for Interdependent) instead of Ltd. or Inc.. The 'Idt.' would signal membership of 'The Interdependence' – an identifier that could connect and make visible the scale of community economy initiatives. The interdependence is a response to the naysayers who respond to our examples of community economy practices and initiatives by saying "that's nice, but is it scalable?" In response we can say ubiquity is our scale … join The Interdependence … a multi-local contagion.

Currently, the Idt. is being formalised as an international network of likeminded initiatives, with its own site and identity. Moreover, the Idt. – as an organisational model and an expression of intent – sets its focus on the economic foundations of self-organisation, which is far too often overtly reliant on underpaid and voluntary labour (→ P is for poor). An exemplary solution of interdependence in action is offered by Company Drinks, an artistic enterprise based in Barking and Dagenham in London, established by an artist, activist and entrepreneur Kathrin Böhm (discussed in the entry → M is for mutualising).

Adopting the notion of interdependency for the realm of contemporary art, we can reimagine modes of thinking and acting that move beyond obsessively individualistic pseudo-independency. This conceptual and practical shift opens up new avenues for interdependent curators and artists to embed their practices within the organisational ecosystems engendered and maintained by → art workers, collectives and institutions, to which interdependent cultural producers owe their allegiance. This shift of optics – from an individual to an ecosystem – has ethical and political consequences, as art workers cease to be invested solely in 'their own' trajectories, but are rather indebted to others, with whom they share bonds of mutual obligations. Such interdependent practice recognises and fosters systems of social collaboration that always underpin artistic circulation, but that are otherwise exploited in pursuit of individual profits. The notion of interdependence also suggests such values like loyalty, empathy, firmness of convictions and devotion to a cause (→ S is for struggles), at odds with the political and ethical flexibility of the networked world, where convictions are peddled, ideals swapped and loyalties transactional.

K   is for...

K   is for (no) kids

One of the most glaring examples of the inequality prompted by the → winner-takes-it-all economy is the gender-related injustice that pervades in both higher echelons of the commercial art world and the daily grind of circulation. Though students of artistic schools are mainly female, only few are commercially represented, feature in collections, or score record auction prices (Fard 2017; Judah 2019). Male artists (if they manage to win the competition where most are doomed to fail) tend to celebrate their success as if it were owed solely to their innate talents, and not related to their gendered privilege. At the same time, the feminised workforce of educators, facilitators and assistants is symbolically downgraded, due to the structurally imposed invisibility of the → labour of love.

This problem is endemic not only to the commercial art market. As evidenced by the report on gender imbalances in Polish academies of fine art (Gromada et al. 2015), female students still tend to be less promoted, their access to more prestigious opportunities is limited, and they are often put down and discriminated against by male professors. Due to highly gendered role models, they are also less prone to extreme displays of confidence when it comes to presenting their projects or promoting themselves, the vices almost 'indispensable' in competitive networks that gratify → entrepreneurial artists who pursue their own artistic careers at all cost.

The problem gets even starker after young artists graduate and decide to have children. Hettie Judah argues that motherhood is taboo in the art world (Judah 2019; 2020b), as having kids is often related to a long pause in artistic careers, from which only few women are able to recover fully. If there are kids, women artists are usually more willing to accept a larger share of familial responsibilities than their male partners, at the cost of individual career. Women often experience problems with combining studio-based artistic practice with tasks undertaken in the domestic sphere, and these are only amplified in the → expanded field of art and artistic circulation. Because artists have to move from one project to another, and often between different places, these types of careers are fundamentally intermittent, a condition described vividly by Angela Dimitrakaki:

> The mobility requirement embedded in artistic labor at present (including retreats and the ubiquitous 'residency' culture) is in direct conflict with the work of family-focused social reproduction still expected from women—and where women are single mothers, entire 'components' of the contemporary art work culture (such as residencies) may become impossible. Although we lack statistical figures, many women artists opt (as in the past) to not have children so as not be homebound—and this can apply more in cases where artistic labor (and its output) involves weeks or months spent in 'real' social relations encountered outside the home, the studio, one's town, or one's country (Dimitrakaki 2018).

Typically, women artists feel more obliged to perform the labour of caring, and thus are less eager to → apply for projects, residencies, positions or jobs abroad. The gender-based inequality does not only involve formal aspects of making and applying for projects, but also or even especially the informal, social life that is indispensable for making it in the worlds of art (commercial and non-commercial alike). Hettie Judah, whose analysis is based on numerous accounts of artists-mothers, points out that:

> Few aspects of the art world better illustrate its power structures than the persistence of the witching hours, the six to eight pm private views, during which, artists, gallerists, collectors and the press socialise, exchange gossip and do business. Making art can be a solitary occupation and these periods away from the studio, building and maintaining a network are important. Spending time with a peer group has an impact on an artist's career: this is an industry that relies to a large degree on word of mouth, and that legendary, intangible quality of 'buzz.' Artists who are respected by their peers will often in turn attract the attention of dealers and collectors. Out of sight risks being out of mind. To put it simply, six to eight pm is when artists come into contact with their industry. For parents of nursery and primary school aged children, six to eight pm are witching hours of

a different kind, occupied by the immovable trinity of supper, bath and bedtime (Judah 2019: 16).

Attending yet another opening or all-night art-bash might have an impact on the professional prospects in the art world, where inequalities accumulate over time. They are even more insidious, as the processual character of this inequality is hard to grasp and yet not any less dramatic in its outcomes. In highly competitive networks, failure does not result from one failed selection, rejected application, missed deadline, biennale or a party, but rather dozens of them, in which one missed opportunity makes finding a new one in the future less likely, thus creating a chain of failure that drags down personalised trajectories. This is exclusion-by-a-thousand-little-cuts.

It is not surprising that some of the very well recognised female artists, like Marina Abramović, decided not to have kids, publicly declaring that

> I have no husband, no family, I'm totally free (...) In my opinion that's the reason why women aren't as successful as men in the art world. There's plenty of talented women. Why do men take over the important positions? It's simple. Love, family, children – a woman doesn't want to sacrifice all of that (Marina Abramović quoted in Neuendorf, 2016).

It should also be said that in artistic circulation it is totally normalised not to have kids, and to establish a variety of non-standard relations, experimenting beyond the model of the typical, heterosexual, nuclear family. It is extremely important in societies exposed to authoritarian backlash, such as Poland (which at the end of 2020 enacted a total ban on abortion, in an abhorrent feat of right-wing ideology), which aims at casting women solely in the roles of child-bearers and mothers. But, as Angela Dimitrakaki argues, the problem with the → neoliberal arrangement of networks is an actual absence of choice, disguised as free will:

> if an employer in an 'advanced' economy of liberal reproductive laws tells a pregnant woman to get an abortion or she will lose her job, the woman would be expected to take the case to a court of law. If an artist has so internalized the production requirements of her profession as to exclude the possibility of pregnancy, it is seen as the free choice of a liberated woman. Women artists can believe that they are making such a free choice (practicing the feminist 'refusal

to procreate') as liberated women. Yet such choice can be pure ideology – indeed, an ideology necessary for submitting to the demands of the labor market as organized in capitalism, even (as in the case of art) wages may well be absent and the woman is asked to practice self-management towards the promise of procuring income (Dimitrakaki 2018).

The Free/Slow University of Warsaw's study of the conditions of artistic labour in Poland evidenced the practical consequences of this ideology. When asked about the causes of inequality experienced in contemporary art, only a tiny minority of respondents identified gender as a decisive factor (Kozłowski, Sowa and Szreder 2015). These results were rather surprising, at odds with everyday observations and other studies alike. They were even revoked during consecutive research phases of the same study, as artists participating in qualitative group interviews presented a much more familiar vision – of the art world ridden with gender-based inequality, just as described above (Figiel 2015). This apparent contradiction can be partially explained by the make-up of the research sample. As the study focused on people who were actively in circulation through making projects and participating in exhibitions, they proved to be a very specific cohort – young (90 percent were under 35 years old), and childless (only 15 percent had any kids). It is telling that another factor of inequality – which is age – was also totally ignored by the respondents, as almost none of them identified youthfulness as a condition of possibility of their own participation. But in competitive circulation, which is permeated by the cult of youthful enthusiasm and constant mobility, having kids or getting old might become a first step in the downward tumble to → exclusion. It looks as if the bodily matters – like age and gender, but also being fit and healthy – that actually restrict or grant access are ideologically supressed to sustain the illusion of openness and access.

L   is for...

L   is for labour of love

Labour of love is a key term in the feminist critique of economy, covering the care labour and work of maintenance that keeps the economy going. It is mostly conducted by women and just as often remains unpaid and undervalued (Federici 1975; 2012; Finch and Groves 1983; Gibson-Graham and Cameron 2003; Weeks 2011;). It also informs many of the most acute analyses of contemporary art (Child, Reckitt and Richards 2017; Child 2019; Dimitrakaki 2013; 2018; Kunst 2015; Stakemeier and Vishmidt 2016), due to its theoretical potential and political viability. As Angela Dimitrakaki argues, this cross-usage owes to the similarities between housework and artwork, as both are unrecognised as productive work by mainstream economies, both implicate emotional and imaginative investments and both are rarely paid (Dimitrakaki 2018).

One of the first artists who consequently applied this analysis to the realm of artistic labour was Mierle Laderman Ukeles, who in her *Manifesto of Maintenance Art* (1969) explored the structural similarities between the work of woman artists and the daily maintenance work of cleaners, sanitation workers, janitors, nurses and carers. In her manifesto, she asked a very pointed question: 'The sourball of every *revolution*: *after the revolution*, who's going to pick up the garbage on Monday morning' (Ukeles 2014, italics by author). Her response as both an artist and a maintenance worker was to act in solidarity with other maintenance workers and become an artist-in-residence of the Sanitation Department of New York City.

Following this diagnosis, one needs to analyse the economic underpinnings and reputational hierarchies of artistic circulation by acknowledging the different types of work involved. On the one hand, there is the authorial work of artists or writers, often underpaid, but just as often still considered as prestigious – or at least credited. And then comes the work of facilitators, fabricators, supporters, educators, that is just as hard, just as underpaid and yet often also not-as-prestigious, unrecognised and uncredited. The underbelly of artistic production has been brilliantly analysed by Danielle Child in her book *Working Aesthetics*, where she discusses the fabrication of the grand works of classical land art, the production offices supporting Young British Art and the recent rebellions of this reproductive, aesthetical labour, related to the ecological movements of the 2010s (Child 2019). This anonymous labour of love, performed by the mostly unpaid and invisible inhabitants of the → dark matter of art, maintains the infrastructure of artistic circulation, enables the realisation of projects and supports individual trajectories.

One example of how this operates in practice is George Yúdice's case study of InSite, a large public art event that was organised at the USA/Mexican border in the late 1990s and early 2000s (Yúdice 2003). Like feminist scholars before him, George Yúdice applies the notion of the labour of love to analyse the production structures of this project. As he says:

> staff members also make an enormous personal investment into the projects and the artists, including ferrying them to sites and suppliers, having long discussions with them into the wee hours, and investing the unmeasurable labor of love (of art) and the labor of producing process. This investment includes critical work that does not always surface in the exhibition materials like the catalogue and guide (Yúdice 2003: 327–28).

The importance of this type of labour usually remains unnoticed as no authorial credits are attributed to the support personnel, a category proposed by Howard Becker to denote groups of people whose labour is socially necessary for the execution of any artistic endeavour, but who are not regarded as authors of a given project or piece of art (i.e. technicians, assistants, etc.) (Becker 1984: 17). The depreciation of support labour harks back to the art field-specific system of beliefs, which sanctifies authorial positions as imbued with social value (Bourdieu 1996: 166–73). The Free/Slow University of Warsaw's research into the conditions of artistic labour clearly confirms this. When respondents were asked to indicate who contributed most of their time to a given project, all professional groups equally named artists and support personnel. However, when respondents were asked who contributed most to the success of an exhibition and should be honoured as such, only artists and curators were named (Kozłowski, Sowa and Szreder 2015: 208–34).

This ideologically skewed assessment was voiced by everyone, without any significant differences between artists, curators or assistants.

But in project-based production, like site-specific commissions, public art projects or any artistic endeavours in the → expanded field, support personnel not only organise and support, but also participate in the creative exchange (not that it should matter, as the distinction between 'creative' and 'uncreative' are also entirely arbitrary). This situation was very convincingly analysed by Sara Buraya, Paula Moliner and Manuela Pedron who wrote about the exhibition *Really Useful Knowledge*, organised in the Museum of Queen Sofia in Madrid in 2014 (already mentioned in the entry → B is for belt-tightening). As the exhibition required advanced negotiations between the museum and social movements, whose activist knowledge was to be brought into the institution, the engagement of facilitators (usually disregarded as mere 'assistants') was paramount to its success (Buraya, Moliner and Pedron 2018). If not for their diplomatic skills, knowledge and contacts with social movements, this exercise would have utterly failed. Responding to this challenge, Buraya, Molina and Pedron propose a new 'ethics of coordination' which requires a transformation of institutional viewpoints to attribute far greater value to an unrecognised interpersonal labour of care, negotiation and maintenance.

Similar exercises in institutional transformation were undertaken by the team at the CASCO Art Institute in Utrecht. Engaging in a long action research process with artist-researcher Annette Krauss, they transformed the internal division of labour to bridge the gap between highly regarded creative labour and the usually disregarded labour of maintenance, trying to share even such menial tasks as cleaning the office and involving everyone in the programmatic activities of CASCO (CASCO 2018). In the process, they actualised the legacy of Mierle Laderman Ukeles, not only citing her *Manifesto of Maintenance Art*, but also re-enacting her iconic performance *Washing/Tracks/Maintenance: Outside* (1973).

The work of art educators is similarly undervalued and invisible, as explained by feminist curator Helena Reckitt:

> Institutionally, art educators have been treated as if they occupy the lowest ranks of curatorial and programming teams. This hierarchy no doubt stems from educators' primary contact with the 'unschooled'

general public, and their association with reproductive, rather than productive, labour, which doesn't leave a tangible – or saleable – trace. That art education has historically been a female-dominated field, and thus devalued, can't be accidental, either! (Helena Reckitt in: Child, Reckitt and Richards 2017: 156).

The low status, diminished earnings and → precarity of the labourers of love came to the fore in the context of the 2020 global pandemic, when art educators, facilitators and technicians were first in the line to have their contracts terminated. Many larger institutions, faced with lockdowns and budget cuts, decided to make savings by laying off their frontline staff (Steinhauer 2020). In a feat of institutional hypocrisy, some institutions did not miss an opportunity to signal their own virtue by organising exhibitions lauding frontline workers of the pandemic – nurses, carers, doctors – while at the same time busily axing their own workforces. Hettie Judah commented on the exhibition *Everyday Heroes* that was opened in September 2020 in the Southbank Centre in London:

> Cognitive dissonance infects our cultural sector. Turner prize-winner Tai Shani wrote blisteringly this week about the 'bewildering ethical paradoxes of the art world' in which an 'expansionist, market and state-driven managerial approach' is cloaked in a facade of liberal centrism [see → A is for art workers]. Southbank Centre employees are currently protesting threatened redundancies. Some 400 jobs are on the line, overwhelmingly among the organisation's lowest-paid sectors, including the very same front-facing roles celebrated in the portraits quite literally cloaking the complex's facades. It displays brass neck in the extreme for an organisation to glorify key workers so publicly at the very moment it threatens its own with redundancy (Judah 2020a).

Such cases only support the argument that the organisational grammar of contemporary art is able to accommodate any project, even ones at odd with the structural logic of hosting institutions (→ C is for curatorial mode of production). It proves that the global circulation of art remains a field of struggle, which needs to be further radicalised to correct the structural disfranchisement of the labour of love.

M is for...

M is for mutualising
(risks and economies)

Veteran freelancers never keep all their eggs in one basket. They distribute risks by always making too many applications, getting involved in too many projects, chasing too many opportunities, just in case a projects fails, an application is rejected, an opportunity falters. This urge to diversify investments seems to be a sensible strategy in the world deprived of more stable support structures. However, these safety nets are very fragile, as most projectarians, unless they were born with a silver spoon, are three months of bad luck away from impoverishment and → exclusion. The COVID-19 pandemic only proved that these seemingly reasonable strategies are built on shifting sands, as it is not possible to individually distribute systemic risks: this can be done only collectively by creating sound safety nets through coordinated, political action. However, everybody is too busy spreading their individual risks to engage in political action, running in vicious circles.

The side effect of unbridled individualism is overextension, as freelancers are spread too thin to fully commit to their projects. Every mobile → art worker has their fingers in too many pies. For example, once I found myself organising a festival in Berlin, attending a conference in London, conducting a project in Warsaw, in between writing an application to make yet another project elsewhere, and preparing research reports for my PhD. Even if short-term risks are diversified as a result, the long-term probability of mishaps, → burn-outs and → precarity rises exponentially.

Only collective strategies of mutualisation can work effectively, ideally at a systemic level, in combating the → neoliberal individualisation of responsibility. But even on a micro scale, people can get together and establish support structures, cooperatives, associations and other forms of radical → patainstitution that would support them in time of need. Responding to the conundrum of the need to de-individualise systemic risks, Angela McRobbie advocates for establishing radical social enterprises that in order to sustain themselves have to diversify their operations, reaching outside of the stereotypically understood field of art and its reputational economies which only impoverish people in the long run (McRobbie 2011). Company Drinks is an example of such a radical social enterprise, located in Barking and Dagenham, in East London. Established by artist Kathrin Böhm, Company Drinks is both an artistic project and a fully-fledged company that specialises in producing drinks and cordials, delivering workshops and providing space for local community groups and artists (Böhm and Pope 2015). On the one hand, Company Drinks is exhibited and commissioned as an artistic project, partaking in the circulation of artistic idioms. On the other, it is embedded in other economic circuits, distributing drinks, providing services to schools and cultural centres and cooperating with a local council. This rich ecosystem provides sustenance for a couple of art workers, who cooperate on securing future incomes. Company Drinks does not exist in a social vacuum: it is very well connected with other likeminded organisations across Europe, such as La Foresta / Communitas Frizante in Rovereto (Italy), Feral Trade in Bristol (UK) or AAA in Paris (France). Together, they work as part of the Communities Economies Research Network, that advocates for diversifying economic systems to empower local communities (→ I is for interdependence).

The term 'diverse economies' was itself established by the feminist economists J.K. Gibson-Graham in order to criticise and deconstruct monetised and capital-centric notions of the economy 'in which capital-ist economic activity is taken as the model for all economic activity' (Gibson-Graham 2006: 56). In introducing this term, Gibson-Graham emphasise the open-ended and complex nature of an economy, which cannot just be conflated with capital accumulation, wage labour, monetary investment, profit making and extraction of rent. These diverse economies are 'the economic landscape (...) populated by a myriad of contingent forms and interactions' (Gibson-Graham 2006: 54), encompassing both monetary and non-monetary, capitalistic and non-capitalistic, waged and non-waged, mainstream and alternative modes of transactions, types of labour and forms of resources. In the case of artistic networks, financial inputs constitute only a fraction of its economy. Equally important are human time, emotional engagement, artistic ideas, social connections, infrastructure or in-kind provisions. Consequently, both individuals and collectives utilise a variety of monetary and non-monetary support systems to realise their projects and sustain themselves.

Some of the diverse economies prompted by artistic circulation are exploitative, unequal and unsustainable. In relation to economy in general, Graham-Gibson give the feminist view that:

> on both sides of the market/non-market, paid/unpaid, capitalist/ non-capitalist divides there are opportunities for economically exploitative and emotionally oppressive conditions as well as fair and emotionally creative ones (Gibson-Graham 2006: 156).

Graham-Gibson refer to housework or childcare that can be framed as an 'economically exploitative' and yet non-market, unpaid and non-capitalist activity (→ L is for labour of love). Similarly, independent curators or artists, despite the non-commercial nature of their projects and progressive politics, might reproduce systems based on (self-)exploitation of unpaid or underpaid labour, which is an endemic problem of both artistic and academic circuits.

Quite a lot of independent undertakings are dependent on the free labour of their supporters, their willingness to cooperate, ideas and enthusiasm. Jakob Jakobsen, from Copenhagen Free University, explains in detail how the economics of such self-organised platforms function:

> The university was run within our household economy. So we didn't apply for any project funds. But, on the other hand, we didn't pay anyone, so it was no cost activity. Anyone who participated did it out of their free will and desire. The booklets we did as print on demand. So it was a minimal economy or no economy at all. Of course, we had to earn money in other ways, but we had to pay the rent anyway (Jakobsen and Pyzik 2009: 1).

The decision to rely on voluntary provisions are partially pragmatic, motivated by the lack of available resources. Sometimes it is political, purposefully avoiding exposure to grant systems and the endemic opportunism of artistic circulation. However, the main problem with such reliance on voluntary contributions is related to the systemic exploitation of free labour in the sector of contemporary art. Refusal to reimburse artists and other cultural producers is a popular strategy among both official art institutions and informal arts organisations (such as artist-run spaces, independent galleries or smaller arts institutions). Hans Abbing argues that such practices reproduce what he calls provocatively 'exploita-tion of poor artists', beneficial solely to the art establishment that feeds on a special status of the art, acquired and maintained due to the sacrifices made by artists and curators in the name of artistic autonomy (Abbing 2014: 338–40). As he argues, self-organised initiatives reproduce the structural causes of poverty, even if they do not benefit from them directly. According to Abbing, such complicity with exploitation is not excusable by the ethos of self-organisation or belief in independence.

I locate myself somewhere in the middle between these two responses to the persistent problem of unpaid labour. I am not as vehement as Abbing in criticism of unpaid labour in the arts. He does not make a distinction between the art establishment, which utilises the unpaid labour of artists in order to reproduce its own privilege, and politicised organisations, which rely on voluntary labour in order to wage their → struggles, uncover and criticise systems of exploitation (and it would be unrealistic to expect that such activities would be fully funded or commercially viable, just as INCITE! quipped – 'revolution will not be funded'). Furthermore, it is questionable whether → patainstitutions directly benefit from such exploitation. Frequently, people who self-organise are as un- or underpaid as those who participate in them. In the case of such self-organised collectives, it would be more appropriate to understand exploitation as self-exploitation, but often people establish these platforms to mutualise the risks inherent to artistic circulation, to question the structural conditions of exploitation and to organise to combat them.

N is for...

The emergence of the globalised circulation of art is paired with the rise of neoliberalism as a political project, and this profoundly impacts on the daily worries, aspirations and structural limitations faced by → projectarians. Even after the coronavirus pandemic, neoliberalism prevails, in its own zombie form, reanimated by public funds injected into the financial bloodstream, staggering levels of debt and the regimes of intellectual property. Patents regulating access to COVID-19 vaccines are a telling example of the privatisation of what has been generated in → common (i.e. in the international research community), and in effect of the huge public stimuli (a recent study shows that the costs of researching and developing the technology used in the Oxford-AstraZeneca vaccine were 97% covered by the public and charitable funds (Cross et al. 2021)). The patents limit access to vaccine programmes to all but most affluent countries, a situation labelled by Hadas Thier as 'vaccine apartheid' in the context of the early 2021 pandemic outburst in South Africa (Thier 2021). The primacy of private ownership and accumulation of capital over human lives and social welfare is neoliberalism at its worst. Naomi Klein analyses this socio-economic formation as 'corona-capitalism', a new iteration of disaster capitalism that has dominated the globe since the early 1980s (Klein 2007; 2020).

Neoliberalism as such can be defined – after Jeremy Gilbert – as both an aggregate of ideas and a social and economic programme that encompasses several heterogeneous yet interconnected policies (Gilbert 2013). Just as David Harvey argued, advocates of neoliberalism use whatever means at their disposal to reinstate the dominance of the capitalist class at the expense of other sectors of society (Harvey 2005). As a result, neoliberalism reduces living standards for the majority of populations while amassing wealth at the top tiers of the social pyramid, raising economic inequality to levels unseen since the Second World War, as analysed by Thomas Piketty (Piketty 2017). This goal is achieved by privatising public services, cutting social welfare, weakening trade unions and other forms of collective organisation, and lowering work and environmental standards. Neoliberalism is an ideology that expands the rules of economic rationality to other, previously not-economised, social fields (Foucault 2010: 218–19), based on crude social Darwinism founded on the notion of entrepreneurial and competitive individuals, whose actions are driven by self-interest and narrow, instrumental utilitarianism.

More to the point, neoliberalism configures the socio-economic environment in which → independent curators and artists circulate. As argued by Jim McGuigan, the emergence of neoliberalism has 'saturated culture with a market-oriented mentality that closed out alternative ways of thinking and imagining' (McGuigan 2005: 229). In other words, neoliberalism prompts the emergence of specific policies, socio-economic regimes and ideologies, which directly and indirectly influence artistic circulation. For example, when public healthcare is privatised as an effect of neoliberal policies → precarious and intermittent workers suffer, as they are not able to cover the costs of private insurance. When wages stagnate and the costs of housing increase in cities such as New York, London, Berlin or Warsaw, only the most affluent are able to afford to live and work in the centres. Thus, cities are turned into hotbeds of gentrification rather than cradles of new artistic ideas. When the costs of artistic education raise exponentially, as has been the case in the USA or UK, it not only limits access to higher education to a privileged few, but also impacts on the forms of art that are being taught there. Precisely in this context, the USA-based art-activist collective bfamfaphd asks pointedly – 'what is a work of art in the age of $120.000 degrees?' (bfamfaphd 2014). The privatisation of education leads to the commercialisation of art, as people burdened with debt are pressured to orient themselves to commercially viable artistic production that only reinforces the hegemony of the art market, dominated by rich collectors, dealers, art fairs and auctions. The affluence of this sector is proportional to the levels of social inequality and the amounts of wealth accumulated at the very top of social hierarchy, as it closely depends on the patronage of financial oligarchies (Fraser 2011). The supremacy of this compromised – and yet influential – sector is sustained by the politics of austerity that have a negative impact on the public institutions and informal collectives alike. Neoliberalism siphons the resources from the bottom layers of society to the top, where it trickles down only to the → one percent of privileged artists, gallerists or auctioneers. Public art institutions operate on shoestring budgets, their programmes depending on scarce public funding, private sponsorship, low wages and precarious enthusiasm. When → art workers are barely able to make ends meet, due to the constant neoliberal pressure on their welfare, they are often too tired and overworked to engage in patainsitutional self-organisation. Furthermore, project-related → apparatuses are strategically functional to the neoliberal hegemony, moulding projectariats' ways of thinking, living and working in accordance with the neoliberal credo. For example, neoliberalism shapes desires for independence and autonomy, innate to flexible labour regimes, in the form of possessive, competitive and cynical individualism. Neoliberalism enforces competition (especially in the middle and lower classes) as the general rule, regulating access to opportunities and resources so that only the fittest (or rather – most privileged) survive. The fundamental precarity of the majority of projectarians imposes on them the need to constantly organise one project after another. Last, but not least, are the implicit hierarchies of privilege and access embedded in the intersecting structures of class, gender, ethnicity and citizenry, underpinning the superficial meritocracy of the → winner-takes-it-all economy.

However, this kind of structural junction does not constitute an enclosed, totalitarian system that would prohibit dissent and cannot be changed; it is rather a 'totalising' tendency within social systems, to refer to Gene Ray's observations:

> (...) critical and autonomous subjects who do emerge are increasingly blocked from any practice *that could change the dominant trend or aim radically beyond it*. In this sense, the system is 'totalizing'. But totalizing does not and cannot mean *totalized*, as in actualized with an exhaustive completeness that would, once and for all, eliminate every gap and permanently block critical subjects from ever emerging again (Ray 2011: 172, italics by author).

Projects, networks, clusters and individual trajectories are all constituted on tensions and inconsistencies, which do not have to be articulated in accordance with the hegemonic programme of neoliberalism. There is always the possibility to resist, and to articulate these conflicts by following alternative ideals and values, such as → interdependence or the → commons.

The networker is above all a strawman, or (in the words of Max Weber) an ideal type built here not only to deliver a couple of punchlines, but to support a critical analysis of the patterns of behaviour endemic within artistic circulation. A networker is not who you are but rather a type of personality that some of us assume. Real life tends to be populated by complex people with their dilemmas, compromises and occasional feats of heroism, rather than caricatures or ideal types. Artistic circulation is no different, so what follows should be taken with a pinch of salt.

The networker is a native of artistic circulation, as having a knack for networking is indispensable for every projectarian. Making contacts with ease, perfecting small talk, catching stuff on the fly, following human traffic, going where others flock and avoiding places where nothing is going to happen, the networker is adept at predicting trends and fashions. Such skills facilitate survival in the world of networks and provide access to → opportunities (→ O is for opportunism).

For networkers, to stay in circulation is both an end in itself and a way to achieve it. The networker is a perpetual motion machine, connecting in order to stay in touch, doing projects to make even more of them, moving to keep moving. They embody artistic circulation, blending into the world of flows so much that there is nothing else to see. This corroded character is a derivate of trends and a relative of connections, without opinions of their own, but never missing an opportunity to pass on what they have overheard. And as they move constantly, such titbits possess an aura of freshness, easily mistaken for acute insights. Networkers pose as a contemporary person without qualities, a decadent being whose psyche mirrors the world of continuous acceleration. But in fact, networkers succumb to a reality of a second sort: that of non-places such as Airbnbs, condo hotels and airports. As networkers leapfrog from one non-residual place (cluster or event) to another, they rarely have a place of their own. They make a virtue out of necessity, following the elusive discursive fashions, as uprooted as they are, avoiding any obligations and narrations larger than their own precious egos, resistant to anything but a rudimentary post-modern credo of routine scepticism.

With the portfolios of professionalised hipsters, some networkers, especially celebrity curators or artists, would like to imagine themselves as trend setters. But in fact they are more like alpha sheep: just because their bleating is loudest, they think they lead the flock. Unfortunately, just because someone is able to sense what others will think before they are aware of it, does not imply leadership. Networkers are uber-conformists, avoiding risks, anxious about social rejection. A failed prediction or a misread fashion can result in a collapse of reputation, a couple of botched projects lead to an atrophy of contacts. As the circulation → turns, it is easy to become as outdated as the last season. There is a short fall from mobility to → exclusion. For this reason, even uber-networkers feel compelled to be continuously on the move, always stretched too thin, in the state of mind of travelling salesmen, brilliantly dissected by Hito Steyerl when she mocks the demands of being unceasingly present, and always somewhere else, inherent to the global art world (Steyerl 2017, already quoted at length in → A is for apparatus).

It is a sad, pseudo-individualistic existence marked by emptiness, because networkers in order to thrive need to capitalise on themselves and others, while denying the parasitic plagiarism of their own character. Even though networkers seem to be perfectly convergent with the → apparatuses of circulation, artistic circulation as such cannot be composed solely of networkers. Somebody needs to do the job, while others are on the move (→ L is for labour of love and → P is for pollination). Boltanski and Chiapello describe the networker as an ethically compromised person, who 'seizes on all the actually or potentially useful connections (...) in order to divert them to the end of personal profit' (Boltanski and Chiapello 2005: 94). Networkers professionalise freeloading, as for the atomised → entrepreneurs of the self, capitalising on the labour of others is more beneficial than investing in prolonged collaborations. Of course, such privatisation of gains is possible as long as there is a cooperatively constituted resource to be exploited, the reproduction of which depends on the constant and hidden labour of the multitudes. For this reason, in order to protect the → common, the commoners have to fend off networkers, or use them for the benefit of all, helping them to help others.

As artistic circulation is painted in all shades of grey, even the networkers have an array of positive functions. In the best possible case they are like bees who → <u>pollinate</u> by moving between contexts and places, in what can be intellectually fertilising and artistically inspiring. Networkers are often excellent companions, telling good and engaging stories from remote corners of the earth, travelling so that others do not have to move so much. Radicants, those plants that thrive on the roots of others, might become beneficial for the entire ecosystem, but only if they manage to establish an actually symbiotic and not parasitic relation. Otherwise, they just professionalise → <u>cynicism</u> and → <u>opportun-ism</u>, instead of propagating the common by sharing connections and expanding networks.

N   is for numbers and
measures

Projectarians are exposed to all the silly rituals of audit societies, a term introduced by Michael Power to denounce the neoliberal bureaucratisation of public institutions and private enterprises alike (Power 1997). The propensity to quantify is intrinsically linked with the fundamental rules of societies of → control, which form 'a system of variable geometry the language of which is numerical' (Deleuze 1992: 3). This tendency has only accelerated recently, as technologically advanced societies are run on bullshit jobs, processing nonsensical data and monitoring directionless processes (Graeber 2018).

Grant systems inherent to circulation exemplify this drive for unchecked bureaucratisation. The universal language of → applications is numerical. Each idea can be calculated and accounted for, especially under the ubiquitous and penetrating view of gate keepers. → Grant art is best expressed in the medium of spreadsheets, carefully arranged tables and colourful PowerPoints. Every applicant is tasked with counting numbers of events planned, viewers expected, impact reached. Such calculations copy the commercial paradigm, where success is evidenced by sales, the share of viewership, the scope of coverage. As Negri and Hardt suggest:

> Modern bureaucracy is a particularly adequate complement to the rule of capital, in other words, because capital, too, functions primarily through measure (the measure of value) and, like bureaucracy, capital is threatened by the immeasurable. One primary function of capitalist money (…) is to fix the measure of values, and increasingly today, through complex financial instruments such as derivatives, to stamp measures on social values that threaten to escape calculation (Hardt and Negri 2017: 115).

In networks of contemporary art, calculations are also mechanisms of numerical → capture of otherwise uncapped values. They are not just ordinary numbers; they perform a couple of crucial functions. As they are plugged into the → apparatuses of networked production, they have the power to shape projectarians and their projects alike, moulding them into their own numerical image.

Quantifiable indicators enable comparison, assessment and verification of otherwise incompatible and idiosyncratic projects, replacing judgements based on deliberative negotiation of values. Swapping quality with quantity is a matter of bureaucratic convenience. The emphasis on numbers and measures legitimises the power of grant providers by presenting arbitrary decisions as if they were based on objective and thus unquestionable evidence. Bureaucratic authority manifests itself in its ability to define criteria, on the basis of which decisions are made. There is nothing obvious in considering the size of the audience or the number of quotations as indicators of value. Quantifiable criteria promote dull results, accounting for only short-term effects and dismissing more balanced reflection on the long-term impact of any undertaking. Measures are taken of the geographical scope of a project, but not the value of partnerships thus established; the numerical size of audiences, but not of people's engagement; the range of media coverage, but not of social impact; the number of reviews, but not of artistic quality. This kind of quantitative abstraction and the general arbitrariness of cultural bureaucracies is criticised by Pascal Gielen because 'once the abstraction is made, literally anything can be related to anything else, and relationships therefore become relative and interchangeable too' (Gielen 2013: 26). However, Gielen's criticism of neoliberal systems of measurement supports a preference for institutionalised value regimes, as for him 'rising up, or creating something (...) needs a solid cultural ground to stand on. And that is exactly what the classic institutions provided' (Gielen 2013: 26). It is hard to agree that bureaucratic discipline and ideological enclosure, these intrinsic traits of traditional institutions, is in any sense better than the free-floating numerical control of projects and networks. Living in Poland, one is inherently sceptical of any calls for 'solid cultural ground', as they resemble propagandistic slogans used by the right wing to wage their culture wars. I do not think that we are dealing with a binary choice between neoliberal bureaucracy (using quantification to express everything in capitalist value form), and conservative values, grounded in such notions as nation or religion. Having said all this, the obsession with numbers and measures is a neoliberal articulation of a more fundamental and essentially positive capacity of project-related apparatuses. After all, these apparatuses are able to traverse and connect various social universes, and if released from the numerical yoke, could have strong emancipatory potential.

O   is for...

O   is for one percent

In 2014, Illuminator, an artistic collective from New York affiliated with the art-activist campaign Occupy Museums, occupied the facade of the Guggenheim Museum in New York by projecting onto it the slogan 'Museum of 1%', thus creating one of the most iconic images of the Occupy movement (Vartanian 2014). It was a rallying cry against the inequality haunting the mainstream art world, rearticulating the demands for democratisation that animated occupations and protests that attempted to overtake public spaces in the aftermath of financial crisis. Writing in the similar vein, Andrea Fraser in her self-reflective essay *L'1%, c'est moi* dissects the complicity of major galleries and boards of larger art institutions with contemporary forms of capitalism. As Fraser points out, it is enough to look at the boards of leading art institutions in New York to spot many people who are also mentioned on the Forbes 500 list, and the prices of art works are closely correlated with the indicators of inequality (Fraser 2011: 114–16). The top tiers of mainstream art world – artists, curators and gallerists – serve financial oligarchies as the new dance masters of financial capitalism, providing new items to speculate with, trophies to showcase, playgrounds to play in and laundries in which to art-wash tarnished reputations. And yet, the circulation of art is far from being entirely subdued, because what appears like a playground when viewed from the top, is a social factory when seen from the ground, manned by precarious creatives and maintained by the unremunerated and unrecognised labour of artistic → dark matter, a hotbed of art-activism and occupy movements. The vast majority of projectarians are definitely not of the One Percent; in fact, only a tiny cohort of ultra-privileged artists, curators or directors could even aspire to be counted amongst them.

Even if the mainstream art world is rigged against ninety-nine percent of projectarians, they identify cracks in artistic systems that can be exploited to survive. One example of such exercise is a humorous comic *London's Art Economies* created by Rosalie Schweiker (2018).

She depicts the London art world as ridden with inequalities, where poor artists rent shitholes for hundreds of pounds, are too busy to meet with each other and have to compete for access. This art world is underpinned by a vast inequality of wealth and access. As she writes in one of her comic strips: 'Some of my cash comes from teaching at many of London's art schools. Recently I did an exercise with my class when we all showed what we have in our wallets. Many of the students had a credit card given to them by their parents. Most people who survive as London artists have been or are subsidised by family wealth, partners or patrons. Making it in London is not based on merit' (Schweiker 2018). From the throngs of young artists or independent curators roaming the network, those who can really 'make it' usually come from a more privileged background. The illusory flatness of networks is in fact a fluid hierarchy, as in the chaos of circulation only a few win while many lose, and success depends on having access to various forms of → capital, and privileges of gender, race, citizenship or class. Artistic circulation offers unbridled mobility for those who can afford it, but it can easily descend into a nightmarish dependence on fleeting opportunities for those who cannot.

This artistic universe is superficially founded on an ideology of meritocracy and talent, which disguises class hierarchies (Malik 2013; Phillips and Malik 2012). The inequality enmeshed within a seemingly left-liberal artistic mainstream has moved recently to the centre of focus in the UK, denounced in actions and condemned by reports such as *Panic! Social Class, Taste and Inequalities in the Creative Industries* that paints a condemning picture of the British art world, where most of the higher positions are taken by people who come from privileged back-grounds – white, privately educated elites (Brook, O'Brien and Taylor 2018; Jeffreys 2018; Judah 2018). Adding insult to injury, most of the people in these high positions believe that they owe their success solely to their own talent and hard work, stubbornly oblivious to the networks of privilege upon which their advancement relies. This kind of class distinction is nothing new. In the 1980s, it was analysed in detail by Pierre Bourdieu, who dissected how the seemingly meritocratic universes of art, academy and education are underpinned by class hierarchies, while representing the outcomes of privilege as a matter of taste and merit (Bourdieu 1984).

Within the global circulation of art, despite its apparent flatness, inheriting a portfolio of economic, social and symbolic capital also proves to be tremendously helpful if you want to 'make it'. Only with family backup, like a credit card or a place to live, is one able to survive long periods of unpaid or underpaid labour in culture and academia. Only by having social networks are freelancers able to secure better opportunities. Being born to cultured and wealthy families grants access to private education, imbues young projectarians with confidence and exposes them to relatable role models. All these factors make it easier for them to enrol in more prestigious universities, or even to make the risky decision to pursue a precarious career in contemporary art and academia – choices which never cease to appear as a luxury for those brought up poor. But this privilege should not only be understood solely in the context of class, though it obviously matters, as it intersects with the divisions established by political geography, race (→ B is for (no) borders), and gender (→ K is for (no) kids). In any case, the creatives should heed one of the suggestions for the better art world, proclaimed by the White Pube on a series of billboards exhibited on the streets of Liverpool and London in early 2021: 'people across the creative industries need to declare if they have rich parents who helped them get where they are today' (Bourton 2021).

O   is for opportunism

Opportunism is not a moral stance, but a highly individualistic relation of production, arising because → art workers, who are always moving between projects, need to chase interchangeable opportunities. In this respect, they are like other uprooted workers who roam the post-Fordist networks looking for temporary jobs and assignments, for any chance to ensure their own survival. Here, I take inspiration from a non-judgemental definition of opportunism used by Paolo Virno:

> The roots of opportunism lie in an outside-of-the-workplace socialization marked by unexpected turns, perceptible shocks, permanent innovation, chronic instability. Opportunists are those who confront a flow of ever-interchangeable possibilities, making themselves available to the greater number of these, yielding to the nearest one, and then quickly swerving from one to another (Virno 2004: 86).

People chase the flow of interchangeable opportunities by → capitalising on their reputations, social contacts, skills and emotions. This enables them to gain access to future opportunities and helps them to stir networks in a desired direction, thus harnessing social and individual labour within those networks as privatised → capital. In this manner, structural opportunism moulds art workers into → entrepreneurs of the self.

Taking into consideration the basic dependency of independent curators or artists upon their clever utilisation of opportunities, I partially agree with Gielen's observation that in the contemporary art network 'cynicism and opportunism have become necessary modes of operation' (Gielen 2009: 36). Gielen portrays the contemporary curator as an 'optimistic joy rider', who:

> (...) enjoys the pleasures afforded by today's widespread neoliberal market economy, and seizes every opportunity to tell a critical, engaged or unique story. In other words, such a curator is always a big opportunist (Gielen 2009: 36–37).

Even though Gielen rhetorically recognises that opportunism should be understood 'in a neutral sense of the ability to grab opportunities' (Gielen 2009: 38) and that contemporary curating includes 'balancing exercises' between opportunism and ethical concerns (Gielen 2009: 37), he doesn't draw consequences from Virno's insights and his 'structural, sober, non-moralistic' definition of opportunism. For Gielen, cynicism and opportunism are morally condemnable outcomes of post-Fordism, by default linked with other vices of → neoliberalism, such as widespread egoism, lack of social solidarity, crumbling ethical norms and instrumental rationality (Gielen 2013: 33–51).

But these networked forms of opportunism could be understood more on Virno's terms by harking back to the ancient etymology of the word, since the Latin word 'opportunus' denotes a favourable, advantageous wind that pushes sailors to a friendly harbour. Similarly, contemporary opportunists try to navigate the treacherous seas of tumultuous networks, anxiously looking for sparse havens and temporary shelters. Projectarians have to find favourable winds and navigate hazardous waters. While the wind is there for all, opportunities are only for the selected few and cannot be taken for granted. As a result of neoliberal → belt-tightening, opportunism becomes a perilous way of life for everyone but the → one percent, who can simply enjoy the flow without a care for the risks of → precarity, → poverty and → exclusion so prevalent for everyone else.

P   is for...

P   is for patainstitutions

The term 'patainstitution' is coined after Alfred Jarry, a nineteenth-century bohemian writer and proto-surrealist, who in his novel *The Exploits & Opinions of Doctor Faustroll, Pataphysician* (1898) describes pataphysics as a science of exception and uniqueness, of poetry and heightened stances of perception. According to him, pataphysics is a mode of reflection motivated by the belief that 'the virtual or imaginary nature of things as glimpsed by the heightened vision of poetry or science or love can be seized and lived as real' (Jarry 1996: 9). This concept was picked up by writers, poets, artists, surrealists, mad scientists and serious researchers alike. Pataphysics proved to be an inspiration for organisational innovation, with several pataphysical institutions emerging in the following decades. The most famous of these was the College of Pataphysics, established in Paris after the Second World War, and closely followed by pataphysical institutes and journals in places like Buenos Aires, London and Vilnius.

However, this legacy is only of secondary import to the analysis of artistic circulation, as the very notion of patainstitutionalism, as proposed and used here, is a result of more recent curatorial innovation and creative translation. 'Patainstitutionalism' is an English translation of the Polish term *patainstytutcjonalizm*, a neologism created to denote the plethora of 'mock institutions' (Sholette 2011), 'institutions of exodus' (Raunig 2009a; 2009b), 'monster institutions' (Universidad Nomada 2009), 'plausible art worlds' (Basekamp Group & Friends 2013), 'art sustaining environments' (Wright 2013), 'open organisations' (Critical Practice 2011) and 'undercommons' (Harney and Moten 2013), which have entered international debates about artistic self-organisation since the early 2000s. To add even more complexity, patainstitutionalism was framed after the concept of pataeconomy, popularised by Goldex Poldex, an anarcho-artistic cooperative from Kraków, in their inquiries into imaginative economies. Janek Sowa, a sociologist affiliated with the cooperative and an active member of the → Free/Slow University, proposed to think about this imaginary mode of self-instituting as representative of what he called the Sector π (Sowa 2009). This mode of self-organisation exists at an angle to the conventions of the bourgeois public sphere. The paradoxical immeasurability of the number π, whose digits stretch out infinitely (3.14159265358979 ...), is a useful symbol for Sowa's claim for a surplus sociality specific to the Sector π, distinguishing it from the so-called Third Sector of non-governmental organisations which are currently mired in market logic and neoliberal bureaucracy (→ G is for grant art). After all those twists and turns, the notion of patainstitutionalism emerges as a semi-peripheral revenge on the dominant language of art theoretical debate, a linguistic blowback in the predominantly English-speaking universe.

But it is not just a pun, just as pataphysics was not just a joke. Patainstitutionalism proved to be a handy conceptual tool to support curatorial inquiries into the vast realm of alternative modes of sustaining art beyond the field of art. One of these we conducted with Sebastian Cichocki during the exhibition *Making Use. Life in Postartistic Times*, organised in the Museum of Modern Art in Warsaw in 2016 (Szreder 2017). During this exhibition, the → Free/Slow University of Warsaw assembled the First Warsaw Patainstitutional Convention. This international summit, modest in size but not wanting in ambition, gathered representatives of various self-organised collectives active in and beyond contemporary art from all over Europe.

In any case, patainstitutions are akin to mock institutions – described by Gregory Sholette as organisational forms embedded in the artistic → dark matter – research institutes, informal universities, collectives of urban gardeners, tribes of eco-artistic-nomads, temporary service points – that tend to operate in an institutional landscape ravaged by the hostile forces of late capitalism, filling in the vacuum left after the demise of public institutions, and which, according to Sholette:

> superimpose two different states of being in the world – one deeply suspicious of institutional authority (...) and therefore informally organized, and one mimicking (...) the actual function of institutions (Sholette 2011: 13).

When he describes the results of his survey of 67 mock institutions from around the globe (mostly from the USA and Western Europe) he underlines that mock institutions adopt a variety of institutional formats:

sometimes borrowing aspects of traditional not-for-profit organizations, at other times looking more like temporary commercial structures, and still other times appearing as a semi-nomadic band or tribe stumbling across a battered social landscape (Sholette 2011: 13).

Consequently, the social architecture of mock institutions is 'discontinuous and contradictory', a description that perfectly matches the organisational paradoxes embraced by patainstitutions. But these paradoxes are of a fundamentally productive nature, as patainstitutions pave the way for new institutions of the common (→ I is for instituting the commons), which emerge beyond the tired opposition of public institutions and private enterprise (a division based on the bourgeois concept of individual ownership), often in protest against the structural pressures of artistic circulation. Patainstitutionalism is a form of self-defence against the privatisation of collectively generated capital, against short-termism and prevalent → opportunism. Patainstitutions are constructed as basic support structures to shelter their affiliates from the risks of → precarity and → exclusion and unfix the individualistic psychopathology responsible for depression and → burn-outs. In the context of rising fascism, → instituting the commons represents an institutional bulwark against micro-fascism, articulating new left politics (Szreder and Majewska 2016) (more in the entry → A is for Anti-fascist Year). The best practical example of such resistant patainstitutionalism in action is the OFF-Biennale in Budapest, Hungary, a biannual grassroots event, the first edition of which was organised in 2015 (Zafiropoulos 2017) in protest against the right-wing takeover of all major artistic institutions in Hungary (András 2014). The OFF-Biennale, despite lacking official support, is able to pull off a very ambitious programme, composed of projects and actions self-organised by a patainstitutional coalition of individual artists, collectives, associations and private galleries. In its form, it is more akin to social movements than to official events, providing a bit of breathing space for the art scene otherwise suffocating under the authoritarian stranglehold of Victor Orbán's government.

Patainstitutions are 'monstrous' in a sense given to this term by Universidad Nomada from Spain, who pictured self-organised collectives that emerge in the crucible of social movements, as many-headed, unexpected mutants which appear grotesque in their refusal to conform to the institutional frameworks of the bourgeois public sphere. These movement-originated monster institutions were subsequently planted in the world of institutions, mutating their hosts, giving rise to new institutions of the common (Universidad Nomada 2009). Commenting on the cooperation between the Reina Sofia Museum in Madrid and Fundación de los Comunes, Jesus Carillo suggests that we think about these emergent assemblages – composed from social movements, collectives and public institutions – in terms of a shared conspiracy, aimed at resisting neoliberal and authoritarian onslaught:

> We are conspirational institutions endowed with highly sophisticated tools to engage in actual processes of social transformation. We may just have to assume that conspirational, collective breathing, attitude in the way we organize ourselves, the way we administrate our budgets, the way we address our constituencies and the way we design our programmes (...) Conspiracy, with all its subversive power, is at work when we take part in the collective and cooperative endeavour of resisting expropriation, segregation, commodification and banalisation (Carrillo 2017).

I find his concept of conspirational institutions very inspiring, as he shifts the debate from the realm of self-organised initiatives to the public institutions proper, patainstitutionalising them in the process. Carrillo suggests that institutions need to conspire with social movements to undo their own dependency on state powers, mass tourism and cultural industries. Along the way, they invent new models of constituent museums and institutions of the common that, as he explains, are instigated to support activist groups – such as Casa Invisible from Malaga, a squatted cultural centre, the eviction of which was prevented by the partnership with the Reina Sofia Museum.

While thinking about these patainstitutions, it is important to shift the focus away from a singular institution to the larger landscape of the interlocking configuration of many kinds of structure that might engage also larger museums or art centres. There is always more than one patainstitution, and monster institutions come in swarms, networks, assemblies. That's what makes them monstrous. Their molecular motions accelerate until the moment of fusion, when a creative surplus ruptures the artistic circulation and an immeasurable element of social energy is released that begins the work of constituting new institutional configurations, revamping existing institutions in the spirit of the common.

P   is for pollination

As the → <u>labour of love</u> denotes the – often anonymous and invisible – work of maintenance and care, the labour of pollination is the general social labour involved in generating the human knowledge and social connections that are indispensable for the global → <u>circulation</u> of ideas and projects. The concept of this work of pollination was coined by Yann Moulier Boutang in his analysis of the business models characteristic to late capitalism (Boutang 2007: 16). To explain what he means by the 'work of pollination', Boutang provides the following example: a majority of people believe that the main economic function of bees is to produce honey. But this conviction is misleading, as the true role of bees in an economic cycle is to pollinate orchards and plantations. Honey is only a by-product of a more economically significant process. Analogically, in cognitive capitalism the symbolic product emerges only as a result of long and distributed processes of multifaceted exchange – as a result of the socially dispersed 'work of pollination'. The business models characteristic for this phase of capitalism → <u>capture</u> socially produced values 'on the move'. They try to control social processes of valorisation and distributed symbolic production. The main mode of profit making is crowdsourcing: attracting communities of users who do unpaid work. They pollinate portals, web pages, blogs and search engines, creating values harvested by their owners and administrators. Negri and Hardt expand on this argument, while discussing the dispersed labour of the multitudes that generates the common, subsequently extracted by capitalist businesses in search of profit (Hardt and Negri 2009) (→ <u>I is for instituting the commons</u>).

Generally speaking, multifaceted, frenetic and informal exchanges are at the core of artistic and academic production. People team up, pool their knowledge and create collective surplus value for the sake of their existential satisfaction, research interests and professional progress. This labour of pollination exceeds what can be formalised and attributed to the group of identifiable individuals. The flow of inspiration that allows people to do research and art cannot unfold on a lonely island – be it in the mind of a genius or in a collective of supremely talented creatives. These activities are derivative of situated exchanges, links, contacts, relations, flows, chats, readings, seminars, summer camps – formal and informal, authored and anonymous. The situation is even more nuanced, as the majority of these exchanges are not stereotypically viewed as 'creative' or 'authorial': ideas often emerge in the most mundane places and in unexpectedly convivial situations, not only at writers' desks, in artistic studios or in the sanitised white cubes of exhibition halls. Artistic ideas or idioms might be put into formal shape during these more solitary moments, but originate somewhere else, in the mesh of → interdependent exchange and communication.

P   is for poor (artists)

The notion that artists are poor is so deeply rooted in the romantic mythos of art that it is virtually unquestionable. After all, as the bohemian stereotype goes, 'a starving artist is a better artist'. Or, as Klaus Wowereit, Mayor of Berlin between 2001 and 2014, quipped, the city of Berlin, just like its artists, is 'poor but sexy' (at least to a degree). Not surprisingly, the → art workers themselves are not very eager to subscribe to this received wisdom. These economic difficulties are an object of their everyday concerns and complaints, as relative pauperisation is a shared fate of the artistic projectariat in its different guises – independent artists, writers, curators and producers.

In his book *Why Are Artists Poor?* Hans Abbing, an artist and economist from Amsterdam, presents a convincing analysis of artistic poverty (Abbing 2002). Based on a number of statistics, mainly from Western European countries, Abbing argues that almost 80 percent of artists earn below average, and more than half earn less than the official poverty level in countries like the Netherlands. As Abbing writes, the artists' situation is a derivative of the cruel economy of contemporary art (→ W is for winner takes it all) and their willingness to work for free (→ A is for Artyzol).

His findings about the economic situation of artists are corroborated by many other studies, even if most of them do not share his explanations of the structural causes of artistic poverty. In 2010, W.A.G.E., an advocacy group from New York, commissioned a short report about the appalling working conditions in the arts, where most artists are not paid exhibition fees (W.A.G.E. 2010). Similar conditions, but in European contexts, were denounced in Ireland (Falvey 2020), Scotland (Gordon Nesbitt 2008), the UK (Kinsella 2017), Germany (Haben und Brauchen 2012) and in Poland (Ilczuk et al. 2018; Kozłowski, Sowa and Szreder 2015).

As evidenced by the daily observation and sociological research of the → Free/Slow University of Warsaw, people working in the artistic sectors in Poland often receive low remuneration for participating in artistic projects (Kozłowski, Sowa and Szreder 2015). They are not paid with money, but rather with → visibility, reputation and contacts (→ C is for capital) or even with the possibility of staying in → circulation. At first glance, the artistic projectariat enjoys a number of privileges, such as education, mobility and contacts, which create an unofficial and yet functional safety net partially compensating for lower incomes and deficits in welfare. In addition, a large proportion of the people working in the artistic sectors are able to count on the help of their parents or partners. Some own the apartments they live in. In this way, their available income increases in the short term, while accumulating existential risks (associated with a lack of support structures in the event of sickness and old age) in the long run. But such superficial analysis misses the point, as most of those people are not really privileged: in terms of income, they are located in the lower strata of the middle classes, often living on the threshold of poverty, as low wages in the cultural sector are often paired with other factors, such as → precarity and general lack of security. These shortcomings became even more obvious in the time of COVID-19, when artists, curators and other art professionals shared the fates of other freelancers: not being able to access rescue packages, whilst their projects or other jobs were suspended ad infinitum. Not surprising, then, that often they are riddled with debt. Depending on the welfare system, one of the consequences of not having regular employment is lack of access to medical services and pension funds. This difficult situation mobilises more militant sectors of the artistic projectariat to unionise and struggle for the structural transformation of social welfare, so that they would include all precarious people, artists or not. The prudence of such organising is proved in the event of crisis, like the one caused by the coronavirus pandemic, when relative privilege crumbles into a baseline of → precarity, as projectarians are exposed to the same risks as other precarious people with whom they share basic interests.

P

is for precarity

As befits a saint, San Precario revealed himself to an unexpecting crowd in 2004. Appearing first in Milan and other towns across Northern Italy, his cult followed the pilgrimage routes of the EuroMayDay movement, which organised a series of anti-neoliberal protests in the first decade of the 2000s in various cities across continental Europe. The icons, shrines and figures of San Precario appeared everywhere: in squats, at demonstrations, on walls. His figure was on show in the Museum of Modern Art in Warsaw during the exhibition *Making Use. Life in Postartistic Times* (2016), accompanied by a short entry that read:

> Tapping into the Catholic traditions deeply entrenched in their social environment, a group of activists from Northern Italy have used artistic competence to call into being a figure that embodies their own concerns, while simultaneously setting Italian sacral iconography in a new context. San Precario's gender identity remains undetermined, which makes the saint an even more perfect figure to confront the volatile and undefined face of the era of liquid capital and unstable employment. In practicing the incantation 'a proper saint for the current times,' San Precario began to embody a typical representative of the precariat; they who struggle with obstacles posed by flexible employment, diminishing welfare, and poor working conditions. The unique cult of this newly invented saint materializes in group actions, joint demonstrations in defence of labor rights, as well as individual 'prayers' meant to offer protection against free market pathologies. The figure of San Precario appears in a broad array of iconographic variations, in figurines and devotional images. The saint has also conquered the Internet, which is used as yet another strategy for labor rights evangelisation and a platform of protest. San Precario's Day, on February 29, is celebrated every four years (Cichocki and Szreder 2016).

San Precario is the patron saint of all precarious people, who compose, according to economist Guy Standing, a 'new dangerous class', which he refers to as the precariat (Standing 2014). The term 'precarity' is commonly used to denote instability, low wages, lack of security and thwarted possibilities of advancement, all related to adverse modes of employment, such as zero hours, part-time and flexible contracts. More generally, as feminist scholars such as Isabell Lorey and Judith Butler argue, precariousness is a fundamental condition of vulnerability, lack of protection, exposure to risks and violence, inherent not to any specific class of workers, but to whole populations, such as *sans-papiers* or women exposed to sexual violence (Butler 2006; Lorey 2015). And precisely this form of existential precariousness is revealed by such major upheavals as the coronavirus epidemic, as it first and foremost impacts negatively on people lacking fundamental security, such as flexible workers, victims of domestic violence, people with mental disorders, racial minorities and migrants.

All of these theories, despite their differences, refer to the etymological roots of the word 'precarious', which in the seventeenth century meant 'held through the favour of another', originating from the Latin *precarius* 'obtained by asking or praying'. The notion of dependence on the will of another led to the extended sense of 'risky, dangerous, uncertain' by the late seventeenth century (Online Etymology Dictionary n.d.).

This etymological genealogy resonates in the current uses of the term 'precarity' and 'precariousness', as they denote unwanted and perilous forms of dependency. The precarisation of vast segments of society is triggered by several systemic trends characteristic of → <u>neoliberalism</u>. Andrew Ross identifies precarity as the general condition of labour under neoliberalism, signifying the dominance of employers over employees, as the latter become, as Ross dramatically puts it, 'forced to beg and pray to keep one's job' (Ross 2009: 34). Precarity, according to him, is directly related to one's 'social and economic insecurity (…) which not only gives employers leeway to hire and fire workers at will, but also glorifies part-time contingent work as "free agency," liberated from the stifling constraints of contractual regulations' (Ross 2009: 34).

Precarity is widely referenced in the context of intermittent and insecure positions prevalent in the contemporary art world (Aranda, Vidokle and Wood 2011; Precarious Workers Brigade 2011; 2017). The field of contemporary art is notorious for contracting freelance labour, enforcing self-employment, outsourcing even basic jobs like cleaning or exhibition supervision for nominal fees and either not paying or delaying payment for artistic work. As emphasised by Susuana Amoah, a researcher, curator and an initiator of the digital exhibition platform #GallerySoWhite, contemporary art is a hostile environment to the people of colour, who are much more exposed to the risks of precarity (Amoah 2020). She quotes one of the anonymous respondents, who speaks about work in a London gallery:

> Where interacting with galleries becomes exploitative is when you look at the number of Black and brown people on zero hours contracts or working freelance. From curators to gallery assistants, being Black in the art world means that you would have to come to terms with, and participate in, your own precarity. It is demoralising (Amoah 2020).

Similar findings are presented in the research report on the conditions of migrant labour in the cultural sector, published in 2019 by Migrants in Culture. The organisers speak about themselves as people who 'work in economically and legally precarious workplaces, where we are invisible (as there is little understanding or care of how immigration regimes impact our lives) or hypervisible (co-opted as tokens of internationalism and diversity) in a monoculture' (Migrants in Culture 2019). Migrants in Culture address this conundrum by collective self-empowerment. They campaign against precarious conditions of artistic labour that are particularly harmful to more vulnerable social groups, who cannot rely on their privileges to offset professional risks (→ O is for one percent).

While the elite of the projectariat resembles a class of people Guy Standing calls 'proficiens' – highly skilled professionals working in the law, media and IT who are able to enjoy all the benefits of flexible work arrangements – the vast majority of projectarians are at systemic risk of chronic precarity, which the COVID-19 crisis only amplified. For them, precarity derives from the lack of existential and economic security, inherent to a world run on projects and short-term assignments, which aligns them – at least partially – with the lower strata of the precariat, occupied by people who are forced to pursue badly paid and chronically unstable jobs. In the spring of 2020, all over the world artistic freelancers (artists, curators, educators, lecturers, technicians, etc.) found themselves overnight without any source of income, with no savings, patchy access to health care and no right to maternity/paternity leave. Most art institutions, faced with temporary closure, instinctively offloaded these (unpayable) costs onto its precarious workforce. Even in times of 'prosperity' most freelancers barely make ends meet and do not earn enough to save for the hour of need. When coronavirus struck, some were left with literally a couple of Euros in their accounts.

Under 'normal' circumstances, freelancers are precarious due to their structural dependency on the flow of interchangeable opportunities and/or badly paid jobs. When this flow stutters, they are left with nothing, especially if they are not lucky enough to be residents of one of the privileged European welfare states, like Germany, with its still-functioning safety nets. But this exception only confirms a universal law: that precarity is a long-term consequence of the general individualisation of responsibility for securing potential projects and future employment. Under neoliberal mismanagement, the chances of projectarians of finding new opportunities depend on what Boltanski and Chiapello call 'employability':

> employability refers to the capacity people must be equipped with if they are to be called upon for projects. The transition from one project to the next is the opportunity to increase one's employability. This is the personal capital that everyone must manage, comprising the total set of skills people can mobilize (Boltanski and Chiapello 2005: 93).

Employability as a term is ideologically charged, as it suggests some sort of due process of securing employment. In reality, it is a euphemism used to gloss over the individualisation of risks imposed on projectarians in the context of structural insecurity. The temporariness of employment forces freelancers to migrate constantly between projects, while being personally responsible for the success of their migrations. In such circumstances, only an unhindered trajectory constitutes a resemblance of stability. Such a career is always precarious, as nobody can be sure of whether or not they will be engaged in any projects in the scope of two, three or five years. This kind of precarity is especially noticeable when somebody is economically dependent on churning out one project after another, as the absence of projects seriously undermines their chances of survival.

One of the main challenges for politicising projectarians is the seemingly self-elected character of precarity (→ E is for enthusiasm). The intrinsic relationship between individualistic → opportunism and project-related freedom hampers collective attempts to combat the causes and effects of precarious conditions. This complexity was unpacked by Lorey, who analysed the self-elected character of precarity in the creative professions, arts and academia by discussing what she terms as 'self-precarisation' (Lorey 2006). She describes self-precarised cultural producers as 'subjects easily exploited' who 'seem able to tolerate their living and working conditions with infinite patience because of the belief in their own freedoms and autonomies, and because of the fantasies of self-realisation' (Lorey 2011: 86–87). In the long term, self-precarisation results in 'experiences of anxiety and loss of control, feelings of insecurity as well as the fear and the actual experience of failure, a drop in social status and poverty' (Lorey 2011: 87). The self-imposed lack of security entraps cultural producers in a vicious cycle, as they 'constantly support and reproduce the very conditions in which one suffers and which one at the same time wants to be part of' (Lorey 2011: 87). Trying to find a response to this tendency, Lorey picks up on the theoretical and activist work of the feminist collective from Madrid, Precaria de la Deriva, and proposes to establish communities of care, founded on shared precariousness. She sees this as a potentially unifying rather than atomising process:

> The focus on care has, above all, two strategic components: on the one hand, it is intended to enhance the status of care work with a new understanding and make this the starting-point for political-economic considerations. The traditional evaluation is not thereby simply reversed, rather, the gender-specific and heteronormative distinction between production and reproduction is to be divested of its foundation, just like the separation between a private and a public sphere. On the other hand, the focus on care is intended to 'return to the initial moment of anxiety' and acknowledge our relationality with others – and thus also 'our vulnerability and ... our situated, partial and unfinished constitution within the weave of relationships in which we live' (Lorey 2015: 94–95).

Similarly, to combat precarity, projectarians need to unmake their fixations on the → entrepreneurial self and, at the same time, challenge the system of exploitation that is based on the privatisation of the common (→ C is for capture), embracing the distributed → labour of love. Thus, these communities of mutual care are essential to the maintenance and growth of the fundamental → interdependence of projectarians.

P   is for productive
                withdrawals

A wave of art strikes, boycotts and occupations engulfed global artistic circulation in the first two decades of the twenty-first century. These protests have directly or indirectly targeted artistic infrastructures like museums, biennales and art fairs (→ H is for herding cats). Organising an → art strike, partaking in a boycott or occupying art infrastructure are best understood as acts of → productive withdrawal. The withdrawal of labour or the refusal to circulate-as-usual should not be confused with idle disengagement. Instead, it should be read in the way that Antonio Negri and Michael Hardt look at social strikes:

> The social strike, however, must be not only a refusal but also an affirmation. It must, in other words, also be an act of entrepreneurship that creates or, better, reveals the circuits of cooperation and the potentially autonomous relationships of social production that exist inside and outside waged labor, making use of social wealth shared in common (Hardt and Negri 2017: 150).

People engaging in social strikes are not targeting any particular industry, but rather recognise that their very lives are being exploited by mechanisms such as debt, rents, tuition fees, gentrification and so on. The social strike is an emergent mode of action that is as distributed as the apparatuses of extraction that it resists. In the context of contemporary art, there are many forms of social strike, such as the exhibitions and actions against the educational debt of artists in the USA organised by the collective Occupy Museums (Debtfair 2015), or the reclamation of an abandoned theatre Embros in Athens in 2011, which had been closed as a result of imposed austerity and squatted by its former workers alongside other cultural producers (Argyropoulou 2018). These acts of productive withdrawal challenge the distributed mechanisms of artistic circulation, an imperceptible but tangible system of connections that link individual → networkers, institutions, → projects, embedding them all in the → neoliberal policies of austerity (→ B is for belt-tightening).

There is another substantial convergence between forms of protest inherent to circulation and social strike: the ethos of unrestrained social creativity, so fittingly expressed by Negri and Hardt.

The projectarians who refuse to simply go with the neoliberal flow instead engage in artistic self-organisation, which produces new → patainstitutions, social assemblages that sustain artistic creativity beyond its ossified forms (→ D is for demonstration of paintings). Far from destroying artistic circulation, the refusal of art workers in moments of productive withdrawal allows for its resumption at some point in the future and under better terms (→ T is for time machines). Without moments of collective refusal, there would be nothing to circulate under the name of art but luxurious objects and flashy projects, emptied of sense and value.

Productive withdrawals refer to the collective actions of → art workers who make the usual bohemian demands of freedom, creativity and mobility, but rearticulate them in the context of artists' fronts, trade unions and associations (→ H is for herding cats), with reference to the legacy of → art strikes. The → art workers themselves are changed by the process of transforming the system, becoming more embedded in the collective and moving further from entrepreneurship of the self (Apostol 2015). They target artistic circulation as a site of work and extraction, not motivated by the nostalgia for artistic autonomy (and its exceptionalism), but rather driven by a collective demand for better wages and social security, where creative freedoms are underpinned by solidarity and equality. Precisely such responses to networked modes of production → institute the common, since, instead of → cynicism, → opportunism and → fear, the striking multitude institutes solidarity and → mutualises social production.

Acts of productive withdrawal emphasise a dialectical relationship between projectarians and the distributed apparatuses of artistic circulation, which freelance curators contest while working within them, comparable to how 'regular' workers resist Fordist factories, trying to socialise them in the course of political action. Striking projectarians refuse the personalised trajectories offered by the structures they are resisting, targeting the problematic aspects of their industry that cannot be resolved individually, but only as a result of collective struggle. Paraphrasing Foucault, when projectarians strike, they definitely do not want to be 'governed like that, by that, in the name of those principles, with such and such an objective in mind and by means of such procedures, not like that, not for that, not by them' (Foucault 1997: 28).

Sometimes striking → art workers are painted as if they have merely disengaged from responsibility and are typically presented as idle or lazy. Such 'idling' art workers are contrasted with those members of the artistic workforce who 'engage' by diligently replicating institutional routines. But such accounts are mistaken, as a withdrawal from circulation is paired with institutional creativity, which relies on and strengthens alternative → support structures. Speaking about the decision to boycott Manifesta in Saint Petersburg in 2014, a member of the Russian collective Chto Delat? (→ P is for patainstitutions), Dmitry Vilensky, stated:

> We made our work *as local artists* who have the resources to continue and make a public program completely outside of the Manifesta framework. We realized a mobile platform for communication between Russian and Ukrainian artists, and it was our priority. We did a big-scale performance with our school in public space, without any authorization, and all this stuff was quite visible (Vilensky 2017).

It is important to underline that Chto Delat? is explicitly against boycotts, as they are committed to liberating the means of production for the sake of art workers and their radical politics (Chto Delat? 2009). Neither can they be dismissed as marginal outsiders. They are well reputed internationally, and connected to various global networks (for example, art-activist movements, academic networks and the biennale circuit). Their decision to boycott was informed by the statements of Kasper König, chief curator of Manifesta, after he expressed his admiration for artistic autonomy and a reluctance to sustain a more politicised platform, a statement especially striking in the context of Russian annexation of Crimea and the war in Ukraine. Chto Delat? quite sensibly took the situation for what it actually was and deemed the links between Manifesta, the Russian government and global art circulation to be too firmly knotted to allow them to engage on terms that would be acceptable to the collective. But they did not withdraw idly. Instead, they organised alternative programmes and a series of events for both local and international audiences. They were able to do so precisely because their access was not dependent on Manifesta: they had their own distributed means of collating resources, mobilising fellow art workers and broadcasting their message in a way which would not distort its meaning beyond recognition, → <u>repurposing</u> infrastructures instead of being instrumentalised by them.

Productive withdrawals utilise the organisational grammar of projects to contest the competitive underpinnings of global artistic networks. Pulling them off requires a hefty amount of organisation, of collating resources, finding allies and rallying other projectarians. They usually have pretty visible outcomes. When activists from G.U.L.F. (Global Ultra Luxury Fraction) temporarily occupied the Guggenheim in New York to protest against the appalling conditions of labour for workers constructing the Guggenheim Abu Dhabi (2011), the museum management responded to this action by closing their premises to visitors and emptying the exhibition halls, while art-activists engaged in fervent discussions and ad hoc assemblies. When Decolonize This Place protested the involvement of Warren Kanders in the board of the Whitney Museum in 2019, their calls for a boycott of the Whitney Biennale were paired with performances, interventions, symposia and community organising (Penny 2019). During the Days Without Art in 2012, Polish art workers not only convinced institutions to close their premises in protest against artistic precarity, but also published newspapers, distributed flyers and organised a professional media campaign, prompting an animated discussion that has reverberated ever since.

In light of such practices, it is clear that deviations from institutional routines should not be mistaken for a lack of productivity. The suspension of routines implies liberation of time, to be quickly filled with an activity of a different sort: political actions, discussions and media campaigns, the aim of which is to ensure that business as usual will not continue. If artistic circulation is in itself an interruption of a steady flow of time characteristic to a Fordist assembly line, striking art workers interrupt the interruption with festivals of orgiastic, self-directed creativity (to borrow the words of Gerald Raunig (2013)). The interruption of the interruption creates the conditions for an industrious filling of interrupted time. This industriousness harks back to the genealogical core of the word 'industria', understood as an inventive re-appropriation of time, a moulding of excess collective energy to shape new social universes. These moments of social creativity influence the ways in which art is practised, produced and theorised, in a way similar to how → <u>art strikes</u> recalibrate art as a practice of radical laziness. Just as the New York-based collective MTL suggests, linking artistic practices with a materialist perspective on sustenance and daily reproduction – people 'strike art as a training in the practice of freedom' (McKee 2016). Expanding on this thought, Yates McKee discusses how the term 'art strike' signifies both withdrawing and striking against the current art system, liberating artistic creativity from institutionally induced alienation. He discusses parallel processes of negation and affirmation, unmaking and reinvention:

> [...] this renaissance [of occupations – my addition] involves the unmaking of art as it exists within the discourses, economies, and institutions of the contemporary art system – including its progressive sectors nominally concerned with public participation and civic dialogue. At the same time, it involves the reinvention of art as direct action, collective affect, and political subjectivization embedded in radical movements working to reconstruct the commons in the face of both localized injustices and systemic crises that characterize the contemporary capitalist order (McKee 2016: 6).

The dialectic of making and undoing is at the core of any programme of → repurposing the → apparatuses of artistic circulation, paramount to the politics of projectarians and artistic qualities of their projects alike.

P   is for project

The project is the daily bread of projectarians and a basic unit of circulation. Boltanski and Chiapello define a project as:

> a mass of active connections apt to create forms – that is to say, bring objects and subjects into existence – by stabilizing certain connections and making them irreversible. It is thus a temporary *pocket of accumulation* which, creating value, provides a base for the requirement of extending the network by furthering connections (Boltanski and Chiapello 2005: 105).

As they argue, the project is the centrepiece of the new spirit of capitalism, with its own systems of values, modes of social control and organisation of production, which are widely adopted in so- called post-Fordism (Berardi 2009; Gielen 2009; Gielen and de Bruyne 2009; Hardt and Negri 2005; 2009; Virno 2004). Post-Fordism is usually defined as a social and economic formation, which emerged from the 1970s onwards, replacing the Fordist model of organising the relationship between labour and capital which relied on heavy industries and large bureaucracies. Post-Fordism is characterised by global delocalisation of industries, the growth of the service sector in the core capitalist economies, the flexibilisation of labour markets, the increasingly dominant role of networks and the acceleration of capitalist accumulation.

The use of the term 'projects' to describe artistic and curatorial practices also dates back to the 1970s. Since then, project-related modes of organisation have emerged to take a dominant position in the → expanded field of art. According to Karen van den Berg, in this period the development of artistic projects began to be considered as an alternative to the typical, object-oriented and studio-based artistic practice, facilitating the expansion of the field of art beyond the 'gallery-exhibition nexus' (van den Berg 2013: 66–69). Boris Groys has this kind of artistic project in mind when he proclaims that:

Each project is above all the declaration of another, new future that is supposed to come about once the project has been executed. But in order to induce such a new future one first has to take a period of leave or absence for oneself, with which the project has transferred its agent into a parallel state of heterogeneous time (Groys 2008: 3).

Groys locates a sort of loneliness of the project in the fact that the project isolates its owner(s) for a period of time – and he defines time in a way specific to the twentieth-century political and artistic avant-garde. Groys defines projects as collective or individual undertakings, the main aim of which is to envision and change social or aesthetical order (Groys 2008: 2). When Groys speaks about projects, he clearly does not define them in the context of management. On the contrary, he is critical of project-related systems of funding cultural production. Instead, he sees them as a bureaucratic formalisation of what ought to be avant-garde undertakings, which corrupt the fundamental premises of daring aesthetical or political projects (Groys 2008: 1). For rank-and-file projectarians, their own projects veer between the avant-garde promise of a more interesting future, and the daily grind of → applications and → deadlines.

P   is for projectariat

The projectariat are people who, in order to survive, have no choice but to make and implement projects, as many of them do not own much beyond their own capacity to move in artistic → circulation. In this situation, they are both similar and distinct from proletarians, who have to sell their own labour force in order to survive. Similar to proletarians, projectarians are forced to chase temporary possibilities of employment provided by projects or jobs structured as if they were projects (i.e. temporary and task-oriented assignments). On the other hand, projectarians are → entrepreneurs of the self, because projects enable them to capitalise on their skills, social connections and reputations in exchange for opportunities and other future gains. In this sense, they are owners of their own means of production, capitalising not only on themselves, but also on the labour of others.

The term 'projectariat' is a theoretical *détournement* of the classical Marxist term. I owe this terminological feat to the linguistic creativity of Szymon Żydek, a friend and comrade from the → Free/ Slow University of Warsaw. Despite its somewhat ironic resonance, the term informs a materialist, critical and dialectic effort at understanding the labour conditions of the highly mobile artistic workforce. It is not specific to the global networks of contemporary art but is more generally referenced in critical management studies and analysis of international NGOs, wherever people work on a project-to-project basis (Baker 2014; Greer, Samaluk and Umney 2018; Jałocha 2016). Projects are adopted not only in the world of contemporary art, but also dominate sectors such as contemporary dance (van Assche 2020) and theatre (Ćwikła 2016; Kunst 2015), which are also frequented by projectarians.

The elites of the projectariat are similar in their social composition to the class of highly skilled professionals described by economist Guy Standing as proficiens (Standing 2014). Proficiens work in similarly flexible arrangements to precarious workers but are able to benefit from their mobility due to owned → capital, contacts and skillsets, and who manage to situate themselves among the higher echelons of the labour market. However, the majority of projectarians are as precarious as other precarious workers, and only a tiny elite among professional → networkers enjoy the spoils of circulation. In the → winner-takes-it-all economy specific to global networks of contemporary art, most circulate, but only few earn decently, usually predestined to higher positions by their inherited privilege (→ O is for one percent).

Project-related forms of production share many similar traits with what Maurizio Lazzarato calls 'immaterial labour' (Lazzarato 1996), which involves the intellectual and emotional capacities of working subjects. According to Lazzarato, the term 'immaterial labour' was conceived as a contribution to the wider political project, to accentuate the hybrid nature of new forms of labour, from which new political alliances and forms of collective intelligence could potentially emerge. Lazzarato does not suggest that 'immaterial labour' does not have a material component, i.e. that it is somehow 'spiritual' (Cvejić and Lazzarato 2010: 12). The concept of 'immaterial labour' points towards the differences between old forms of industrial work, which reduce workers to their manual capacities, and new forms of labour, which engage subjects cognitively and affectively. In a similar vein, Paulo Virno suggests that contemporary workers are similar to 'virtuosos', because of the systemic emphasis on workers' individual performance, public self-presentation and their cognitive involvement in the execution of tasks (Virno 2004: 53–66). According to Virno, such 'virtuosity' is not just a form of work but also social cooperation and communication, the synthesis of which facilitates the emergence of what – in reference to Marx's famous 'fragment on machines' – Virno calls the 'general intellect'. By this he means a form of collective intelligence, embodied in both machines and the bodies of people, that gives a basis for political mobilisations under post-Fordism (Virno 2004: 66).

In short, projectarians are both 'immaterial workers' and 'virtuosos' of projects, as the practice of making projects involves a bundle of intertwined activities, such as looking for opportunities, connecting, proposing, applying, relating, assembling, reporting. But more fundamentally, the projectariat is defined by its intrinsic dependency on the flow of interchangeable opportunities, and thus exposed to the risks of → opportunism, → cynicism, → precarity and → fear. On the other hand, certain forms of political mobilisation are available to projectarians, including → <u>productive withdrawals</u>, establishing of → <u>patainstitutional</u> support structures, → <u>interdependent</u> unmaking of the individualistic fixations and creating lasting affiliations with the social and political → <u>struggles</u> of other groups of precarious workers.

R   is for...

R   is for radical
pragmatism

Radical pragmatists talk the talk while walking the walk. They are radical, because they look for radixes, the roots of the problem at hand, identifying the structural causes of their own plight. But in contrast to armchair revolutionaries, they are not afraid of getting their hands dirty. They vouch for a non-moralistic approach, to deal pragmatically with the challenges identified. But their pragmatism is informed by the radical deconstruction of the entrepreneurial self, confronting the → neoliberal hegemony that underpins it. And they use various → opportunities at their disposal to pursue this cause. Thus, the → art workers summit in the Museum of Modern Art in Warsaw was used to jumpstart a coalition spearheading such undertakings like the → Anti-fascist Year, and a micro-grant from the EU was utilised to organise the first meeting of the international alliance of the interdependent organisations (→ I is for interdependence), and an artistic commission was → repurposed to establish Company Drinks, a sustainable artistic enterprise (→ M is for mutualising). In this sense, radical pragmatism is neither only radical nor merely opportunistic. Instead, it is a hybrid stance, which negotiates between pragmatic challenges, ethical concerns and political engagement, acknowledging its own incompleteness and not aspiring to political or moral purity.

Politicised projectarians are radical pragmatists, because it is impossible to enact socialism in one project, even less so than it was to establish communism in one country. But it is perfectly plausible to embed the flow of projects in social movements that struggle for other, better, more equal social systems. Radicalised projectarians approach the 'here and now' of a project as a pragmatic challenge, informed by the radical analysis of a given situation and its strategic dimension to contribute to a potentially cumulative movement towards change. They operate at both tactical and strategic levels, surmounting the division between tactics and strategies, in the meaning defined by Michel de Certeau. According to de Certeau, tactics differ from strategies to the extent that 'strategies are able to produce, tabulate, and impose (...) whereas tactics can only use, manipulate, and divert' (Certeau 1984: 30). In other words, strategies set the stage for action, while tactics react to given circumstances. For example, when the authoritarian government of Hungary took over most of the artistic institutions in the country by installing directors affiliated with the ruling party, it imposed a new structural landscape. When → art workers organise OFF-Biennale, they are not able to reclaim the institutions in question, but rather to 'use, manipulate, and divert' resources at their disposal to build a temporary pocket of autonomy. However, OFF-Biennale is a good example of radical pragmatism, as it partially eludes the distinction between strategies and tactics. Because of its own international → visibility, it establishes new connections and repositions Hungarian art on the global stage, for example by partaking in the curatorial network of Documenta 15, one of the most prestigious art exhibitions in the world, curated in 2022 by the Indonesian art collective ruangrupa.

As Stephen Wright puts it in the context of usership, radical pragmatists 'have neither the time to be revolutionary – because things have to change – nor the patience to be reformists, because things have to stop' (Wright 2013: 27), and so they change how their projects operate, here and now, while addressing the systemic conditions in which they act. For example, in 2017, together with Greg Sholette and Marco Baravalle from S.a.L.E. Docs, we curated *Dark Matter Super Collider*, an open exhibition structure organised in parallel to the opening of the Venice Biennale. The *Collider* featured dozens of examples of political art from the entire world, solicited by activating networks of mutual trust between artists and activists on a global scale. Thanks to the open call we made, dozens of examples of political art were donated to S.a.L.E., either sent by post, uploaded to the Internet or brought in suitcases by people attending the opening. Because the *Super Collider* accelerated social energies accumulated previously in art-activist networks, it was possible to put up the exhibition with a very modest budget, using construction materials recycled by the team of S.a.L.E. Docs from the decommissioned exhibition pavilions from previous years.

These artistic and social energies were circulated on the basis of a gift economy – people agreed to partake in the *Collider* because of shared political affiliations and comradery. In this manner, we received a brick from an artistic cooperative called New Linthorpe Pottery from

Middlesbrough (Morgan 2018), as well as the slogans and masks of the Bison Girls, a collective protesting patriarchy in Warsaw, and the poster 'Art historians against fascism' that had been paraded a couple of months earlier at the pickets outside New York's MoMA. Those who managed to visit S.a.L.E., did so because they had come to visit the Biennale anyway, as we deliberately organised the event around the Biennale's opening to make it easier for people to attend while not spending extra carbon miles (→ F is for footprint). Those who came had a chance to meet other likeminded people from elsewhere and partook in various open forums organised during the course of the exhibition. Typically, the Venice Biennale is based on limiting access – visibility is an exclusive currency that is traded there in the form of closed openings, invite-only parties or dinners with important people. In the *Collider* it was free for all – everybody could add their contribution and everyone was invited to attend. Of course, not everyone who sent their contributions was able to fly to Venice. But on the other hand, those who did contribute acquired → visibility that is reserved for the privileged few during an event such as the Biennale.

It is pretty simple: to rent a space for the period of the Biennale costs thousands of Euros – and organising a pavilion even more. It is not surprising, then, that only national states, bigger institutions or larger foundations can afford such investments. Activists from all over the world – under normal circumstances – cannot. To pay social movements or art-activists in visibility might seem like a reinforcement of the cruel economy of the arts (see → P is for poor) and, obviously, the *Collider* is not an example of the revolutionary takeover of the Venice Biennale nor of the total rearrangement of artistic circulation. Instead, it was radical pragmatism. Pragmatic in the sense that we achieved what we could on the scale that was possible, and we found the best ways available to deal fairly with networks based on friendship and comradery. We took care to ensure that the costs of participation were reduced to a bare minimum, both in financial and labour terms, asking only for the handing-out of a flyer, passing of a model, carrying of a brick in a suitcase, sending of a bison mask, or donation of an already-printed slogan. None of these donations were taken against empty promises of future gains, but rather in the clear understanding of the benefits of shared political affinities and trust generated through various → struggles. And under the rules of the gift economy, all of those contributions had to be paid back in kind – the → interdependent system of mutual obligations that allowed *Super Collider* to happen did not start with this project, and nor did it end there.

Even more importantly, *Super Collider* was made possible because S.a.L.E. managed to secure long-term access to space, resources and collective labour. These came from its firm alliance with the social movements in Venice, such as the ecological campaigns aimed at preventing the destruction of the lagoon, and art workers' struggles for bettering working conditions in creative industries, including the Venice Biennale itself, and those combating fascism and responding to the rise of new authoritarianism (Baravalle 2018a). Baravalle argues that this connection to a struggle (or struggles) makes all the difference between radical alter-institutions and a typical NGO that multiplies projects for projects' sake. Following his argument, when radicalised → art workers engage in → productive withdrawals or establish their → patainstitutions, they do so in order to → repurpose the apparatuses of cultural production in the service of social → struggles, some of which have a strategic dimension, like the → Anti-fascist Year.

In this sense, projects animated by radical pragmatists can be struggle-specific, to riff on the term introduced by Bert Theiss. Theiss was one of the initiators of the Isola Art Centre in Milan who mobilised the potential generated within artistic circulation as part of the struggle against the gentrification of a post-industrial district in their home city of Milan (Isola Art Center 2013). The art specific to the Isola's struggle spanned almost two decades, including dozens of exhibitions, performances and direct actions, often organised in teams that brought together artists, curators, urbanists, activists, town folks, urban gardeners and workers from defunct factories. In order to put on their campaigns and projects, often with scarce or no money at all, they had to be very efficient and radically pragmatic → repurposing social energies, reputations, ideas and resources gleaned from the global circulation of art and embedding them in their struggles. Even though the Isola has not managed to turn the neoliberal wave, it evolved and created spaces of its own – an urban garden Pepe Verde, a series of actions *Isola Utopia* – and had many offshoots, such as the autonomous art centre Macao, that planted their roots in other sites and engaged in subsequent struggles.

This radical approach to material and immaterial properties, and the distributed → apparatuses regulating the flow of projects alike, constitutes a difference between the → <u>entrepreneurs of the self</u>, who cynically capitalise on the work of others, and the entrepreneurial multitudes that socialise opportunities for the sake of many. However, one has to be pragmatic about the situation, should not assume the moral high ground and should view radical pragmatism with a sense of proportion. As such activities focus on the micro-scale of a collective or a project, they only create the conditions for engagement in political movements or parties with a strategic reach, the success of which is definitely not a given.

R   is for repurposing

Alternatives such as → <u>productive withdrawals,</u> → <u>patainstitu-</u>
<u>tions</u> and other forms of → <u>instituting the commons</u> are examples of
repurposing the apparatuses of cultural production that Walter Benjamin
discussed in his seminal essay about literature, *Author as Producer*
(1934). Repurposing often unfolds in the wake of grand social struggles – proletarian revolution in times of Benjamin – social movements
such as Black Lives Matter, anti-fascist fronts or Occupy, nowadays.
For example, in 2011, during Occupy in New York, a studio artist could
decide to bring his works to an ongoing occupation, organise assemblies,
discuss issues of art and labour, start new inquiries into artists' debt
and engage in new aesthetic experiments. Yates McKee recalls these
events:

> The camp is a challenge to describe, provoking many participants
> and commentators alike to draw upon the language of art and even
> religion to capture the experience of this remarkable environment.
> Organizer Gan Golan overtly described the occupation as an 'artistic
> spectacle.' Along with his characterization of the park as a 'canvas
> on which a new world was being painted' and 'a living artwork,'
> Nathan Schneider called it 'sacred space' in which a 'new messiah'
> seemed to be on the verge of apocalyptic arrival. Anthropologist
> Michael Taussig described the camp as a 'strange and fabulous land'
> between waking and dreaming, a magical, enchanted, 'surreal zone'
> in which the dictates of capitalist realism were suspended as new
> forms of life emerged. Veteran activist-artist Martha Rosler called
> it 'a grand public work of process art with a cast of thousands,'
> highlighting the affinity between the 'process over product' ethos
> of sixties sculpture, such as Robert Morris's Continuous Process
> Altered Daily (1968), and the 'means without ends' of Occupy in its
> putative privileging of democratic processes over finite end-goals or
> demands. Yet if 'process' is typically thought of as being immanent,

which is to say, grounded in its own temporality and power rather than some external model, Rosler's figure of the 'cast' interestingly evoked theatre, spectacle, and representation. Also attuned to this oscillation between immanent process and spectacular image were Hardt and Negri, who, when noting the importance of art to the overall unfolding of Occupy, remarked that 'an occupation is a kind of happening, a performance piece that generates political affects (McKee 2016: 100).

Occupiers made use of artistic and organisational competences to forge new links between the occupying collective, the occupied spaces, the politics of occupation and various emergent aesthetical idioms. When a similar path is taken by many, a new social assemblage emerges: at first ephemeral, but if attractive and persistent enough it becomes a new centre of social gravity, twisting social trajectories and forging new patterns of social flows. On a patainstitutional level, an alliance of collectives, NGOs, progressive institutions, media outlets and channels of formal and informal communication created the conditions of possibility for Occupy Wall Street. These networks reflected the ripples made by the Occupy movement, reverberating in future political campaigns, like Bernie Sanders' in 2020. Movements like Occupy have their well-documented legacies, institutional structures, value systems and aesthetic conventions, which are transversal to the dominant orders, neither totally external (unwaveringly oppositional) nor subsumed (pathetically peripheral). Collectives and institutions like Not an Alternative, 16 Beaver and Creative Time are not located totally outside the art system – however defined – but neither are they subsumed by an inherently corrupted mainstream. While analysing such situations one has to manoeuvre between the Scylla of totalised critique and the Charybdis of the romanticised vision of the realm of the institutional outside, as a pristine territory of unspoiled righteousness and human spontaneity. The repurposing of social apparatuses unfolds within contested territory, frequently making use of resources, institutions or agents specific to that territory, slightly and yet significantly transforming the orderings of the assemblages in question.

Taking a cue from Walter Benjamin, I propose to think about such events as repurposing means of artistic production, as → art workers instead of simply 'transmitting the apparatus of production, change it to the maximum extent possible in the direction of socialism' (Benjamin

1970: 3). The central aim of Benjamin's essay is to politicise authors as producers by defining the apparatus of literary production as a site of political intervention, scrutinising the position of authors inside the literary apparatuses of the time, and their embeddedness in the class relations of bourgeois societies (Benjamin 1970: 2). For the sake of his argument, Benjamin differentiates between authorial 'tendency' and 'technique' (Benjamin 1970: 2). According to Benjamin, authors who represent the correct political tendency and use the unchallenged apparatus to disseminate politically engaged contents (like, for example, works of socially engaged photographers of his time, who beautified poverty instead of addressing its causes), merely reproduce the current form of class relations (Benjamin 1970: 8). The authorial technique, in contrast, aims at revolutionising the apparatus in solidarity with the political struggle of the proletariat, thus transforming its social and aesthetical functions. For Benjamin, the radicalised avant-garde, like the Berlin Dadaists, were proper allies of the proletariat in its struggle against fascism, linking aesthetic experiments, technological innovation and political engagement (Benjamin 1970: 8).

It would not be theoretically insightful to simplify the notion of functional transformation as a mere 'takeover' of existing infrastructures (→ A is for assemblage or apparatus). When Stephen Wright advocates for 'repurposing' as one of the tactics of usership, he embeds it within an idea of all users, geared against all forms of ownership (Wright 2013). Moreover, the apparatuses at play have clearly aesthetical components and these go on to inform and influence the modes of art that arise from repurposing. A good example of this process is Pablo Picasso's *Guernica*, the copies and fragments of which have been carried to thousands of peace demonstrations worldwide since the moment of its first presentation in the Republican Spanish pavilion during the World Exhibition in Paris in 1937. It is often exhibited as a masterpiece of modern art, but just as often repurposed as the most famous anti-war poster of all time, used as a means of protest and brought to → demonstration of paintings.

The networked → apparatuses of contemporary art cannot be simply retaken, but they might be repurposed by changing the relationships between their component parts and introducing new elements. This process can be imagined in a diagrammatic manner, as a shift from the vicious cycle of networking to the cycle of struggles animated by the radicalised art workers.

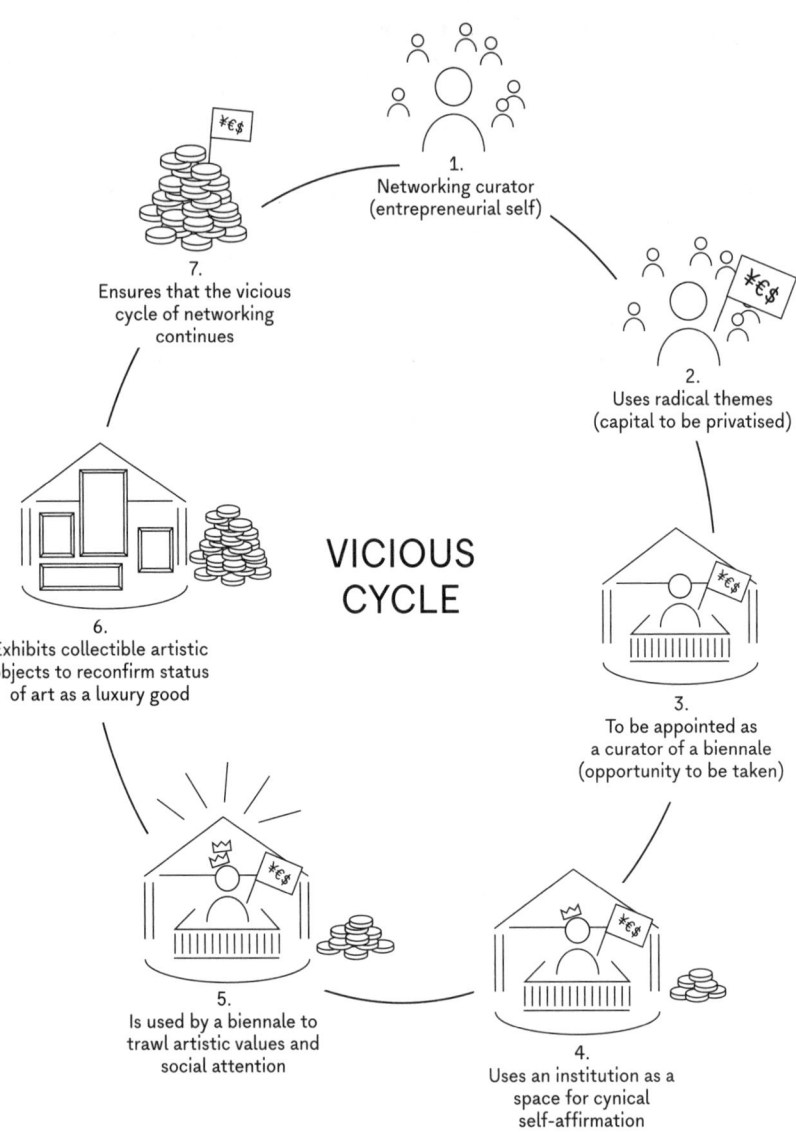

1.
Networking curator
(entrepreneurial self)

2.
Uses radical themes
(capital to be privatised)

3.
To be appointed as
a curator of a biennale
(opportunity to be taken)

4.
Uses an institution as a
space for cynical
self-affirmation

5.
Is used by a biennale to
trawl artistic values and
social attention

6.
Exhibits collectible artistic
objects to reconfirm status
of art as a luxury good

7.
Ensures that the vicious
cycle of networking
continues

VICIOUS
CYCLE

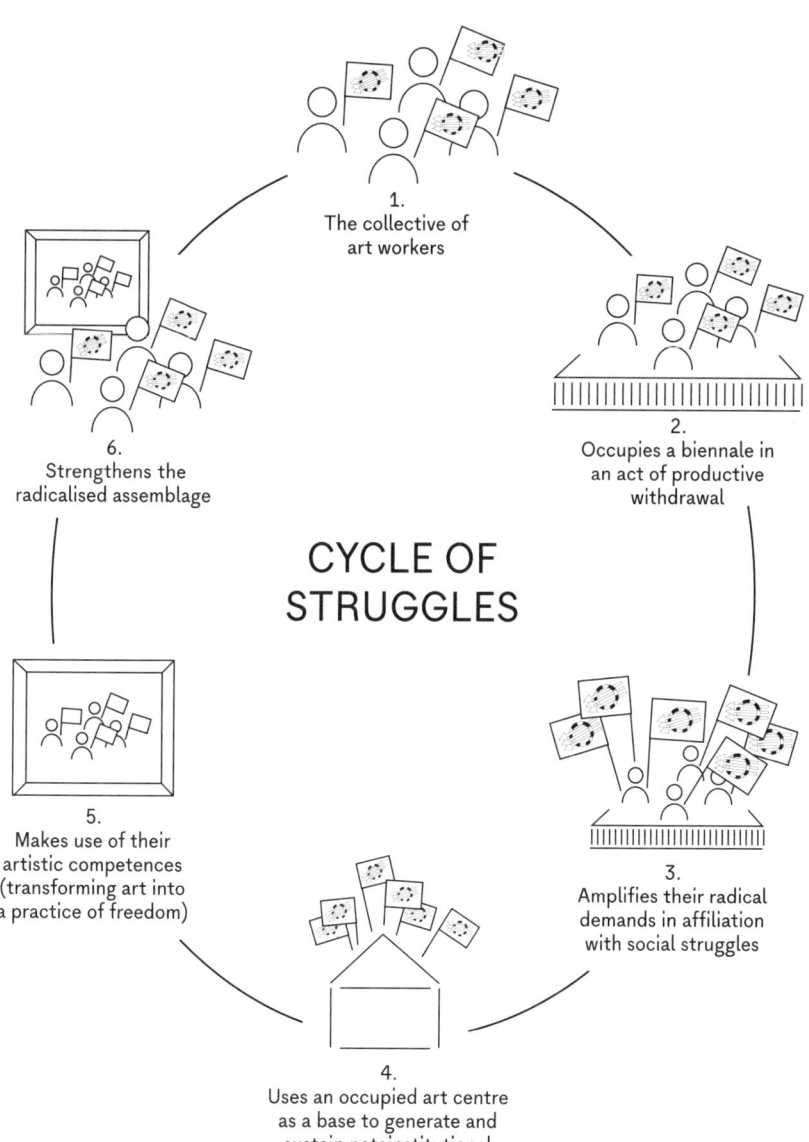

1.
The collective of
art workers

2.
Occupies a biennale in
an act of productive
withdrawal

3.
Amplifies their radical
demands in affiliation
with social struggles

4.
Uses an occupied art centre
as a base to generate and
sustain patainstitutional
infrastructures

5.
Makes use of their
artistic competences
(transforming art into
a practice of freedom)

6.
Strengthens the
radicalised assemblage

CYCLE OF
STRUGGLES

In this way, art systems are unmade and reinvented together with their inherent aesthetical concepts, modes of justification and institutional infrastructures. In the process of unmaking–remaking–repurposing, social energy is released, reinvented and moulded into new institutional, intersubjective and subjective forms. This social re-composition sustains art in multiple different guises, catering to different needs and tastes, and operating according to varied economic principles – the market logic regulating the circulation of projects and objects being just one system among many. Art thus produced rarely resembles what is called and peddled as art in the blue chip gallery nexus: it does not need to be an authored object of aesthetical contemplation, and such art actually might be put to collective use (→ D is for demonstration of paintings). It is sustained by the repurposed infrastructures and apparatuses that coalesce into new examples of the → common.

S   is for...

S
is for seeing everything twice, or the catch 22 of the projectariat

In order to avoid military service during the Second World War, captain John Yossarian, the main protagonist of *Catch 22*, one of the most vehemently anti-war novels of all time, pretends to see everything twice (Heller 1994: 232). Yossarian is simulating the affliction of a fellow soldier hospitalised along him and, after the soldier dies, scared Yossarian stops pretending and is released from hospital. When he tries to argue against his release, the friendly doctor explains to him the paradoxes of catch 22: anyone who would like to resign from military service due to mental breakdown thus proves their sanity and fitness for service, as 'anyone who wants to get out of combat duty isn't really crazy'. The catch 22 of contemporary networks is that projectarians who are perfectly well aware of the glaring contradictions of artistic circulation are nevertheless mobilised to circulate even more due to the contradictory nature of their own experience. They are motivated by the same enthusiasm that is used to justify their poverty, attracted by freedom that easily leads to precarity, and enticed by fleeting opportunities, the chase of which wears them down.

This section of the *Catch 22* finishes on a sombre note, as Yossarian is asked to dress up as the soldier who-saw-things-twice who had just died a day before. He is offered the task of impersonating the dead man in front of his working-class family, who have come to visit from America, re-enacting the moment of his death. Yossarian's objections are subdued by a doctor who threatens to reveal that he had faked all his afflictions. When the astonished Yossarian asks the doctor why he has not turned him in, the doctor responds: 'Why the devil should I? (...) we're all in this business of illusion together. I'm always willing to lend a helping hand to a fellow conspirator along the road to survival if he's willing to do the same for me' (Heller 1994: 234). Despite this humane attitude, or possibly because of it, the bureaucratic military machine moves on. Respecting the obvious, enormous difference between the nightmares of war and the joys of networking, there is a more universal lesson on the nature of bureaucracy and social systems to be learned from Yossarian, who became a kind of counter-cultural hero of the 1960s. Just as bureaucracies tend to, the global networks of art keep circulating viciously despite, or even possibly due to, the human gestures and flickers of sanity of people who are totally aware of the systemic mishaps they experience on a daily basis.

It is possible that the → projectarians native to the eastern peripheries of European Union are more attuned to the paradoxes of global networks of contemporary art. They are connected and privileged enough to revel in the sweet promises of mobility, enjoying the bliss of visa-free travel and unlimited access to the capitalist centres. But they are not privileged enough to be sheltered from the risks inherent to circulation, as they reside in countries fraught with precarious labour markets, unfinished infrastructures, relatively weak welfare systems and ridden with chronic political unpredictability. Poles, Hungarians, Latvians, Slovenians or Croatians are poor members in the rich men's club. Still richer than most, but poorer than some. They can afford mobile phones and computers, have access to Internet and health care, and live outside of a war zone, but booking an intercontinental flight, which costs more than the average monthly income, or studying in London, which requires sound financial backup, is beyond their means. So, this ragtag team of Sunday → sprinters test their mettle on the racetracks designed by and for professional runners, who constantly brag about their own innate talents and hard work – to which they supposedly owe everything – whilst being predestined for this job by the merit of inheritance and citizenry. It is a shared condition of global semi-peripheries, located somewhere on a transversal line between North and South: definitely not in the West, slightly offbeat, somewhere East of the centre.

Observing the nationalist demonstration that she witnessed in Warsaw in November 2018 (for the record: attended by almost 100,000 people, making it one of the largest nationalist demonstrations in Europe), Imani Jacqueline Brown, an artist, writer and activist from New York, succinctly commented on the weird psychopathology of semi-peripheries:

Historically, and even to this day Poles and other central and eastern Europeans are often considered not-quite-white-enough by Western European nations and the USA. Perhaps the far-right loves Donald

Trump so much because he's offered them open tickets to USA-style whiteness (I. J. Brown 2020: 113).

This would explain why the Polish authoritarian state TV channel was possibly one of the last media outlets on earth to concede the defeat of Trump in 2020 presidential elections. In any case, these kinds of racist identifications are protested by many (→ A is for Anti-fascist Year) and cannot be considered as either a Polish national trait, or a speciality of this region.

For slightly older people, who still remember Polish jokes traded by our Western neighbours only two decades ago (like: why should you go on holiday to Poland? Your car is already there), this aspiration towards Western whiteness is both misguided and repugnant. Especially irritating is the claim for racist privilege of people who are bearers of the not-as-white-as-properly-bourgeois-Western-white whiteness, which should be rebuked and challenged, using both political and artistic means (→ D is for demonstration of paintings).

Such critical interventions are necessary as Central-Eastern Europe struggles with its own semi-peripheral status, never really modern, always modernising, desperately trying to catch up, whilst succumbing to an entirely ungrounded superiority complex. This wildly nationalistic self-belief sits strangely in a region more colonised than colonising, more conquered than conquering, aspiring to move as far West as political geography allows (that's why it is called Central-Eastern Europe and not just Eastern Europe), but never really fitting in, dreaming the stalled dreams of long forgotten defeats and victories, fighting battles already lost centuries ago. Currently, it is a landscape spotted with Special Economic Zones, where workers assemble appliances or cars designed and sold elsewhere, and logistical centres that sort wares to be distributed on Western markets (Pobłocki 2017). It is not too badly organised, but still rather unpredictable, as a region where in one lifespan people can experience a couple of revolutions that can on each occasion profoundly transform how things are.

In fact, Poland, Hungary and other countries of the region are much more normal than Western Europe, if we take normality to mean the global, statistical norm. Similar fates are shared by many non-Western nations. In a world that is actually characterised by permanent crisis and continuous disruption, the semblance of stability offered by the countries of global West and North is rather unique, stemming from the metropolitan privilege that manages to export instability elsewhere.

At its worst, this semi-peripheral condition can descend into aspirational racism and homebrewed authoritarianism. At its best, it can root for new, trans-border imaginaries and solidarity networks. Being semi-connected, hovering at the borderlines, in flight from one temporary project to another, might prompt the radicalised projectarians of the region to change this sentiment into action and move towards the constitution of an actually-existing and not merely illusory, borderless world.

S   is for sprint

Projectarians are natural sprinters. They rush from one project to another, with acute understanding of the transitory character of their own ventures. As the end of every project is nigh, they deal with the temporariness imposed by → deadlines by proliferating their activities. They need to make sure that they will never find themselves at a dead end, with no project in sight. They run forward to escape the looming angst of → exclusion. Even in the context of the general stoppage caused by the coronavirus pandemic, they responded with yet another rush of overproduction, shifting their activities to social media and channels of e-communication. Moving fast, they → capture and → trawl ideas, reputations, contacts and connections. This penchant for multitasking embodies structural tendencies of the network to expand, which is the cause and reason for the proliferation and temporariness of projects:

> the project is a transient form (...) adjusted to a network world by multiplying connections and proliferating links, the succession of projects has the effect of extending networks. The extension of the network is life itself, whereas any halt to its extension is comparable to death (Boltanski and Chiapello 2005: 111).

Commenting on this imposed short-termism, Gerald Raunig suggests that the contemporary industries of creativity adopt project-related temporality in order to prompt flexible yet efficient structures of production (Raunig 2013: 102). In industries of creativity and factories of knowledge 'time can no longer be clearly assigned according to dual parameters like work and leisure, production and reproduction, employment and unemployment, but is striated and smoothed beyond these designations' (Raunig 2013: 102). This temporality, 'striated' and 'smoothed' by project-driven interruptions, enables new forms of exploitation which expand beyond the work-place and consequently beyond working-hours, as the punch-clocks of creative workers 'know no on and off but only countless versions of on' (Raunig 2013: 142). As a consequence of this apparently unchained temporality, the engagement and → <u>enthusiasm</u> of projectarians is subsumed as a 'veritably endless source of new possibilities for commodification' (Raunig 2013: 103).

Thus, the projectariat's fondness for uninhibited mobility (→ <u>I is for independence</u>) is not a flight of fancy, but rather one of the basic laws of social physics regulating artistic circulation. Move or perish, says this rule, → <u>enthusiastically</u> obeyed by the legions of sprinters whether they like it or not. At the beginning of the run, early in their careers, freelance artists and curators often enjoy the thrill of the chase. It is simply exhilarating to run after projects, get the buzz, grab opportunities and move on in search of the next ones. But how many projects can one do before succumbing to → <u>burn-outs</u>, especially if racetracks are rigged by inherent privilege (→ <u>O is for one percent</u>) and where odds work against many (→ <u>W is for winner takes it all</u>)? All in all, running fast over short distances does not bode well for participating in marathons. Dazzled by the flurry of short-term assignments, projectarians miss the strategic dimension of their fight and plight and their capacity to establish durable alliances is weakened. The projectarians' psyche becomes as distributed, capricious and multiplied as the projects they chase, the tendency countered by → <u>free/slow</u> collectives and other support structures that serve as new, better → <u>time machines</u>.

S   is for squabbles

When even grand ideas, political idioms, radical theories and artistic experiments are captured as cultural → capital, petty squabbles follow. Instead of becoming politicised, the affects, desires and bodies of projectarians are capitalised, just to secure cynical advancements for micro → entrepreneurs. The artistic circulation is populated by huge egos, eager to take the moral high ground and put themselves before others, legitimising their pursuits by donning robes of radical politics – not to → repurpose the apparatuses for the sake of many, but rather to get on with business as usual. Such pseudo-radicals are ready to correct others, while never missing an → opportunity for their own advancement. They are an awful crowd, to be avoided at all times, possibly even worse than → networkers, who are at least fun and amiable compared to these hypocritical champions of pseudo-radicalism, who are usually insufferably uptight.

However, uncovering hypocrisy can easily devolve into yet another sectarian witch hunt, destroying movements by eradicating trust. Paradoxically, a key method of attack in such squabbles is reproaching others for being petty careerists. Considering huge amounts of energy wasted on such personalised politics, a radical → generosity and → interdependent inclusivity seem to be a much better option, granting fellow → art workers the benefit of the doubt. The general rule of thumb is to focus on actions rather than words, especially considering that both genuinely concerned projectarians and → cynical operators may use very similar vocabularies and theoretical references. In any case, camaraderie is forged in struggles, mettle tested in → productive withdrawals and trust generated in → patainstitutional networks.

It is important here, I think, to underline this systemic perspective. Otherwise, instead of developing a sharp dialectical analysis of circulation, we end up describing a typical tit-for-tat wherein networkers squabble with each other for bits and pieces of prestige and connections. Most of those interpersonal conflicts are squabbles rather than struggles, symptoms of the systemic arrangement that turns people into → entre-preneurs of the self, obsessed with their own investments. Projectarians-as-entrepreneurs get totally paranoid that somebody will 'steal' their precious ideas, grab opportunities before they do or cut them out of the loop. This anxiety is not entirely ungrounded, no doubt about it, as artistic circulation is full of → cynical opportunists. However, just as Rasheed Araeen said (see → G is for generosity), ideas should never become a property of any individual (Araeen 2010). Everybody can then relax a bit, because it is more or less certain that any idea of theirs has been already thought by someone else – and that for every opportunity out there, hundreds of equally competent individuals will be competing, most of whom are fellow → art workers. So better to have done with those squabbles and focus our energies on bringing about a world where all those talents will not go to waste – and where ideas can multiply in the process of → generous exchange. But to get this done, projectarians need to engage in a project larger than themselves, stay with the → struggle and exercise their shared → interdependence in practice and not only in theory.

S   is for struggles

The organisational grammar of circulation supports everything, even projects openly hostile to networked capitalism or authoritarian politics, as long as they do not last too long. One can make projects about the common, equality, socialism, real democracy, feminisms, environmental justice, against racism and xenophobia. And move on soon after, to make yet another project about yet another fashionable topic (→ T is for turns). The obvious problem arises that structural change – however understood – will not materialise as a result of such short-term undertakings, despite the best intentions of their initiators. In particular, the climate catastrophe is the trouble that we will have to live with because, as Donna Haraway discusses in her recent book, it will stay with us, whether we like it or not (Haraway 2016).

The challenge for projectarians is to stay tuned to a problem and embed the flow of projects in a social or political struggle, animated by distributed multitudes, social movements or political parties, despite the short-termism embedded in circulation, reversing the logic of fashion that organises its daily operations. And projectarians do in fact often rise to this challenge, → repurposing the circulation for the sake of what Martha Rosler termed the 'artistic mode of revolution', responding to the global wave of occupations from the early 2010s (Rosler 2011) (→ C is for curatorial mode of production/revolution). Rosler keenly observed the radicalisation of bohemian hipsters, previously cherished by neoliberal propaganda as useful idiots of gentrification, who during Occupy Wall Street became politically active, protesting against inequality and demanding real rather than nominal democracy. After the occupation dissipated, the multitudes engaged in organising numerous other projects and campaigns, keeping up with their radical credo.

The first iconic poster of Occupy featured a ballerina dancing on the massive bull of Wall Street, her pirouette an expression of defiance and imagination, transgressing the self-referential logic of financial circulation. Her dance had both a spin and a thrust, driven by hope, similar to the one about which Rebecca Solnit wrote:

> Hope is not like a lottery ticket you can sit on the sofa and clutch, feeling lucky [...] Hope is an axe you break down doors with in an emergency; because hope should shove you out the door, because it will take everything you have to steer the future away from endless war, from the annihilation of the earth's treasures and the grinding down of poor and marginal. Hope just means another world might be possible, not promised, not guaranteed. Hope calls for action; action is impossible without hope (Solnit 2016: 4).

Change needs hope, time, a movement and a political organisation that can address and transform the dynamics of power. Even though the late 2010s saw the rise of a number of new left parties, like Podemos in Spain, Razem in Poland, Momentum in the UK, Diem25 in the EU or the movement around Bernie Sanders in the USA, most of those parties have failed at gaining much political traction, and their strategic reach is still too small to ensure a lasting political transformation, especially in comparison to the scale of the far-right political offensive.

Nevertheless, the relationships between nomadic assemblages, social movements and (or) political organisations have to be stabilised in order to direct the flows of social energy for the sake of social change. One might think that such stabilisation could be provided by an institution, as they are supposedly more vertically organised, and stay intact despite transitory projects. Such is the argument of Pascal Gielen, who perceives institutions as stabilisers of values in the otherwise overtly fluid world of networked capitalism (Gielen 2013).

The problem is that institutions, especially of an artistic ilk, are prone to the logic of fashion (→ T is for turns), turning around in search of new ideas, anxious about losing significance. That is why museums have to be → repurposed to become socially useful and to serve their publics, who are treated as constituents – i.e. as collective political subjects, rather than mere customers – an institutional model advocated by the editors and authors of two seminal tomes published in the framework of L'Internationale Coalition of European Museums (Aikens et al. 2016; Byrne et al. 2018). Manuel Borja-Villel, the director of Reina Sofia Museum in Madrid, one of the largest museums in Europe, advocates for the institutions to learn from social movements, embedding their exhibitions, collections and educational programmes in the struggles for real democracy, while trying to democratise themselves in the process (Borja-Villel 2018). This was the aim of the exhibition *Really Useful Knowledge*, curated by the collective What, How and for Whom in 2014, which not only featured examples of art and knowledge generated in the context of social struggles, but also hosted activist groups. This included the anti-austerity campaign White Wave, who opposed what they termed austerocide, i.e. an austerity-driven genocide (→ B is for belt-tightening), including the privatisation of the Spanish health service. During the exhibition, the activists of White Wave voiced their concerns using the format of a Greek chorus, an action that they repeated on multiple other occasions during assemblies and protests (for more examples of this kind of action, see → D is for demonstration of paintings). An activist group of facilitators and coordinators called subtramas, who worked at the Museum, have suggested that such activities negotiate between two different logics – of an institution and a movement – hybridising them both (subtramas et al. 2018). As Claire Bishop argues, museums can be radicalised by → repurposing the means at their disposal; for example, the Reina Sofia Museum's collection was rehung to contextualise *Guernica* by Pablo Picasso to tell the story of the anti-fascist struggles of the Spanish Civil War (Bishop and Perjovschi 2014). Similar ways of affiliating with social struggles were tested during the → Anti-fascist Year in Poland. Such activities are always linked, both within the struggle itself and internationally, with other networks and coalitions. The Anti-fascist Year, for instance, established and maintained strong connections with campaigns like the Anti-fascist Coalition in Poland, collectives like the UK-based Keep it Complex, which emerged in the context of anti-Brexit advocacy and continued after, and institutional alliances like the L'internationale. In order to stay with the struggle and establish lasting alliances, individual projectarians, their → patainstitutions and institutions proper have to unlearn their own habits, moving away from their current aim of staying competitive in the dense symbolic jungle of global circulation.

T   is for...

T

is for time machines

Radical segments of the projectariat aim at → repurposing time machines of artistic → circulation. The → common is not only a material or immaterial resource but also a different arrangement of the → apparatuses that regulate the flow of social time. Artistic circulation is organised into patterns of what we can call the speculative time complex, which remixes future, present and past, removing all the moments in which human reflectivity and agency could potentially unfold, a phenomenon analysed by Suhail Malik and Armen Avenessian in the general context of digital capitalism (Avanessian and Malik 2016). The time of circulation is comparable to the time of stock exchanges, where values and stocks are flipped in nanoseconds. In artistic networks, and especially on the global art market, people speculate about future values of artistic trajectories and art objects, commodifying them both. Every project shreds time into bits and pieces. Past achievements are recycled to secure future prospects while applications entomb artistic processes by formulating schedules into the future, well before anyone involved could ever begin to experience anything. For precarious art workers, every passage from one project to another, every passing → opportunity, every → deadline and every → application is a time machine that eradicates the present. To grab opportunities, one has to capitalise on the past that is reinvested into new futures. Caught in the never-now, projectarians are deprived of agency, as this involves not only following the flow, but having the capacity to stir its direction.

Having a successful career means that one gets more of the same: a celebrated art worker needs to circulate even more, make more projects, answer more emails and attend more events, as Hito Steyerl sensibly points out (Steyerl 2016). It sounds like an awful lot, unless one can afford to hire studio assistants. But even this might not mitigate the feeling of being spread too thin, mired in a messy tangle composed of fragments of the past, desires for the future and momentary impulses.

Art workers, when integrated into the global circulation of art, expect returns on their current precarity. But in the → <u>winner-takes-it-all</u> economy, many artists will never get anything except what they already know: precarity and debt. This nexus forges an iron link between debt and the art market which is mediated, at least in some countries, by student loans, as is succinctly analysed by Sholette, who takes up the collective research done by such groups as Occupy Museums (and their project Debt Fair), Strike Debt or bfamfaphd to analyse the political economy of this bare art world (Sholette 2017: 53–77). Caught in the capitalist debt loop, which Lazzarato and David Graeber analyse (Graeber 2012; Lazzarato 2012), artists are forced to compete for access to opportunities and the art market – from which they are not able to escape, but in which they are not able to succeed.

→ <u>Productive withdrawals</u>, as modes of instituting the common, are also, or especially, important because they interrupt these routines, building new, better social time machines, to reuse a term coined by Suhail Malik during one of his lectures in London. The multitudes on strike try to establish different relationships between present and future as they struggle to come up with alternatives to the deadened productivity of artistic circulation, in which everything moves so that nothing can change. When Liberate Tate worked with the purpose of ending the partnership between the Tate and British Petroleum, they operated within a clearly strategic horizon (Evans 2015). They transgressed the logic of temporary projects by embedding each of them into a carefully planned campaign. So, every one of their actions, such as the *Gift* from 2014 when they donated a discharged wind turbine to the collection of the Tate Modern in London, was aimed strategically at dismantling the ties between the Tate and BP. Liberate Tate organised the *Gift* by efficiently applying models of project management. They researched artistic conventions, found a good idea, mobilised activists and artists to carry out an action, procured a turbine, brought it to the Turbine Hall, made a press release, invited media, ticking all the boxes of a successful artistic project. But instead of simply dispersing soon after, satisfied with a job well done, Liberate Tate carried on and stayed with the → <u>struggle</u>. Eventually, in 2016, BP officially resigned from their partnership with the Tate after 26 years of sponsorship, citing challenging business conditions (Khomami 2016). Even after that sponsorship ended, Liberate Tate carried on with lobbying other cultural institutions, like the British Museum and the Royal Shakespeare Theatre, to cut their ties with extractivist industries.

Liberate Tate and others like them demand that public art institutions are → repurposed, transformed from being mere outlets devoted to 'art washing' to being → institutions of the common. Such repurposed institutions should propose a vision of a sustainable future, which can be democratically discussed with the aim of preventing the climate mayhem and mitigating its effects. Instead of expecting individual returns on their precarity, members of campaigns like Liberate Tate and Art not Oil invest themselves in collective futures, dismantling neoliberal time machines.

These better social time machines are put in motion to gain collective access to the means of subsistence. The main demand of the organizers of Art Strike in Poland in 2012 was to introduce retirement programmes for artists, who are currently excluded from participating in the public pension and healthcare systems due to their intermittent working patterns (Figiel 2014). Art Strike disrupted any social illusions that such a miserable condition is the individual responsibility of entrepreneurial artists. In this way, Polish art workers resonated with other advocacy groups, like the American W.A.G.E. (Working Artists and the Greater Economy), who state in their Womanifesto: 'W.A.G.E. believes that the promise of exposure is a liability in a system that denies the value of our labor. As an unpaid labor force within a robust art market from which others profit greatly, W.A.G.E. recognizes an inherent exploitation and demands compensation' (W.A.G.E. 2021b). Members of these collectives debunk the ideology of return-on-precarity and unmake the concept of artists as → entrepreneurs of the self. To advocate for more reasonable policies, politicised art workers underscore the strategic and general character of artistic contributions to the cultural common, advocating for a collective right to the future (spelled out in basic terms as pension, health care and social welfare).

T   is for trawling

Whereas → <u>entrepreneurs of the self</u> specialise in capturing snippets of reified social energies as their own → <u>capital</u>, larger players are in the wholesale trade of trawling the flow of social value. Just as Internet giants are not interested in our individualised content – who posted what where – but in big data, larger artistic events and global institutions go for the big game, by anticipating global trends, attracting thousands of subscribers, catering to audiences of millions and making millions' worth of sales pitches. Luc Boltanski compares this capitalist form of artistic circulation to the world of finance, where big traders set the investment trends and are followed by throngs of smaller investors, who flock to those attractors with their petty capital, reconfirming the decisions taken by the movers and shakers (Boltanski 2014: 29). In this theoretical perspective, the multitudes play only derivative roles, conforming to decisions taken by bigger players, deprived of their own agency. The difference between stock markets and art networks is that bigger players in contemporary art are still vulnerable to the stoppage of social flow, like the one caused by the COVID-19 crisis, whilst the stock markets appeared untouched (because of the infusion of speculative capital, released by central banks). Museums were still dependent on ticket sales and mass tourism, larger events were suspended, and even auctions are not the same online.

In any case, tracing the connections between artistic → <u>commons</u> and privatised → <u>capital</u> unearths the relative character of those hierarchies, because to trawl social energy on the move, even the bigger players have to take note of where smaller fishes swim. As such, this situation is extremely volatile, exposed to the whimsical nature of fashions, and the bigger players have to manage this human traffic by encroaching upon alternatives, assuming the position of trend setters and gate keepers. The easiest and most popular strategy of assuming domination is to exclude the alternatives and strip them of visibility (→ <u>D is for dark matter</u>). This strategy is often seen throughout Eastern Europe, as provincial players secure their own privileged access to global networks by side-lining anyone but their own cliques. When networks grow and get more complex, such narrow-minded strategies become less plausible, as larger artistic institutions are expected to keep up appearances, stay tuned and never lose the cool factor. As not everything can be done in-house, and it is hard to be both hierarchically managed and vibrant, larger institutions need to outsource, commission and co-opt. Just as Internet giants buy out promising start-ups in order to thwart the competition before it is too big to sell out cheaply, the global museums try to co-opt alternatives, always on the look out for the next big thing that appears up-and-coming or threatening enough. This is an interesting situation, as what at first glance seems to be a show of strength in fact exposes institutional vulnerability. It might be perceived as an opportunity to be taken by radical projectarians, but far too often this social game of co-optation is won by those with greater clout.

Instead of playing the cat-and-mouse of institutional critique – where 'radical' artists pretend to address deficiencies of the mainstream art world while working hard to get integrated into it, as described by Andrea Fraser (Fraser 2006), it is much more productive to create lasting alliances with the aim of establishing the → common by liberating institutional infrastructures (MTL Collective 2018).

This tendency of supporting the common can be observed especially amongst the more progressive public institutions, who are losing their traditional grounding in conventions of artistic autonomy (→ C is for circulation) and are either not able or not willing to corporatise themselves as global museum brands. They find their footing by creating alliances with non-traditional audiences and extra-institutional entities (as already discussed in → I is for instituting the commons and → S is for struggles). But the corporate museums and larger events adopt more predatory strategies. They cater to social flows only to exploit them and reinvest capital thus trawled for their own benefit. They are not interested in sustainable symbolic economies, but rather indulge in overfishing, depleting one artistic niche after another, always in search of new fishing grounds to satiate their appetites and their urge for expansion, replicating the patterns of behaviour we associate with financial capital.

T   is for turns, or on the vicious cycle

The artistic circulation turns in a rhythm of passing fashions. Everybody looks where others flock, to identify the trend when it is still *en vogue*. Professionalised trend spotters announce yet another – social, educational, curatorial – turn almost every season. Unfortunately, spinning around their own self-referential axis, the denizens of global art worlds easily become turncoats, as following the latest fashion is more important than staying with the → struggle. Ideologues of unapologetic networking spin post-modern mantras to make a virtue out of necessity, because every projectarian, willingly or not, has to chase the flow of interchangeable → opportunities by capitalising on political idioms or artistic ideas. Institutions, on the other hand, have to cater to capricious audiences who need to be fed with 'something new' every season, even if it is the same old stuff under a new guise. Passing intellectual trends deliver on that front, especially given that their announcers can always count on the short attention span and even shorter memory of their publics. In the end, in circulation, people are only as good as their last projects – and the turnover of people and ideas is so fast that nobody cares. Paradoxically, the centrifugal power of this vortex is so enormous that even when social machines of remembrance, such as museums or academia, get into circulation, they also tend to capitulate to structurally induced amnesia. Even if they are established as custodians of memory, they are forced to come up with new exhibitions, papers and conferences every season, revisiting old themes only if they look like something new, paralysed by their own fear of irrelevance. Thus, the cult of youthful → enthusiasm flourishes, even if its main virtue is to repeat old mistakes. The artistic → dark matter, a spinning underbelly of this turning universe, is too engulfed in its own atomised resentment to serve as a repository of memory. Thankfully, not everybody turns, and this circular logic is resisted by those configurations of institutions, collectives, projectarians and movements who aim at establishing better social → time machines. Their refusal to forget is all the more important in the age of returning fascisms, as social amnesia is one of the prerequisites of their success (→ A is for Anti-fascist Year).

T

is for twilight, or support structures against exclusion

The paradox of circulation, organised by the → winner-takes-it-all economy, is that those who suffer most are → excluded from the platforms where protests against injustice can be staged. The → dark matter of the art world is invisible, thus voiceless, and would remain so if only gate keepers were able to exercise full control over the means of visibility and articulation. Fortunately, the vessels of circulation leak and the network, in its expansionistic drive, is a realm of always shifting shadows, a multiplication of twilight zones. This architecture of semi-visibility is one of the factors motivating projectarians in their entrepreneurial efforts, justifying their → enthusiasm. In the end, all of those people who circulate are never entirely invisible, even if not very famous, and thus always in → fear of being entombed in darkness, without next projects to move onto.

Instead of succumbing to the logic of competitive individualism, underpinned by anxiety, radicalised projectarians create collective support structures for those who are not-yet or already-not excluded. An interesting aspect of Gregory Sholette's analysis of the artistic dark matter is his keen observation of the patainstitutional entities that try to mobilise it politically (Sholette 2011: 152–86). All the mock institutions he describes are located on the fringes of the mainstream art world and its informal support networks, occupying the twilight zones of reputational hierarchies. As a result of their activities 'the dark matter is getting brighter' (Sholette 2011: 3), challenging the cruel economy of visibility that characterises the mainstream art world. They constitute what the Basekamp collective from the USA names as plausible art worlds, that not only grant their own specific visibility to those involved, but also sustain artistic production beyond the conventions of the gallery-exhibition nexus (Basekamp Group & Friends 2013).

Artistic trade unions, collectives and brigades of precarious art workers gather those who are neither totally invisible nor really famous, mutualising their visibility, thus creating platforms for voicing their concerns. By collectivising, they unmake the fixation with individual status and constitute fragile yet real safety nets of mutual sympathy and → generosity that engender trust and facilitate friendships. This social glue brings critical practitioners together, not reliant on the competitive mechanisms of global artistic circulation, exercising their → interdependence in the real world. One example of such a support network is the Pirate Care group that emerged in the transitional zone between Croatia and the UK in 2019 and riffs on the legacy of both → art workers and hackers' movements. This is how the group presents itself:

> Pirate Care is a transnational research project and a network of activists, scholars and practitioners who stand against the criminalization of solidarity & for a common care infrastructure. Pirate Care researches, gathers & nourishes those care initiatives which are taking risks by operating in the narrow grey zones left open between different knowledges, institutions and laws, inviting all to participate in an exploration of the mutual implications of care and technology that dare to question the ideology of private property, work and metrics. Neoliberal policies have for the last two decades re-organised the basic care provisions that were previously considered cornerstones of democratic life – healthcare, housing, access to knowledge, right to asylum, freedom of mobility, social benefits, etc. – turning them into tools for surveilling, excluding and punishing the most vulnerable. The name Pirate Care refers to those initiatives that have emerged in opposition to such political climate by self-organising technologically-enabled care & solidarity networks (Pirate Care 2019).

The Pirate Care network showed its mettle in the midst of the coronavirus pandemic, immediately starting to generate an online repository that catered to the needs of self-help groups that organised in response to the crisis. This self-generated syllabus featured practical advice for doorstep activism and facilitated theoretical discussions to make sense of this crisis of social reproduction. The Pirate Care network is just one example of the wider trend of establishing support structures that do not replace universal welfare, but rather aim to strengthen it. Another example is a Precarity Office based in Vienna, established in 2013, a space for precarious workers 'to get and give informal advice, meet and discuss, hear about our respective struggles and develop them further' (Precarity Office Vienna 2013), that during the migration crisis of 2015–16 engaged in solidarity actions with refugees trying to find shelter in Europe (→ B is for (no) borders).

The ability of such initiatives to sustain contact and friendships, regardless of the → exclusion perpetuated by the → winner-takes-it-all economy, is important for a potential political mobilisation of not-yet or currently-not excluded projectarians. Within the social architecture of circulation, the excluded are also atomised. Disconnected projectarians not only disappear from the horizon of the network, they also become disconnected from each other and much more often fall prey to → burn-outs and depressions, those pathologies of individualised responsibility. Interdependent support structures link people who are under direct threat of → exclusion, and enable them to publicly discuss their shared problems, exchange information and self-organise. Thus, they contribute to the emergence of nascent, counter public spheres, an example of what Ewa Majewska terms as weak, non-heroic resistance (Majewska 2017), that addresses not only grand political structures, but also dwells in the twilight zone of social reproduction, creating spaces of self-articulation and self-organisation.

V is for...

V   is for visibility

The projectarian obsession with visibility and exposure is not merely a matter of individual vanity, but rather a factor of survival in the global networks of contemporary art, where access is mediated by reputations. If projectarians are not seen for too long, they are quickly forgotten and → excluded, not connected and not generating any further connections. For this reason, taking a longer break, for whatever reason, fills people with dread (→ K is for (no) kids). Personal visibility is a halo of the → entrepreneurial self. Capturing ideas as individual → capital is done by being 'seen on the scene', to use Pascal Gielen's expression (Gielen 2009: 50–54). Only communicating openly and announcing ideas in public, in front of a peer group, secures recognition. In this way, ideas become more or less formally attached to their announcers, prompting and propelling their reputational advances. The louder the announcement is, and the more people hear it, the greater the chances are that this act of attribution will be appreciated. Most projectarians do not have a lot of opportunities to announce their ideas on the global scene, so they have to satisfy themselves with much smaller audiences. Even if they are the 'first' to formulate a ground-breaking idea, all the clout goes to perhaps less creative but more visible peers who promote their – sometimes even derivative – concepts on the global stage. In the → winner-takes-it-all economy, people who occupy central positions and are already recognised are much more eligible to promote any ideas as 'their' own. Moreover, they cherish access to publishing channels that grant global recognition of their acts of → capture. In this system, gate keepers are able to extract their toll by regulating the flow of communication. Global institutions, publishers or newsletter lists guarantee the public staging of ideas, rubberstamping authorial assertions and personal reputations. For this reason, those institutions are able to either charge directly for their services or exhort free contributions from projectarians, → trawling their energies.

This economy of visibility depreciates invisible labour, enabling its exploitation. In any given project, the gains are never distributed equally, and it is the → labours of love and of → pollination that are most often both invisible and underpaid (a feminist economist analysis of the role played by invisibility in the capitalist economy is explained in → A is for apparatus). The gains do not directly relate to the workload, but rather to a professional profile in the network, which is reciprocally based on access and visibility, i.e. some people play the authorial roles and get recognised as such, while others are pushed into subservient positions.

But visibility is a double-edged sword, as artists or curators are often 'paid' only in exposure. Consequently, artists are expected to work for free, only for the promise of symbolic recognition that may contain the potential to turn into access to jobs, projects and other → opportunities. However, they often end up working for nothing, because only very few mechanisms exist for converting their reputations into 'real' money; the majority of projects are unpaid, jobs are scarce and the art market serves the ideological function of arousing aspirations rather than of providing the means of subsistence (at least for all but a commercially successful few). The majority of artists work for mere visibility: they circulate in order not to disappear – and show off just to stay in circulation.

W is for...

W   is for wages
(for artwork)

The fixation with individual → <u>visibility</u> only seemingly works in favour of artists or people who struggle to generate their own portfolios, such as independent curators. They often end up with neither money nor opportunities, paid instead in empty promises of delayed rewards. The structural crisis caused by the coronavirus pandemic only proved how vain these hopes are, unattainable at the best of times – and outright ridiculous when prosperity plummets.

This architecture of postponed gratification is structurally embedded in what Cynthia and Harrison White termed as the critic-dealer system, and what Luc Boltanski analysed as the domestic mode of circulation (Boltanski 2014; White and White 1993). In this mode, artists produce art works in their studios, and after a while these works are 'discovered' by critics, put on sale by dealers and finally bought by collectors. The exchange of money is secondary to the rhythms of symbolic appreciation, and everything takes a long time. This was mapped into the social architecture of symbolic capital, as analysed by Pierre Bourdieu who wrote about the autonomous fields of art from the nineteenth and twentieth centuries (Bourdieu 1996). Symbolic capital is a field-specific token of reputation and an embodied capacity to make future gains (→ <u>C is for capital</u>). Symbolic capital, according to Bourdieu, is based – at least superficially – on giving up direct material benefits. Artists were expected to make art for the love of art (→ <u>A is for Artyzol</u>). Money came into this equation, but at later stages, and often mystified by the topsy-turvy economy of the art market where art-things cost a lot because they are deemed priceless. The ultra-rapid circulation of art objects and art projects that emerged in the 1970s and 1980s has rewired the social conventions of symbolic capital for the sake of big players. Those players are able to monetise art works on the secondary art market, with its rapid turnover, rewriting artistic reputations as sales pitches. In the case of institutional elites, they use the aura of art to justify their pleas for donations, to attract patrons and sponsors. But, as Hans Abbing argues, the same elites who so eagerly capitalise on the symbolic aura of art are quite willing to solicit the unpaid labour of artists and other art enthusiasts who work for nothing but the love of art (Abbing 2014). They have to 'eat art' as Hito Steyerl once quipped (Steyerl 2016), feeding themselves on the empty promises of symbolic advancements, future recognition and big sales, as if the old architecture of modernist art was still in place. This benefits both the institutional players (who avoid paying in hard cash) and the art market (which positions itself as the only economic outlet for artists), but is devastating for artists and those in other artistic professions. Interestingly, paying in prestige is used as a motivational carrot not only for artists, but also for interns, curators, writers and facilitators, who are often unpaid and instead fed with promises of future gains, as analysed by the London-based Carrot Workers Collective and Precarious Workers Brigade (Precarious Workers Brigade 2017).

To cut through this Gordian knot and unmake the obsession with individual visibility, such groups as New York-based W.A.G.E. and the Polish Civic Forum for Contemporary Art advocate for wages for art work. By the means of voluntary certification (W.A.G.E.) and collective negotiations (Civic Forum), they try to persuade smaller and larger artistic institutions to pay exhibition fees to artists. At least in Poland, this campaign has been successful – and in 2014 major artistic institutions agreed to pay such artistic fees for both group and solo shows, recognising the artists' appalling economic situation (→ P is for poor (artists)). W.A.G.E. also achieved a considerable success as by early 2021 as many as 84 institutions were certified and $7.5 million had been paid in fees (W.A.G.E. 2021a).

The same principles are adopted by → patainstitutions to combat rampant self-exploitation. The most entrepreneurial multitudes – like the activists occupying Macao in Milan – even manage to generate financial gains, which are shared between all involved as a kind of basic income. One only needs to spend enough hours, monthly, on collective undertakings (regardless of whether it involves intellectual or physical labour) to receive a share in revenues – which are equally distributed among everyone involved, incentivising solidarity.

Patainstitutional economies involve mutualising the benefits of projects conducted in the spirit of the common, accounting for all types of labour and forms of capital. Simply speaking, this means paying wages to all, crediting everyone, multi-authoring results and creating non-hierarchical spaces where everybody can mingle together and enact inclusive forms of governance. The introduction of even such basic measures is no small feat and continues to be rare in artistic circulation, which offers a semblance of flatness, while reinforcing hierarchies.

On a more general level, equalised distribution within the network is secured by experiments with open licensing, the creative commons, the art commons and other radical licences, all well recognised and widely discussed as a partial measure against the expropriation of social labour.

On a political level, this kind of equalisation is expressed in the political identification of → art workers, which aims at creating solidarity between professional groups that are otherwise easily exploited for the sake of networked governance, a governance that thrives on atomisation, cynical → opportunism and → entrepreneurialism of the self. Wages for art work is such an important idea, because it disincentivises freelancers from succumbing to competitive entrepreneurialism by creating a baseline of equality, the important side effect of which is to prevent → exclusions, as even the less-recognised projectarians get paid and acknowledged.

The campaign for wages for artwork resembles the strategies of Marxist-feminist campaigners who in the 1970s and 1980s advocated for wages for (and against) housework (Federici 1975). As analysed by Kathi Weeks and J.K. Gibson-Graham, these campaigns were often misrepresented and ridiculed by their political adversaries (from both left and right), as if their demand was to commodify and industrialise the domestic sphere, transform care labour into wage labour (Gibson-Graham and Cameron 2003; Weeks 2011). But, as Sylvia Federici posits, their aim was to positively valorise domestic labour, while undermining capitalist forms of alienated labour and finding means of → commoning social production and reproduction (Federici 2012; 2017). J.K. Gibson-Graham tells us that the aim of community economics is to establish systems of material and social support based on the appreciation of the value of non-monetised labour, instead of monetising it directly. In the case of housework, such support includes: public childcare, which frees women of the burdens of housework; municipal grants for collective childcare; legal rights for paternal and maternal leave; provision of common infrastructure – such as parks, communal housing, community gardens – that facilitate the → labour of love; promotion of collective forms of living and sharing reproductive duties. Similar arguments are made by Angela McRobbie in the context of the creative industries, when she analyses the trajectories of female creatives in Berlin and advocates for much stronger public and cooperative support systems aimed at providing childcare and socialising the burdens of domestic labour (McRobbie 2006; 2015).

In the case of art work (almost) nobody advocates for employing artists or freelance curators as institutional functionaries, but rather for changing the systems of social provision in recognition of the cultural and social value generated by them (as discussed in the entry on → art workers). Often, what works for artists would also work for other people too: universal health care, cheap housing, free education, better wages, less work, unrestrained access to benefits and other forms of social wage. Or, in the most utopian formula, the universal basic income, as advocated by the authors and signatories of the recently published manifesto *Art for UBI*, where they write:

> While the art market confirms his status as a safe-haven assets provider for the financial elite, the current pandemic has highlighted the fragility and precarity of art workers around the world, a condition common to a growing portion of humanity. In this situation a UBI (Universal Basic Income) would then represent a solution and indeed an urgent measure to implement. But UBI is not 'only' a response to poverty, it is a necessary condition in order to rethink our extractivist ecological model, to correct many race and gender asymmetries and, last but not least, to change the art world's present neoliberal structure. UBI must be seen as a tool to open up new subjective spaces, alternative to the dominating entrepreneurial individualism and focused instead on commons and care (Institute of Radical Imagination 2021).

Specifically artistic modes of support, such as exhibition fees, artistic grants, state commissions or such programmes as '1% for arts' (which obliged investors to commission artists as part of every new commercial or public development), should be interpreted in the context of universal social welfare and not as a derivative of the misguided exceptionalism of art.

Artistic circulation is a winner-takes-it-all economy, following Hans Abbing's analysis of what he labels the cruel economy of the arts (Abbing 2002). This economic arrangement causes most projectarians to be → poor, spawning stark inequalities between the select few and the impoverished many (→ D is for dark matter). Adding insult to injury, in the winner-takes-it-all economy, the winners are celebrated as the sole authors of their success, while the losers bear the brunt of systemically imposed failures, naturalised as their own personal imperfections. Obviously, in a system where the majority are doomed to fail, most actually will. However, such inequalities do not derive from natural differences in talent or capacity for hard work. Quite a lot of independent artists and curators are pretty talented, and most of them work extremely hard, but only very few will ever achieve 'success'. The inequalities of the artistic subsystem are amplified by the unrestrained accumulation of resources at the very top of the social ladder on the global scale, which is a long-term effect of → neoliberalism. In this system, costs are socialised and profits privatised, camouflaging the social labour that underpins every fortune. In the same way, in artistic circulation, individual trajectories are supported by different forms of distributed social labour (→ L is for labour of love and → P is for pollination).

The question remains: why do winners win? In the cruel economy of artistic circulation, the acquisition of reputations, securing of positions, sales on the art market or seizing of more profitable opportunities all depend on an individualised portfolio of contextualised capital (reputations, contacts, financial standing). Basically, the rule of thumb is that the person with the largest amount of capital will benefit most from any given project. Even small differences in initial status (of the background privilege of new projectarians, for example) accumulate over time and create skewed hierarchies between art celebrities and artistic dark matter.

Here, a comparison to sport comes in handy. In professional football, there are only relatively small differences between junior footballers when it comes to their skills, talents and results. Due to the processes of selection, the ones who start to play in better leagues have a much higher chance of winning everything, as they have better trainers, more time devoted to training, excellent and demanding peers, confidence and recognition. After a decade or two, this competitive regime produces stark hierarchies between players, especially when it comes to their earnings.

Coming back to artistic circulation, some of these mechanisms can be isolated, even though the field of contemporary art is not as professionalised as sport and the differences in performance are even more relative. Gregory Sholette reminds us, using the example of artistic higher education in the USA, that the careers of young artists are streamlined depending on which college they attend. More prestigious programmes offer not only artistic skills, as those are devalued, but also contact with successful artists, their dealers and peers, ingraining in their alumni a tacit understanding of how the industry operates and imbuing them with the social skills necessary to pursue their careers (Sholette 2017). These students are recommended to more prestigious residencies, selected for biennales and quickly secure their affiliations with better galleries, all of which enhances their chances of success.

These injustices are clearly gendered, as the most prestigious positions in art, academia, the higher echelons of the art market and the curatorial circuits are usually occupied by men (→ K is for (no) kids) and founded on stark inequalities when it comes to class, race and citizenship, because the global networks of art are mostly roamed by privileged people from the global North-West (→ B is for (no) borders).

The basic law of social accumulation, which enables people who have more capital to acquire an even larger share of social labour, is particularly important for maintaining class, racial and gender hierarchies on a global scale in a superficially horizontal or flattened world of networks and flows. When Pascal Gielen criticises freelance curators as 'joy riders' – opportunistic and cynical – who freely roam the globe in search of more interesting and beneficial undertakings (Gielen 2009: 36–37), he is actually describing people who already enjoy fairly privileged positions in the network, while the rest struggle to deal with precarious reality.

But, even more importantly, the meritocracy supposedly underpinning their exploits is a convivial myth. Just as Andrea Phillips and Suhail Malik argue, meritocracy is an organic ideology of neoliberalism, because it naturalises inherited privileges (Malik 2013; Phillips and Malik 2012). This analysis echoes Pierre Bourdieu's critique of education and art as modes of reproducing class hierarchies, where both fields select those who have been already preselected by the privilege of birth and elitist upbringing that imbues people with proper attitudes, habits, confidence, modes of being and accents that are positively valorised in art and academia. Despite its own ideological aspirations to flatness, artistic circulation distributes its benefits mostly to people who already enjoy privileged access because of their class, gender, race or citizenship (→ O is for one percent).

Y is for...

In a system that individualises success, failure must also be suffered in solitude, causing depression to become the professional illness of freelancers, who take individual responsibility for structurally induced risks. In this context, finding and enacting alternatives should entail a shift from → independent careers to → interdependent undertakings. In this way, we can maintain shared → support structures and create bulwarks against → exclusion, sustained by the social trust generated in the course of cooperation and → struggles. When art workers partake in → instituting the commons, they are not alone. And this social approach has political potential because support structures serve as spaces of mutual recognition where people can act in front of their equals, discuss issues of importance and formulate and execute agendas. Otherwise, the excluded, who suffer the most, remain invisible not only at the level of global networks, but also to each other and to other compatriots. Therefore, staying in touch, creating platforms based on trust and mutual respect and caring for the things we hold in common are supremely important. Solidarity among the projectariat is the key condition for positive action within artistic circulation, where all that should be solid tends to melt into flows.

Credits

In writing this book I have used – thoroughly edited and reassembled – fragments of the PhD thesis defended at the Loughborough University School of the Arts (2015), my Polish book *ABC Projektariatu* (2016), academic papers, journal articles and book chapters that have been published between 2013 and 2020 in outlets like the *E-Flux Journal*, *Praktyka Teoretyczna*, *L'internationale Online*. The detailed bibliographic references are provided below:

Szreder, Kuba. 2013. 'Cruel Economy of Authorship.' In *Undoing Property?*, edited by Marysia Lewandowska and Laurel Ptak, 41–56. Berlin; New York: Sternberg Press.

———. 2015a. 'How to Radicalize a Mouse. Notes on Radical Opportunism.' In *Mobile Autonomy: Exercises in Artists' Self-Organization*, edited by Nico Dockx and Pascal Gielen, 195–219. Amsterdam: Valiz.

———. 2015b. 'Politicising 'Independent' Curatorial Practice under Neoliberalism: Critical Responses to the Structural Pressures of Project-Making.' Loughborough: School of the Arts, Loughborough University.

———. 2016. *ABC Projektariatu. O Nędzy Projektowego Życia*. Warszawa: Bęc Zmiana.

———. 2017a. 'Exercises in the Curatorial Open Form: On the Example of Exhibition Making Use. Life in Postartistic Times.' *Art & the Public Sphere*, 2017.

———. 2017b. 'Productive Withdrawals: Art Strikes, Art Worlds, and Art as a Practice of Freedom.' *E-Flux Journal*, December 2017. www.e-flux.com/journal/87/168899/productive-withdrawals-art-strikes-art-worlds-and-art-as-a-practice-of-freedom (accessed 1 April 2021).

———. 2018. 'Instituting The Common In Artistic Circulation: From Entrepreneurship Of The Self To Entrepreneurship Of The Multitude.' *Praktyka Teoretyczna*, no. 27: 194–223.

———. 2020. 'Independence Always Proceeds from Interdependence: A Reflection on the Conditions of the Artistic Precariat and the Art Institution in Times of Covid-19.' *L'internationale Online*. internationaleonline.org/opinions/1021_independence_always_proceeds_from_interdependence_a_reflection_on_the_conditions_of_the_artistic_precariat_and_the_art_institution_in_times_of_covid_19 (accessed 1 April 2021).

———. 2021. 'Interdependent Curating.' *Arts of the Working Class*. artsoftheworkingclass.org/text/interdependent-curating (accessed 8 July 2021).

———. 2021 (forthcoming). 'Projectarians.' In *Anti-Atlas: Towards a Critical Area Studies*, edited by Wendy Bracewell, Tim Beasley-Murray and Michał Murawski, London: UCL Press.

Szreder, Kuba and Kathrin Böhm. 2020. 'How to Reclaim the Economy Using Artistic Means: The Case of Company Drinks.' In *The Handbook of Diverse Economies*, edited by J.K. Gibson-Graham and Kelly Dombroski. Northampton: Edward Elgar Publishing.

Bibliography

A

Abbing, Hans. 2002. *Why Are Artists Poor?: The Exceptional Economy of the Arts*. Amsterdam: Amsterdam University Press.

Abbing, Hans. 2014. 'Notes on the Exploitation of Poor Artists.' In *Joy Forever. Political Economy of Social Creativity*, edited by Michał Kozłowski, Agnieszka Kurant, Jan Sowa, Krystian Szadkowski and Kuba Szreder, 83–100. London: MayFly Books and Bęc Zmiana.

Aikens, Nick, Thomas Lange, Jorinde Seijdel and Steven ten Thije, eds. 2016. *What's the Use? Constellations of Art, History, and Knowledge: A Critical Reader*. Amsterdam: Valiz.

Amoah, Susuana. 2020. '#GallerySoWhite: A Digital Exhibition Exposing Racism in Contemporary Art Spaces.' The Conversation. 2020. theconversation.com/gallerysowhite-a-digital-exhibition-exposing-racism-in-contemporary-art-spaces-153920 (accessed 1 April 2021).

An Architektur, Massimo De Angelis, and Stavros Stavrides. 2010. 'On the Commons: A Public Interview with Massimo De Angelis and Stavros Stavrides.' *E-Flux Journal*, June 2010. www.e-flux.com/journal/on-the-commons-a-public-interview-with-massimo-de-angelis-and-stavros-stavrides (accessed 1 April 2021).

András, Edit. 2014. 'Vigorous Flagging in the Heart of Europe: The Hungarian Homeland under the Right-Wing Regime.' *E-Flux Journal*, September 2014. www.e-flux.com/journal/57/60438/vigorous-flagging-in-the-heart-of-europe-the-hungarian-homeland-under-the-right-wing-regime (accessed 1 April 2021).

Apostol, Corina. 2015. 'Art Workers Between Precarity and Resistance: A Genealogy.' *Artleaks Gazette*, August 2015.

Araeen, Rasheed. 2010. *Art Beyond Art: Ecoaesthetics: A Manifesto for the 21st Century*. London: Third Text Publications.

Aranda, Julieta, Anton Vidokle, and Brian Kuan Wood. 2011. *E-Flux Journal: Are You Working Too Much? Post-Fordism, Precarity, and the Labor of Art*. Berlin; New York: Sternberg Press.

Argyropoulou, Gigi. 2018. 'Destituent Spaces and Improvised Institutions between Collectivity and Critique.' Unpublished manuscript.

Avanessian, Armen, and Suhail Malik, eds. 2016. *The Time Complex: Post-Contemporary*. Berlin: NAME publications.

B

Badovinac, Zdenka. 2020. 'Interdependence, or, Secrecy as the Last Universal Right.' *E-Flux Journal*, June 2020. www.e-flux.com/journal/110/336891/interdependence-or-secrecy-as-the-last-universal-right (accessed 1 April 2021).

Baker, Catherine. 2014. 'The Local Workforce of International Intervention in the Yugoslav Successor States: "Precariat" or "Projectariat"? Towards an Agenda for Future Research.' *International Peacekeeping* 21(1): 91–106. doi.org/10.1080/13533312.2014.899123.

Baravalle, Marco. 2018a. 'Art Populism and the Alter-Institutional Turn.' *E-Flux Journal*, March 2018. www.e-flux.com/journal/89/182464/art-populism-and-the-alter-institutional-turn (accessed 1 April 2021).

Baravalle, Marco. 2018b. 'Alter-Institutions and Art. Between Governance and Autonomy. Capture, Subjectivity, Decolonization, Governance, Acceleration, Queering, Imaginary Economics.' Unpublished manuscript.

Basekamp Group & Friends. 2013. *Plausible Artworlds*. S.l.: lulu.com.

Bauman, Zygmunt. 1998. *Globalization: The Human Consequences*. New York: Columbia University Press.

Becker, Howard S. 1984. *Art Worlds*. Berkeley, CA; London: University of California Press.

Beech, Dave. 2019. *Art and Postcapitalism: Aesthetic Labour, Automation and Value Production*. London: Pluto Press.

Beech, Dave, Mel Jordan and Andy Hewitt. 2011. 'Economists Are Wrong! The Warsaw Manifesto 2011.' In *Joy Forever. Political Economy of Social Creativity*, edited by Michał Kozłowski, Krystian Szadkowski, Agnieszka Kurant, Jan Sowa and Kuba Szreder, 237–249. London: MayFly Books.

Belfiore, Eleonora. 2004. "Auditing Culture." *International Journal of Cultural Policy* 10(2): 183–202.

Belting, Hans, Andrea Buddensieg and Peter Weibel, eds. 2013. *The Global Contemporary and the Rise of New Art Worlds*. Karlsruhe, Germany; Cambridge, MA; London, England: ZKM/Center for Art and Media; The MIT Press.

Benjamin, Walter. 1970. 'The Author as Producer.' *New Left Review*, August 1970. www.newleftreview.org/?view=135 (accessed 1 April 2021).

Berardi, Franco. 2009. *The Soul at Work: From Alienation to Autonomy*. Los Angeles: Semiotext(e).

Berardini, Andrew. 2014. 'How to Survive International Art: Notes from the Poverty Jetset.' Momus. 1 December 2014. momus.ca/how-to-survive-international-art-notes-from-the-poverty-jetset (accessed 1 April 2021).

bfamfaphd. 2014. 'Artists Report Back.' New York: bfamfaphd.

Bishara, Hakim. 2021. 'Over 150 Artists Call for Leon Black's Removal From MoMA's Board Over Jeffrey Epstein Financial Ties.' *Hyperallergic*, February. hyperallergic.com/619709/artists-call-for-leon-blacks-removal-moma-jeffrey-epstein (accessed 1 April 2021).

Bishop, Claire. 2006. 'The Social Turn: Collaboration and Its Discontents.' *Artforum*, February 2006.

Bishop, Claire. 2012. *Artificial Hells: Participatory Art and the Politics of Spectatorship*. London; New York: Verso Books.

Bishop, Claire and Dan Perjovschi. 2014. *Radical Museology or, "What's Contemporary" in Museums of Contemporary Art?* 2, rev. edn. London: Koenig Books.

Böhm, Kathrin and Miranda Pope. 2015. *Company: Movements, Deals and Drinks*. Heyningen: JAP SAM Books.

Böhm, Kathrin and Kuba Szreder. 2020. *Icebergian Economies of Contemporary Art*. www.pirammmida.life/cpe (accessed 1 April 2021).

Böhm, Kathrin and Kuba Szreder. 2020. 'How to Reclaim the Economy Using Artistic Means: The Case of Company Drinks.' In *The Handbook of Diverse Economies*, edited by J.K. Gibson-Graham and Kelly Dombroski, 527–535. Northampton: Edward Elgar Publishing.

Boltanski, Luc. 2014. 'From Object to Œuvre. The Process of Attribution and Valorization of Objects.' In *Joy Forever. Political Economy of Social Creativity*, edited by Michał Kozłowski, Krystian Szadkowski, Agnieszka Kurant, Jan Sowa and Kuba Szreder, 17–49. London: MayFly Books.

Boltanski, Luc and Eve Chiapello. 2005. *The New Spirit of Capitalism*. London: Verso.

Borja-Villel, Manuel. 2018. 'Really Useful Knowledge.' In *The Constituent Museum: Constellations of Knowledge, Politics and Mediation: A Generator of Social Change*, edited by John Byrne, Elinor Morgan, November Paynter, Aida Sanchez de Serdio and Adela Zeleznik, 76–80. Amsterdam: Valiz.

Bourdieu, Pierre. 1984. *Distinction: A Social Critique of the Judgement of Taste; Translated by Richard Nice*. London: Routledge.

Bourdieu, Pierre. 1996. *The Rules of Art: Genesis and Structure of the Literary Field*. Cambridge: Polity Press.

Bourriaud, Nicolas. 2002. *Relational Aesthetics*. Dijon: Les presses du réel.

Bourriaud, Nicolas. 2009. *The Radicant*. New York: Lukas & Sternberg.

Bourton, Lucy. 2021. 'The White Pube Takeover Billboards to Address Systemic Injustices and Inequalities in the Art World.' *It's Nice That*, January 2021. www.itsnicethat.com/news/the-white-pube-buildhollywood-art-campaign-290121 (accessed 1 April 2021).

Boutang, Yann Moulier. 2007. 'Cognitive Capitalism and Entrepreneurship: Decline in industrial entrepreneurship and the rising of collective intelligence.' Conference on Capitalism and Entrepreneurship. Cornell University, Ithaca, New York, 28–29 September 2007.

Bradfield, Marsha. 2020. 'Ordinary Extraordinary: The Para/Pata:Institutionalism of Critical Practice.' *Journal of Visual Art Practice* 19(1).

Braidotti, Rosi. 2015. 'Nomadic European Identity.' In *No Culture, No Europe: On the Foundation of Politics*, edited by Pascal Gielen, 97–115. Antennae Series, no. 15. Amsterdam: Valiz.

Brandenburger, Adam M. and Barry J. Nalebuff. 1997. *Co-Opetition*. New York: Currency Doubleday.

Brook, Orian, David O'Brien and Mark Taylor. 2018. 'Panic! Social Class, Taste and Inequalities in the Creative Industries.' Report. Edinburgh: University of Edinburgh.

Brown, Imani Jacqueline. 2020. 'Them: Reflections on Truth as Theatrical Fiction.' In *Things We Do Together: The Post-Reader*, edited by Marianna Dobkowska and Krzysztof Łukomski, 106–36. Warszawa: CSW Zamek Ujazdowski; Mousse Publishing.

Brown, Kate. 2019. '"Everyone at a Place Like Art Basel Is Complicit": Artists May Be Making Art About Climate Change, But Nobody at the Fair Wants to Talk About It.' *Artnet News*, June 14, 2019. news.artnet.com/market/art-basel-climate-change-1571881 (accessed 1 April 2021).

Bruno, Isabelle. 'Governing Social Creativity Through Benchmarking.' In *Joy Forever. Political Economy of Social Creativity*, edited by Michał Kozłowski, Krystian Szadkowski, Agnieszka Kurant, Jan Sowa, and Kuba Szreder, 143–57. London: MayFly Books, 2014.

Bryan-Wilson, Julia. 2010. 'Art versus Work.' In *ART WORK A National Conversation About Art, Labor, and Economics*, edited by Temporary Services, 4–5. Chicago: Temporary Services.

Bryan-Wilson, Julia. 2011. *Art Workers: Radical Practice in the Vietnam War Era*. Oakland, CA: University of California Press.

Buchloh, Benjamin H. D. 1990. 'Conceptual Art 1962-1969: From the Aesthetic of Administration to the Critique of Institutions.' *October*, 1 December 1990, 105–144.

Buraya, Sara, Paula Moliner and Manuela Pedron. 2018. 'Towards a Coordination Ethic.' In *The Constituent Museum: Constellations of Knowledge, Politics and Mediation: A Generator of Social Change*, edited by John Byrne, Elinor Morgan, November Paynter, Aida Sanchez de Serdio and Adela Zeleznik, 202–6. Amsterdam: Valiz.

Bürger, Peter. 1984. *Theory of the Avant-garde*. Manchester: Manchester University Press.

Butler, Judith. 2006. *Precarious Life: The Powers of Mourning and Violence*. London; New York: Verso.

Butler, Judith. 2015. *Notes Toward a Performative Theory of Assembly*. Cambridge, MA: Harvard University Press.

Byrne, John. 2016. 'Social Autonomy and the Use Value of Art.' *Afterall*, Autumn/Winter 2016: 61–69.

Byrne, John, Gemma Medina and Alessandra Saviotti. 2018. 'Asociación de Arte Útil: A Nomadic and Multiform Platform for Usership.' Unpublished manuscript.

Byrne, John, Elinor Morgan, November Paynter, Aida Sanchez de Serdio and Adela Zeleznik, eds. 2018. *The Constituent Museum: Constellations of Knowledge, Politics and Mediation: A Generator of Social Change*. Amsterdam: Valiz.

C

CAMP. 2020. 'CAMP / Center for Art on Migration Politics / Artistic Visions for a Humane Refugee and Migration Policy.' CAMP / Center for Art on Migration Politics. 2020. campcph.org (accessed 1 April 2021).

Carrillo, Jesús. 2017. 'Conspiratorial Institutions? Museums and Social Transformation in the Post-Crisis Period.'

Wrong Wrong Magazine, 26 June 2017. wrongwrong.net/article/conspiratorial-institutions-museums-and-social-transformation-in-the-post-crisis-period (accessed 1 April 2021).

CASCO, ed. 2018. *Unlearning Exercises: Art Organizations as Sites for Unlearning*. Amsterdam: Valiz, book and cultural projects.

Certeau, Michel de. 1984. *The Practice of Everyday Life*. 3rd edn. Berkeley, CA: University of California Press.

Chayka, Kyle. 2019. 'Can the Art World Kick Its Addiction to Flying?' *Frieze*, 26 December 2019. frieze.com/article/can-art-world-kick-its-addiction-flying (accessed 1 April 2021).

Child, Danielle. 2019. *Working Aesthetics: Labour, Art and Capitalism*. London: Bloomsbury Academic.

Child, Danielle, Helena Reckitt and Jenny Richards. 2017. 'Labours of Love: A Conversation on Art, Gender and Social Reproduction.' *Third Text* 31(1): 147–68. doi.org/10.1080/09528822.2017.1365492.

Choi, Binna and Annette Krauss. 2017. 'Unlearning Institution: Do as You Present (or Preach).' In *How Institutions Think: Between Contemporary Art and Curatorial Discourse*, edited by Lucy Steeds, Paul O'Neill and Mick Wilson, 66–78. Cambridge, MA: MIT Press.

Chto Delat? 2009. 'Declaration by Chto Delat/What Is to Be Done? /// We Are Not Off!' 2009. www.chtodelat.org/index.php?option=com_content&view=article&id=574%3Awe-are-not-off&catid=205%3A02-26-new-commons-living-knoledge-action&Itemid=454&lang=en (accessed 1 April 2021).

Cichocki, Sebastian. 2019. 'In Search of Impact (yet Again). Postartistic Practices in Twenty-First Century Poland.' In *On the Edge: Culturescapes Poland 2019*, edited by Kateryna Botanova and Wojciech Przybylski, 111–23. Warsaw: Culturescapes Poland.

Cichocki, Sebastian and Kuba Szreder. 2016. 'San Precario.' MAKING USE. 2 February 2016. makinguse.artmuseum.pl/en/san-precario (accessed 1 April 2021).

Citizens' Forum for Contemporary Art. 2020. 'Obywatelskie Forum Sztuki Współczesnej: Stanowisko OFSW w Sprawie Koronawirusa i Sytuacji Artystycznego Prekariatu.' *Obywatelskie Forum Sztuki Współczesnej* (blog). 14 March 2020. forumsztukiwspolczesnej.blogspot.com/2020/03/stanowisko-ofsw-w-sprawie-koronawirusa.html (accessed 1 April 2021).

Committee for the Radical Change in Culture. 2009. 'Manifesto of the Committee for the Radical Change in Culture.' *Variant*, 15 October 2009. www.variant.org.uk/37_38texts/1ed_2manifest.html (accessed 1 April 2021).

Cossu, Alberto. 2015. 'Mobilizing Art. An Inquiry on the Role of Art in Social Movements: The Case of Macao.' Milan: Politecnico di Milano. air.unimi.it/handle/2434/292851 (accessed 1 April 2021).

Cossu Alberto and Marianna d'Ovidio and. 2017. 'Culture Is Reclaiming the Creative City: The Case of Macao in Milan, Italy.' *City, Culture and Society* 8 (March): 7–12. doi.org/10.1016/j.ccs.2016.04.001.

Critical Practice, ed. 2011. *Parade: Modes of Assembly and Forms of Address*. London: CWC.

Cross, Samuel, Yeanuk Rho, Henna Reddy, Toby Pepperrell, Florence Rodgers, Rhiannon Osborne, Ayolola Eni-Olotu, Rishi Banerjee, Sabrina Wimmer and Sarai Keestra. 2021. 'Who Funded the Research behind the Oxford-AstraZeneca COVID-19 Vaccine? Approximating the Funding to the University of Oxford for the Research and Development of the ChAdOx Vaccine Technology.' Preprint. Health Policy.

Cummings, Neil. 2014a. 'A Joy Forever.' In *Joy Forever. Political Economy of Social Creativity*, edited by Michał Kozłowski, Agnieszka Kurant, Jan Sowa, Krystian Szadkowski and Kuba Szreder. London: MayFly Books.

Cummings, Neil. 2014b. 'Generosity.' In *Truth Is Concrete: A Handbook for Artistic Strategies in Real Politics*, edited by Florian Malzacher, 325–328. Berlin; New York; Graz: Sternberg Press; Steirischer Herbst.

Cummings, Neil, Marsha Bradfield and Amy McDonnell. 2018. 'Three Metonyms for Critical Practice: Jig, Foam and Yield.' Unpublished manuscript.

Cvejić, Bojana and Maurizio Lazzarato. 2010. 'Conversation with Maurizio Lazzarato.' *TkH Journal for Performing Arts Theory*, 17(4–5): 12–17.

Ćwikła, Małgorzata. 2016. *Projekt to Jest Projekt. Specyfika Zarządzania Projektami Kulturalnymi Na Przykładzie Tworzenia Koprodukcji Teatralnych*. Kraków: Attyka.

D

De Angelis, Massimo. 2003. 'Reflections on Alternatives, Commons and Communities or Building a New World from the Bottom Up.' *The Commoner*, 6, January 2003.

De Carolis, Massimo. 1996. 'Toward a Phenomenology of Opportunism.' In *Radical Thought in Italy: A Potential Politics*, edited by Paolo Virno and Michael Hardt, 37–53. Minneapolis: University of Minnesota Press.

De Landa, Manuel. 2006. *New Philosophy of Society: Assemblage Theory and Social Complexity*. London: Continuum.

Debtfair. 2015. 'Debtfair Manifesto.' 2015. debtfair.org/viewer/38 (accessed 1 April 2021).

Deleuze, Gilles. 1992. 'Postscript on the Societies of Control.' *October*, Winter 1992: 3–7.

Deleuze, Gilles and Félix Guattari. 1987. *A Thousand Plateaus: Capitalism and Schizophrenia*. Minneapolis: University of Minnesota Press.

Demos, TJ. 2019. 'Climate Control: From Emergency to Emergence.' *E-Flux Journal*, November 2019. www.e-flux.com/journal/104/299286/climate-control-from-emergency-to-emergence (accessed 1 April 2021).

Depczyński, Jakub and Stefańska, Bogna. 2021. 'Sztuka użyteczna. Praktyki artystyczne wobec kryzysu klimatycznego.' *Quart. Kwartalnik Instytutu Historii Sztuki Uniwersytetu Wrocławskiego* 1(59): 66–86.

Design Museum. 2020. 'TOP 10 WORLD'S RICHEST LIVING ARTISTS.' *Design Museum* (blog). 7 June 2020.

www.designmuseum.me/artists/top-10-worlds-richest-living-artists-nowadays (accessed 1 April 2021).

Diederichsen, D. 2008. *On (Surplus) Value in Art*. Berlin; New York: Sternberg Press.

Dimitrakaki, Angela. 2013. *Gender, Art Work and the Global Imperative: A Materialist Feminist Critique*. Rethinking Art's Histories. Manchester; New York: Manchester University Press.

Dimitrakaki, Angela. 2018. 'Feminism, Art, Contradictions.' *E-Flux Journal*, June 2013. www.e-flux.com/journal/92/205536/feminism-art-contradictions (accessed 1 April 2019).

DIS, and Ecocore. 2019. 'The Carbon Footprint of the Art World.' *DIS Magazine* (blog). 2019. dismagazine.com/dystopia/67560/the-carbon-footprint-of-the-artworld (accessed 1 April 2021).

Dobkowska, Marianna and Krzysztof Łukomski, eds. 2020. *Things We Do Together: The Post-Reader*. Warszawa: CSW Zamek Ujazdowski; Mousse Publishing.

duvaR.english. 2020. 'Prosecutor Seeks Life Sentences for Three Gezi Park Defendants in Final Legal Opinion.' duvaR.english. 6 February 2020. www.duvarenglish.com/domestic/2020/02/06/prosecutor-seeks-life-sentences-for-three-gezi-park-defendants-in-final-legal-opinion (accessed 1 April 2021).

E

Eco, Umberto. 1995. 'Ur-Fascism.' *New York Review of Books*, June 1995: 12–15.

Erdődi, Katalin. 2016. 'A Weird Geography.' *Mezosfera.Org*, no. 1 (April). mezosfera.org/a-weird-geography (accessed 1 April 2021).

Esche, Charles. 2010. 'The Deviant Art Institution.' In *Performing the Institution(al), Volume 1*, edited by Kunsthalle Lisbon. Lisabon: Kunsthalle Lissabon; ATLAS Projectos.

Evans, Mel. 2015. *Artwash: Big Oil and the Arts*. London: Pluto Press.

F

Falvey, Deirdre. 2020. '"Exposure Doesn't Pay Bills": What Artists Say about Freebie Culture.' 12 February 2020. www.irishtimes.com/culture/exposure-doesn-t-pay-bills-what-artists-say-about-freebie-culture-1.4171271?mode=amp&fbclid=IwAR0gCZPp27pCHsEgtdbgzWJBnVDXVLnX9x7B5-cAldvJXJ1giL4O5gbZv0M (accessed 1 April 2021).

Fard, Farah Joan. 2017. 'Women Outnumber Men At Art Schools – So Why Isn't Their Work Being Shown In Galleries Once They Graduate?' *Bustle*, May. www.bustle.com/p/women-outnumber-men-at-art-schools-so-why-isnt-their-work-being-shown-in-galleries-once-they-graduate-55299 (accessed 1 April 2021).

Federici, Silvia. 1975. *Wages against Housework*. Bristol: Power of Women Collective; FaDing Wall Press.

Federici, Silvia. 2012. *Revolution at Point Zero: Housework, Reproduction, and Feminist Struggle*. Oakland, CA; Brooklyn, NY; London: PM Press; Common Notions: Autonomedia.

Federici, Silvia. 2017. 'Feminism and the Politics of the Commons.' In *Former West. Art and the Contemporary After 1989*, edited by Simon Sheikh and Maria Hlavajova, 379–90. Cambridge, MA: MIT Press.

Figiel, Joanna. 2014. 'On the Citizen Forum for Contemporary Arts.' *Artleaks Gazette*, September 2014, No. 2: 27–32.

Figiel, Joanna. 2015. 'Podsumowanie i Komentarz Do Zogniskowanych Wywiadów Grupowych.' In *Fabryka Sztuki*, edited by Michał Kozłowski, Jan Sowa and Kuba Szreder, 274–304. Warszawa: Bęc Zmiana.

Finch, Janet and Dulcie Groves, eds. 1983. *A Labour of Love. Women, Work, and Caring*. London; Boston: Routledge & K. Paul.

Fischer, Noah. 2015. 'Agency in a Zoo: The Occupy Movement's Strategic Expansion to Art Institutions.' *Field. A Journal of Socially-Engaged Art Criticism*, Winter 2015.

Fisher, Mark. 2009. *Capitalist Realism: Is There No Alternative?* London: Zero Books.

Foster, Dawn. 2016. *Lean Out*. London: Repeater.

Foster, Hal. 1995. 'The Artist as Ethnographer.' In *The Traffic in Culture*, edited by George Marcus and Fred Myers, 302–9. Berkeley, CA: University of California Press.

Foucault, Michel. 1980. *Power/Knowledge: Selected Interviews and Other Writings, 1972–1977*. Edited by Colin Gordon. New York; London: Harvester Wheatsheaf.

Foucault, Michel. 1990. *The History of Sexuality, Vol. 1: An Introduction*. Translated by Robert Hurley. New York: Vintage.

Foucault, Michel. 1997. *The Politics of Truth*. Los Angeles, CA: Semiotext(e).

Foucault, Michel. 2010. *The Birth of Biopolitics: Lectures at the Collège de France, 1978–1979*. Edited by François Ewald and Alessandro Fontana. Basingstoke: Palgrave Macmillan.

Fraser, Andrea. 2006. 'From the Critique of Institutions to an Institution of Critique.' In *Institutional Critique and After*, edited by John C. Welchman, 123–37. Zurich: JRP|Ringier.

Fraser, Andrea. 2011. 'L'1%, c'est moi.' *Texte Zur Kunst*, September 2011, no. 83: 114–27.

G

Gibson-Graham, J.K. and Kelly Dombroski, eds. 2020. *The Handbook of Diverse Economies*. Northampton: Edward Elgar Publishing.

Gibson-Graham, J.K. 2006. *Postcapitalist Policies*. Minneapolis, MN: University of Minnesota Press.

Gibson-Graham, J.K. and Jenny Cameron. 2003. 'Feminising the Economy.' *Gender, Place and Culture*, no. 10(2): 145–57.

Gielen, Pascal. 2009. *Pascal Gielen: The Murmuring of the Artistic Multitude. Global Art, Memory and Post-Fordism*. Amsterdam: Valiz.

Gielen, Pascal. 2010. 'Curating with Love, or a Plea for Inflexibility.' *Manifesta Journal*, 2010, no. 10: 14–26.

Gielen, Pascal. 2013. *Creativity and Other Fundamentalisms*. Heyningen: JAP SAM Books.

Gielen, Pascal and Paul de Bruyne, eds. 2009. *Being an Artist in Post-Fordist Times*. Rotterdam: NAi Publishers.

Gilbert, Jeremy. 2013. 'What Kind of Thing Is "Neoliberalism"?' *New Formations: A Journal of Culture/Theory/Politics*, no. 80–81: 7–22.

Gordon Nesbitt, Rebecca. 2005. 'Don't Look Back in Anger.' In *European Cultural Policies 2015: A Report with Scenarios on the Future of Public Funding for Contemporary Art in Europe*, edited by Maria Lind and Raimund Minichbauer, 4–14. Stockholm; Vienna: Iaspis; eipcp.

Gordon Nesbitt, Rebecca. 2008. 'The New Bohemia.' *Variant*, Summer 2008.

Graeber, David. 2012. *Debt: The First 5000 Years*. New York: Melville House.

Graeber, David. 2018. *Bullshit Jobs*. New York: Simon & Schuster.

Graw, Isabelle. 2009. *High Price: Art between the Market and Celebrity Culture*. Berlin; New York: Sternberg Press.

Greer, Ian, Barbara Samaluk and Charles Umney. 2018. 'Toward a Precarious Projectariat? Project Dynamics in Slovenian and French Social Services.' *Organization Studies*, October.

Gromada, Anna, Dorka Budacz, Juta Kawalerowicz and Anna Walewska. 2015. 'Marne Szanse Na Awanse? Raport z Badania Na Temat Obecności Kobiet Na Uczelniach Artystycznych w Polsce.' Warszawa: Fundacja Katarzyny Kozyry.

Groys, Boris. 2008. 'The Loneliness of the Project.' *New York Magazine of Contemporary Art and Theory*, 2008. www.ny-magazine.org/PDF/Issue%201.1.%20Boris%20Groys.pdf (accessed 1 April 2021).

Gulli, Bruno. 2005. *Labor of Fire: The Ontology of Labor between Economy and Culture*. Philadelphia, PA: Temple University Press.

H

Haben und Brauchen. 2012. 'Haben Und Brauchen 〉 Manifesto.' 20 January 2012. www.habenundbrauchen.de/en/category/haben-und-brauchen/manifest (accessed 1 April 2021).

Haraway, Donna. 2016. *Staying with the Trouble: Making Kin in the Chthulucene*. Durham, NC: Duke University Press.

Hardt, Michael and Antonio Negri. 2005. *Multitude: War and Democracy in the Age of Empire*. London: Hamish Hamilton.

Hardt, Michael and Antonio Negri. 2009. *Commonwealth*. Cambridge, MA: Harvard University Press.

Hardt, Michael and Antonio Negri. 2017. *Assembly*. New York: Oxford University Press.

Harney, Stefano and Fred Moten. 2013. *The Undercommons: Fugitive Planning & Black Study*. Wivenhoe: Minor Compositions.

Harvey, David. 2005. *A Brief History of Neoliberalism*. Oxford: Oxford University Press.

Harvey, David. 2006. 'The Art of Rent: Globalization, Monopoly and the Commodification of Culture.' 2006. www.16beavergroup.org/mtarchive/archives/001966.php (accessed 1 April 2021).

Heller, Joseph. 1994. *Catch-22*. London: Vintage.

Holmes, Brian. 2002. 'The Flexible Personality.' *Transversal*, January. transversal.at/transversal/1106/holmes/en (accessed 1 April 2021).

Hudson, Alistair. 2015. 'Middlesbrough Institute of Modern Art. Where Do We Go from Here? Vision Statement 2015-2018.' MIMA (online magazine).

I

Ilczuk, Dorota, Ewa Gruszka-Dobrzynska, Ziemowit Socha and Wojciech Walczak. 2018. 'Szacowanie Liczebności Artystów, Twórców i Wykonawców w Polsce.' Warszawa: SWPS.

INCITE! Women of Color Against Violence. 2009. *The Revolution Will Not Be Funded: Beyond the Non-Profit Industrial Complex*. Boston, MA: South End Press.

Institute of Radical Imagination. 2021. 'ART FOR UBI.' INSTITUTE_of_RADICAL_IMAGINATION. January 2021. instituteofradicalimagination.org/the-school-of-mutation-2020/som-iterations/art-for-ubi (accessed 1 April 2021).

Isola Art Center. 2013. *Fight-specific Isola: Art, Architecture, Activism and the Future of the City*. Berlin: Archive Books.

J

Jakobsen, Jakob and Agata Pyzik. 2009. 'Victory! The Beginning, the Life and the End of the Free University of Copenhagen. Agata Pyzik Talks to Jakob Jakobsen.' In *Culture, Not Profit: Readings for Artworkers*, edited by Katarzyna Chmielewska, Kuba Szreder and Tomasz Zukowski. Warszawa: Fundacja Nowej Kultury Bec Zmiana. www.wuw-warsaw.pl/download/Jakob_Jakobsen_Interview.pdf (accessed 1 April 2021).

Jałocha, Beata. 2016. 'Projectocracy or Projectariat?: How Project Work Shapes Working Conditions in Public, Non Governmental and Business Sectors.' In *9th Annual Conference of the EuroMed Academy of Business: Innovation, Entrepreneurship and Digital Ecosystems*, edited by Demetris Vrontis, Yaakov Weber and Evangelos Tsoukatos, 2022–25. Warszawa: EuroMed Press.

Jameson, Fredric. 1991. *Postmodernism or, the Cultural Logic of Late Capitalism*. Durham, NC: Duke University Press.

Jarry, Alfred. 1996. *Exploits & Opinions of Doctor Faustroll, Pataphysician*. Boston: Exact Change.

Jeffreys, Tom. 2018. 'Survey Shows Extent of Class Divide in Creative Industries.' *Frieze* (blog). 16 April 2018.

frieze.com/article/survey-shows-extent-class-divide-creative-industries (accessed 1 April 2021).

Judah, Hettie. 2018. 'The Art World Is Overwhelmingly Liberal But Still Overwhelmingly Middle Class and White – Why?' *Frieze* (blog). 6 July 2018. frieze.com/article/art-world-overwhelmingly-liberal-still-overwhelmingly-middle-class-and-white-why (accessed 1 April 2021).

Judah, Hettie. 2019. 'Full, Messy and Beautiful.' In *Representation of Female Artists in Britain During 2019*, edited by Kate McMillan, 14–19. London: Freelands Foundation.

Judah, Hettie. 2020a. 'Everyday Heroes: Key Workers Celebrated at Southbank, Where Hundreds Face Sack.' The *Guardian*, September. www.theguardian.com/artanddesign/2020/sep/03/everyday-heroes-review-key-workers-portraits-southbank-centre (accessed 1 April 2021).

Judah, Hettie. 2020b. '"Motherhood Is Taboo in the Art World – It's as If We've Sold out": Female Artists on the Impact of Having Kids.' The *Guardian*, 2 December. www.theguardian.com/artanddesign/2020/dec/02/motherhood-taboo-art-world-sold-out-bourgeoisie (accessed 1 April 2021).

K

Keep it Complex. 2020. '"Competing in a Crisis Is Not a Solution": Arts Activists Want to Form "Solidarity Syndicates" so Funding Can Be Shared.' THE ALTERNATIVE UK. 7 April 2020. www.thealternative.org.uk/dailyalternative/2020/4/11/solidarity-syndicate-arts-funding (accessed 1 April 2021).

Keil, Marta, Igor Stokfiszewski and Agata Adamiecka - Sitek. 2019. 'Feminizacja – Demokracja – Praca. W Stronę Uspołecznionej Instytucji Kultury.' *Didaskalia* 163: 3–5.

Kester, Grant. 2004. *Conversation Pieces: Community and Communication in Modern Art.* Berkeley, CA: University of California Press.

Kester, Grant. 2011. *The One and the Many: Contemporary Collaborative Art in a Global Context.* Durham, NC; London: Duke University Press.

Khomami, Nadia. 2016. 'BP to End Tate Sponsorship after 26 Years.' The *Guardian*, 11 March 2016, sec. Art and design. www.theguardian.com/artanddesign/2016/mar/11/bp-to-end-tate-sponsorship-climate-protests (accessed 1 April 2021).

Kinsella, Eileen. 2017. 'A New Study Shows Most Artists Make Very Little Money, With Women Faring the Worst.' Artnet News. 29 November 2017. news.artnet.com/market/artists-make-less-10k-year-1162295 (accessed 1 April 2021).

Klein, Naomi. 2007. *The Shock Doctrine: The Rise of Disaster Capitalism.* New York: Metropolitan Books.

Klein, Naomi. 2020. '"Coronavirus Capitalism": Naomi Klein's Case for Transformative Change Amid Coronavirus Pandemic.' *Democracy Now!* 19 March 2020. www.democracynow.org/2020/3/19/naomi_klein_coronavirus_capitalism (accessed 1 April 2021).

Kommenda, Niko. 2019. '1% of English Residents Take One-Fifth of Overseas Flights, Survey Shows.' *The Guardian*, 25 September 2019, sec. Environment. www.theguardian.com/environment/2019/sep/25/1-of-english-residents-take-one-fifth-of-overseas-flights-survey-shows (accessed 1 April 2021).

Kortun, Vasif. 2017. 'IN TURKISH THE WORD "PUBLIC" DOESN'T EXIST: Vasif Kortun in Conversation with the Editors.' In *I Can't Work Like This: A Reader on Recent Boycotts and Contemporary Art*, edited by Joanna Warsza, 133–40. Berlin: Sternberg Press.

Kozłowski, Michał. 2019. 'Czym Jest Faszyzm?' *Rok Antyfaszystowski* (blog). 2019. rokantyfaszystowski.org/dlaczego-antyfaszyzm (accessed 1 April 2021).

Kozłowski, Michał, Agnieszka Kurant, Jan Sowa, Krystian Szadkowski and Kuba Szreder, eds. 2014. *Joy Forever. Political Economy of Social Creativity.* London: MayFly Books.

Kozłowski, Michał, Jan Sowa and Kuba Szreder, eds. 2015. *The Art Factory.* Warszawa: Bęc Zmiana.

Krauss, Rosalind. 1979. 'Sculpture in the Expanded Field.' *October*, Spring 1979: 30–44.

Kunst, Bojana. 2015. *Artist at Work, Proximity of Art and Capitalism.* London: Zero Books.

Kwon, Miwon. 2002. *One Place After Another: Site-Specific Art and Locational Identity.* Cambridge, MA: MIT.

L

Lacy, Suzanne, ed. 1995. *Mapping the Terrain: New Genre Public Art.* Seattle, D.C.: Bay Press.

Lafargue, Paul. 1883. *The Right to Be Lazy.* Ardmore, PA: Fifth Season Press.

Lazzarato, Maurizio. 1996. 'Immaterial Labor.' In *Radical Thought in Italy: A Potential Politics*, edited by Michael Hardt and Paolo Virno, 133–51. Minneapolis, MN: University of Minnesota Press. www.generation-online.org/c/fcimmateriallabour3.htm (accessed 1 April 2021).

Lazzarato, Maurizio. 2009. 'The Political Form of Coordination.' In *Art and Contemporary Critical Practice: Reinventing Institutional Critique*, edited by Gerald Raunig and Gene Ray, 161–72. London: MayFly Books.

Lazzarato, Maurizio. 2011. 'The Misfortunes of the "Artistic Critique" and of Cultural Employment.' In *Critique of Creativity: Precarity, Subjectivity and Resistance in the 'Creative Industries,'* edited by Ulf Wuggenig, Gerald Raunig and Gene Ray, 41–57. London: MayFly Books.

Lazzarato, Maurizio. 2012. *The Making of the Indebted Man: An Essay on the Neoliberal Condition.* Los Angeles: Semiotext(e).

Lazzarato, Maurizio. 2014. *Marcel Duchamp and the Refusal of Work.* Los Angeles, CA: Semiotext(e).

Léger, Marc James. 2012. *Brave New Avant Garde: Essays on Contemporary Art and Politics.* London: Zero Books.

Lennard, Natasha. 2019. *Being Numerous: Essays on Non-Fascist Life*. London; New York: Verso.

Lewandowska, Marysia and Laurel Ptak, eds. 2013. *Undoing Property?* Berlin; New York: Sternberg Press.

Lind, Maria. 2018. 'Tensta Museum L'Internationale.' In *The Constituent Museum: Constellations of Knowledge, Politics and Mediation: A Generator of Social Change*, edited by John Byrne, Elinor Morgan, November Paynter, Aida Sanchez de Serdio and Adela Zeleznik, 76–80. Amsterdam: Valiz.

Lind, Maria and Raimund Minichbauer, eds. 2005. *European Cultural Policies 2015: A Report with Scenarios on the Future of Public Funding for Contemporary Art in Europe*. Stockholm; Vienna: Iaspis; eipcp.

Lippard, Lucy. 1973. *Six Years: The Dematerialisation of the Art Object from 1966 to 1972*. London: Studio Vista.

Liscia, Valentina Di and Hakim Bishara. 2020. 'Whitney Museum Cancels Show After Artists Denounce Acquisition Process, Citing Exploitation.' *Hyperallergic*, August. hyperallergic.com/584340/whitney-museum-black-lives-matter-covid-19-exhibition-canceled (accessed 1 April 2021).

Loewe, Sebastian. 2015. 'When Protest Becomes Art: The Contradictory Transformations of the Occupy Movement at Documenta 13 and Berlin Biennale 7.' *Field. A Journal of Socially-Engaged Art Criticism*, Spring 2015.

Lorey, Isabell. 2006. 'Governmentality and Self-Precarization.' *Transversal*, November. eipcp.net/transversal/1106/lorey/en/#_ftn12 (accessed 1 April 2021).

Lorey, Isabell. 2011. 'Virtuosos of Freedom: On the Implosion of Political Virtuosity and Productive Labour.' In *Critique of Creativity: Precarity, Subjectivity and Resistance in the 'Creative Industries,'* edited by Ulf Wuggenig, Gerald Raunig and Gene Ray, 79–91. London: MayFly Books.

Lorey, Isabell. 2015. *State of Insecurity: Government of the Precarious*. London; New York: Verso.

Ludwiński, Jerzy. 2007. *Notes from the Future of Art: Selected Writings of Jerzy Ludwiński*. Eindhoven; Rotterdam: Van Abbemuseum; Veenman Publishers.

M

Maanen, Hans van. 2009. *How to Study Art Worlds: On the Societal Functioning of Aesthetic Values*. Amsterdam: Amsterdam University Press.

Majewska, Ewa. 2017. 'The Non-Heroic Resistance. Singing Mouse, Housewife and Artists in Revolt – Notes from the "Former East."' In *Former West. Art and the Contemporary After 1989*, edited by Simon Sheikh and Maria Hlavajova. Cambridge, MA: MIT Press.

Majewska, Ewa. 2019. 'A Bitter Victory?: Anti-Fascist Cultures, Institutions of the Common, and Weak Resistance in Poland.' *Third Text*, no. 158 (May): 1–17.

Majewska, Ewa and Kuba Szreder. 2016. 'So Far, So Good: Contemporary Fascism, Weak Resistance, and Postartistic Practices in Today's Poland.' *E-Flux Journal*, October 2016. www.e-flux.com/journal/76/71467/so-far-so-good-contemporary-fascism-weak-resistance-and-postartistic-practices-in-today-s-poland (accessed 1 April 2021).

Malik, Suhail. 2013. 'Civic Virtue in Neoliberalism and Contemporary Art's Cartelisation.' In *Mom, Am I Barbarian?* 13th Istanbul Biennial Book, edited by Fulya Erdemici, 630–52. Istanbul: IKSV.

Malzacher, Florian, ed. 2014. *Truth Is Concrete: A Handbook for Artistic Strategies in Real Politics*. Berlin; New York; Graz: Sternberg Press; Steirischer Herbst.

Marazzi, Christian. 2010. *The Violence of Financial Capitalism*. Translated by Kristina Lebedeva. Los Angeles, CA: Semiotext(e).

Mason, Paul. 2015. *PostCapitalism: A Guide to Our Future*. London: Allen Lane.

Mbembe, Achille. 2020. 'The Universal Right to Breathe.' *In the Moment / Critical Inquiry* (blog). 13 April 2020. critinq.wordpress.com/2020/04/13/the-universal-right-to-breathe (accessed 1 April 2021).

McGuigan, Jim. 2005. 'Neo-Liberalism, Culture and Policy.' *International Journal of Cultural Policy* 11(3): 229–41.

McKee, Yates. 2016. *Strike Art: Contemporary Art and the Post-Occupy Condition*. London; New York: Verso.

McRobbie, Angela. 2006. 'Creative London – Creative Berlin.' *Atelier Europa*, 2006. www.ateliereuropa.com/2.3_essay.php (accessed 1 April 2021).

McRobbie, Angela. 2011. 'Re-Thinking Creative Economy as Radical Social Enterprise.' *Variant*, Spring 2011.

McRobbie, Angela. 2015. *Be Creative: Making a Living in the New Culture Industries*. Cambridge, UK; Malden, MA: Polity Press.

Menger, Pierre-Michel. 1999. 'Artistic Labour Markets and Careers.' *Annual Review of Sociology* 25: 541–74.

Mezzadra, Sandro and Brett Neilson. 2013. *Border as Method, or, the Multiplication of Labor*. Durham, NC: Duke University Press.

Migrants in Culture. 2019. 'Migrants in Culture Research Report.' London: Migrants in Culture.

Morgan, Elinor. 2018. 'Middlesbrough's New Communities.' In *The Constituent Museum: Constellations of Knowledge, Politics and Mediation: A Generator of Social Change*, edited by John Byrne, Elinor Morgan, November Paynter, Aida Sanchez de Serdio and Adela Zeleznik, 50–56. Amsterdam: Valiz.

MTL Collective. 2018. 'From Institutional Critique To Institutional Liberation? A Decolonial Perspective on the Crises of Contemporary Art.' *October* 165: 192–227.

N

Negri, Antonio. 2003. 'Constituent Republic.' In *Revolutionary Writing. Common Sense Essays in Post-Political Politics*, edited by Werner Bonefeld. New York: Autonomedia.

Negri, Antonio. 2011. *Art and Multitude: Nine Letters on Art, Followed by Metamorphoses: Art and Immaterial Labour.* Cambridge, MA: Polity.

Neuendorf, Henri. 2016. 'Marina Abramovic Says Kids Hold Back Female Artists.' *Artnet News,* July. news.artnet.com/art-world/marina-abramovic-says-children-hold-back-female-artists-575150 (accessed 1 April 2021).

O

O'Neill, Paul and Claire Doherty, eds. 2010. *Locating the Producers. Durational Approaches to Public Art.* Amsterdam: Valiz.

Online Etymology Dictionary. n.d. 'Precarious.' www.etymonline.com/search?q=precarious&ref=searchbar_searchhint (accessed 1 April 2021).

Ostrom, Elinor. 1990. *Governing the Commons: The Evolution of Institutions for Collective Action.* Cambridge: Cambridge University Press.

P

Penny, Daniel. 2019. 'The Artist-Activists Decolonizing the Whitney Museum.' *The Paris Review* (blog). 22 March 2019. www.theparisreview.org/blog/2019/03/22/the-artist-activists-decolonizing-the-whitney-museum (accessed 1 April 2021).

Petrešin-Bachelez, Nataša. 2017. 'For Slow Institutions.' *E-Flux Journal,* October 2017. www.e-flux.com/journal/85/155520/for-slow-institutions (accessed 1 April 2021).

Phillips, Andrea and Suhail Malik. 2012. 'Tainted Love: Art's Ethos and Capitalization.' In *Contemporary Art and Its Commercial Markets: A Report on Current Conditions and Future Scenarios,* edited by Maria Lind and Olav Velthuis, 209–43. Berlin; New York: Sternberg Press.

Piketty, Thomas. 2017. *Capital in the Twenty-first century.* Cambridge, MA; London: The Belknap Press of Harvard University Press.

Pirate Care. 2019. 'The Pirate Care Project | Pirate.Care.' 2019. pirate.care/pages/concept (accessed 1 April 2021).

Plan C. 2018. 'Acid Communism and Consciousness Raising.' *We Are Plan C* (blog). 22 October 2018. www.weareplanc.org/blog/acid-communism-and-consciousness-raising (accessed 1 April 2021).

Plan C. 2020. 'Pandemic Inequalities, Pandemic Demands.' *We Are Plan C* (blog). 15 March 2020. www.weareplanc.org/blog/pandemic-inequalities-pandemic-demands (accessed 1 April 2021).

Pobłocki, Kacper. 2017. *Kapitalizm: Historia Krótkiego Trwania.* Warszawa: Bęc Zmiana.

Power, Michael. 1997. *The Audit Society: Rituals of Verification.* Oxford: Oxford University Press.

Precarious Workers Brigade. 2011. 'Free Labour Syndrome. Volunteer Work and Unpaid Overtime in the Creative and Cultural Sector.' In *Joy Forever. Political Economy of Social Creativity,* edited by Michał Kozłowski, Agnieszka Kurant, Jan Sowa, Krystian Szadkowski and Kuba Szreder: 211–227. London; Warsaw: MayFly Books and Bęc Zmiana.

Precarious Workers Brigade. 2017. *Training for Exploitation? Politicising Employability and Reclaiming Education.* London, Leipzig, Los Angeles: Journal of Aesthetics & Protest Press.

Precarity Office Vienna. 2013. 'About Precarity Office Vienna.' *Precarity Office Vienna* (blog). 21 August 2013. precarityoffice.wordpress.com/about (accessed 1 April 2021).

R

Ratajczak, Mikołaj. 2014. 'Sztuka i praca. Od ekonomii politycznej produkcji artystycznej do krytycznej filozofii współczesnych form pracy.' In *Skuteczność sztuki,* edited by Tomasz Załuski, 32–56. Łódź: Muzeum Sztuki.

Ratajczak, Mikołaj. 2015. 'Wprowadzenie Do Teorii Kapitalizmu Kognitywnego: Kapitalizm Kognitywny Jako Reżim Akumulacji.' *Praktyka Teoretyczna* 15: 57–95.

Raunig, Gerald. 2009a. 'Instituent Practices: Fleeing, Instituting, Transforming.' In *Art and Contemporary Critical Practice: Reinventing Institutional Critique,* edited by Gerald Raunig and Gene Ray, 3–13. London: MayFly Books.

Raunig, Gerald. 2009b. 'Instituent Practices, No. 2: Institutional Critique, Constituent Power, and the Persistence of Instituting.' In *Art and Contemporary Critical Practice: Reinventing Institutional Critique,* edited by Gerald Raunig and Gene Ray, 173–87. London: MayFly Books.

Raunig, Gerald. 2013. *Factories of Knowledge, Industries of Creativity.* Semiotext(e) Intervention Series 15. Los Angeles, CA: Semiotext(e).

Raunig, Gerald. 2014. 'Occupy the Theater, Molecularize the Museum!' In *Truth Is Concrete: A Handbook for Artistic Strategies in Real Politics,* edited by Florian Malzacher, 76–86. Berlin; New York; Graz: Sternberg Press; Steirischer Herbst.

Raunig, Gerald and Gene Ray, eds. 2009a. *Art and Contemporary Critical Practice: Reinventing Institutional Critique.* London: MayFly Books.

Raunig, Gerald and Gene Ray, eds. 2009b. 'Preface.' In *Art and Contemporary Critical Practice: Reinventing Institutional Critique,* edited by Gerald Raunig and Gene Ray, XIII–XVII. London: MayFly Books.

Ray, Gene. 2011. 'Culture Industry and the Administration of Terror.' In *Critique of Creativity: Precarity, Subjectivity and Resistance in the 'Creative Industries,'* edited by Ulf Wuggenig, Gerald Raunig, and Gene Ray, 167–83. London: MayFly Books.

Relyea, Lane. 2017. *Your Everyday Art World.* Cambridge, MA: MIT Press.

Roberts, John. 2009. 'Productivism and Its Contradictions.' *THIRD TEXT* 23(5): 527–36.

Roberts, John. 2010a. 'Art after Deskilling.' *Historical Materialism* 18. 77–96.

Roberts, John. 2010b. 'The Curator as Producer: Aesthetic Reason, Nonaesthetic Reason, and Infinite Ideation.' *Manifesta Journal* 10: 51–58.

Roberts, John. 2015. *Revolutionary Time and the Avant-Garde*. London; New York: Verso.

Roelandt, Els, Eva Barois de Caevel and Cercle d'art des travailleurs de plantation congolaise, eds. 2017. *Cercle d'art Des Travailleurs de Plantation Congolaise = Congolese Plantation Workers Art League*. Berlin: Sternberg Press.

Rosler, Martha. 2011. 'Martha Rosler, Culture Class: Art, Creativity, Urbanism, Part II.' *E-Flux Journal*, March 2011. e-flux.com/journal/view/219 (accessed 1 April 2021).

Rosler, Martha. 2014. 'The Artistic Mode of Revolution: From Gentrification to Occupation.' In *Joy Forever. The Political Economy of Social Creativity*, edited by Michał Kozłowski, Agnieszka Kurant, Jan Sowa, Krystian Szadkowski and Kuba Szreder, 177–99. London; Warsaw: MayFly Books and Bęc Zmiana.

Ross, Andrew. 2009. *Nice Work If You Can Get It: Life and Labor in Precarious Times*. New York: New York University Press.

Rymsza, Agnieszka. 2005. 'Partnerzy Służby Publicznej? Wyzwania Współpracy Sektora Poza-Rządowego z Administracją Publiczną w Świetle Doświadczeń Amerykańskich.' *Trzeci Sektor* 3: 42–52.

S

Schweiker, Rosalie. 2018. *London's Art Economies*. London: Centre for Plausible Economies.

Sennett, Richard. 1999. *The Corrosion of Character: The Personal Consequences of Work in the New Capitalism*. New York: Norton.

Sevilla-Buitrago, Alvaro. 'Territory and the Governmentalisation of Social Reproduction: Parliamentary Enclosure and Spatial Rationalities in the Transition from Feudalism to Capitalism.' *Journal of Historical Geography* 38: 209–19.

Shani, Tai. 2020. 'Why Art Workers Must Demand the Impossible.' *Art Review*, September. artreview.com/why-art-workers-must-demand-the-impossible (accessed 1 April 2021).

Shaw, Amy and Margaret Carrigan. 2020. 'Reform or Reset? How Cultural Institutions Are Facing a Reckoning over Racism.' *The Art Newspaper*, July. www.theartnewspaper.com/analysis/reform-or-reset-how-cultural-institutions-are-facing-a-reckoning-over-racism (accessed 1 April 2021).

Sholette, Gregory. 2011. *Dark Matter: Art and Politics in the Age of Enterprise Culture*. London; New York: Pluto Press.

Sholette, Gregory. 2017. *Delirium and Resistance: Activist Art and the Crisis of Capitalism*. New York: Pluto Press.

Sholette, Gregory. 2018. 'Optimism of the Will: 2018 FIELD Reports on the Global Resistance to Neoreactionary Nationalism.' *FIELD. A Journal of Socially-Engaged Art Criticism* 12/13. field-journal.com/editorial/optimism-of-the-will-2018-field-reports-on-the-global-resistance-to-neoreactionary-nationalism (accessed 1 April 2021).

Shukaitis, Stevphen. 2014. 'Artstrike and Metropolitan Factory.' In *Joy Forever. The Political Economy of Social Creativity*, edited by Michał Kozłowski, Agnieszka Kurant, Jan Sowa, Krystian Szadkowski and Kuba Szreder, 227–37. London; Warsaw: MayFly Books and Bęc Zmiana.

Solnit, Rebecca. 2016. *Hope in the Dark: Untold Histories, Wild Possibilities*. Chicago, IL: Haymarket Books.

Sowa, Jan. 2009. 'Goldex Poldex Madafaka, or a Report from the (Besieged) Pi Sector.' In *Europejskie Polityki Kulturalne 2015. Raport o Przyszłości Publicznego Finansowania Sztuki Współczesnej w Europie*, edited by Maria Lind and Raimu Minichbauer. Warszawa: Bec Zmiana. www.wuw-warsaw.pl/raport.php?lang=eng#JanS (accessed 1 April 2021).

Sowa, Jan. 2014. 'Poza zasadą skuteczności.' In *Skuteczność sztuki*, edited by Tomasz Załuski, 56–78. Łódź: Muzeum Sztuki.

Spinelli, Aria. 2018. 'Rewriting the History of Art and Activism in Milan. New Forms of Sociality and the Radical Imaginary.' Unpublished manuscript.

Srnicek, Nick and Alex Williams. 2016. *Inventing the Future: Postcapitalism and a World without Work*. Revised and updated edition. London: Verso.

Staal, Jonas. 2019. *Propaganda Art in the 21st Century*. Cambridge, MA: The MIT Press.

Stakemeier, Kerstin and Marina Vishmidt. 2016. *Reproducing Autonomy: Work, Money, Crisis and Contemporary Art*. London; Berlin: Mute.

Stallabrass, Julian. 2004. *Art Incorporated: The Story of Contemporary Art*. Oxford: Oxford University Press.

Stallabrass, Julian. 2006. *High Art Lite: The Rise and Fall of Brit Art*. London: Verso.

Standing, Guy. 2014. *The Precariat: The New Dangerous Class*. London, UK; New York: Bloomsbury.

State of the Arts. 2020. 'A COVID-19 Emergency Fund for the Cultural Sector – State of the Arts.' 17 March 2020. state-of-the-arts.net/2020/03/17/covid-19 (accessed 1 April 2021).

Steeds, Lucy, Paul O'Neill and Mick Wilson, eds. 2017. *How Institutions Think: Between Contemporary Art and Curatorial Discourse*. Cambridge, MA: MIT Press.

Steinhauer, Jillian. 2020. 'A Crisis in Community Reach: MoMA's Arts Educators on the Consequences of Their Contract Cuts.' *The Art Newspaper*, July. www.theartnewspaper.com/analysis/moma-cuts-art-educators-amid-funding-squeeze (accessed 1 April 2021).

Steyerl, Hito. 2009. 'The Institution of Critique.' In *Art and Contemporary Critical Practice: Reinventing Institutional Critique*, edited by Gerald Raunig and Gene Ray, 13–19. London: MayFly Books.

Steyerl, Hito. 2016. 'If You Don't Have Bread, Eat Art!: Contemporary Art and Derivative Fascisms.' *E-Flux Journal*,

October 2016. www.e-flux.com/journal/76/69732/if-you-don-t-have-bread-eat-art-contemporary-art-and-derivative-fascisms (accessed 1 April 2021).

Steyerl, Hito. 2017. *Duty Free Art: Art in the Age of Planetary Civil War*. London: Verso.

Stimson, Blake and Gregory Sholette, eds. 2007. *Collectivism after Modernism: The Art of Social Imagination after 1945*. Minneapolis: University of Minnesota Press.

subtramas, Virginia Villaplana, Montse Romani and Diego del Pozo. 2018. 'Between Acts: Influence, Negotiate, Encounter, Instigate, Narrate. Re-Writing The Relations Between Art And Situated Knowledge Found In Times Of Crisis.' In *The Constituent Museum: Constellations of Knowledge, Politics and Mediation: A Generator of Social Change*, edited by John Byrne, Elinor Morgan, November Paynter, Aida Sanchez de Serdio and Adela Zeleznik, 196–201. Amsterdam: Valiz.

Szadkowski, Krystian. 2015. *Uniwersytet jako dobro wspólne: podstawy krytycznych badań nad szkolnictwem wyższym*. Warszawa: Wydawnictwo Naukowe PWN.

Szreder, Kuba. 2013. 'Cruel Economy of Authorship.' In *Undoing Property?*, edited by Marysia Lewandowska and Laurel Ptak, 41–56. Berlin; New York: Sternberg Press.

Szreder, Kuba. 2017. 'Exercises in the Curatorial Open Form: On the Example of Exhibition Making Use. Life in Postartistic Times.' *Art & the Public Sphere* 6(1–2): 51–67.

T

Teatro Valle. 2012. 'STATUTE OF TEATRO VALLE BENE COMUNE.' 31 October 2012. www.teatrovalleoccupato.it/teatro-valle-occupato-one-year-and-half-of-commoning-english-version (accessed 1 April 2021).

Temporary Services. 2012. 'Independence Proceeds from Interdependence.' In *A Guidebook of Alternative Nows*, edited by Amber Hickey, 11–15. Los Angeles, CA: Journal of Aesthetics & Protest Press.

Terranova, Tiziana. 2000. 'Free Labor: Producing Culture for the Digital Economy.' *Social Text* 18 (2 63): 33–58.

The Anti-Fascist Year. 2019. 'The Anti-Fascist Year.' 2019. rokantyfaszystowski.org/en (accessed 1 April 2021).

The People's Cultural Plan. 2019. 'The People's Cultural Plan Supports 9 Weeks of Art and Action at the Whitney.' *Hyperallergic*, April. hyperallergic.com/492276/the-peoples-cultural-plan-supports-9-weeks-of-art-and-action-at-the-whitney (accessed 1 April 2021).

Thier, Hadas. 2021. 'Vaccine Apartheid.' Africa Is a Country. March 2021 (online magazine). africasacountry.com/2021/03/vaccine-apartheid (accessed 1 April 2021).

Thompson, Nato, ed. 2012. *Living as Form: Socially Engaged Art from 1991-2011*. Cambridge, MA: The MIT Press.

Traverso, Enzo. 2019. *The New Faces of Fascism: Populism and the Far Right*. London; Brooklyn, NY: Verso.

U

Ukeles, Mierle Laderman. 2014. 'Manifesto for Maintenance Art.' In *Truth Is Concrete: A Handbook for Artistic Strategies in Real Politics*, edited by Florian Malzacher, 302. Berlin; New York; Graz: Sternberg Press; Steirischer Herbst.

Universidad Nomada. 2009. 'Mental Prototypes and Monster Institutions: Some Notes by Way of an Introduction.' In *Art and Contemporary Critical Practice: Reinventing Institutional Critique*, edited by Gerald Raunig and Gene Ray, 237–47. London: MayFly Books.

V

van Assche, Annelies. 2020. *Labor and Aesthetics in European Contemporary Dance: Dancing Precarity*. Cham: Springer International Publishing. doi.org/10.1007/978-3-030-40693-6.

van den Berg, Karen, and Ursula Pasero, eds. 2013. *Art Production Beyond the Art Market?* Berlin; New York: Sternberg Press.

van den Berg, Karen. 2013. 'Fragile Productivity: Artistic Activities beyond the Exhibition System.' In *Art Production Beyond the Art Market?*, edited by Karen van den Berg and Ursula Pasero, 45–71. Berlin; New York: Sternberg Press.

Vartanian, Hrag. 2014. 'Activists Take Protest to the Facade of the Guggenheim Museum [UPDATED].' *Hyperallergic*, 25 March 2014. hyperallergic.com/116438/activists-take-protest-to-the-facade-of-the-guggenheim-museum (accessed 1 April 2021).

Vartanian, Hrag. 2017. 'Protesters Demand MoMA Drop Trump Advisor from Its Board.' *Hyperallergic*, February. hyperallergic.com/360236/protesters-demand-moma-drop-trump-advisor-from-its-board (accessed 1 April 2021).

Veblen, Thorstein. 2009. *The Theory of the Leisure Class*. Reissued. Oxford World's Classics. Oxford: Oxford University Press.

Velthuis, Olav. 2007. *Talking Prices: Symbolic Meanings of Prices on the Market for Contemporary Art*. Princeton: Princeton University Press.

Vercellone, Carlo. 2007. 'From Formal Subsumption to General Intellect: Elements for a Marxist Reading of the Thesis of Cognitive Capitalism.' *Historical Materialism* 15(1): 13–36.

Vesić, Jelena and Dusan Grlja. 2007. 'The Neoliberal Institution of Culture and the Critique of Culturalization.' *Transversal* (online magazine). 2007. eipcp.net/transversal/0208/prelom/en (accessed 1 April 2021).

Vilensky, Dmitry. 2017. 'WITHDRAWAL AS INSTITUTIONAL CRITIQUE: CHTO DELAT AND MANIFESTA 10 Q&A with Dmitry Vilensky.' In *I Can't Work like This: A Reader on Recent Boycotts and Contemporary Art*, edited by Joanna Warsza, 233–37. Berlin: Sternberg Press.

Vilensky, Dmitry and Anastasia Chaguidoullie. 2018. '"Anxiety Now Prevails" A Conversation with Dmitry

Vilensky.' *On Curating*, 2018. www.on-curating.org/issue-41-reader/anxiety-now-prevails-a-conversation-with-dmitry-vilensky.html#.Xkk2AUrdiUk (accessed 1 April 2021).

Virno, Paolo. 2004. *A Grammar of the Multitude*. Los Angeles, CA: Semiotext(e).

W

Wade, Gavin and Liam Gillick, eds. 2002. *Strike*. London: Alberta Press.

W.A.G.E. 2010. 'W.A.G.E. Survey.' New York: W.A.G.E.

W.A.G.E. 2010. n.d. "W.A.G.E. HOME." Accessed 11 February 2021a. wageforwork.com/home#top.

W.A.G.E. 2010. n.d. 'Womanifesto.' Accessed 11 February 2021b. wageforwork.com/about/womanifesto#top.

Wallerstein, Immanuel Maurice. 1998. *Utopistics: Or Historical Choices of the Twenty-First Century*. New York: New Press.

Wallis, Brian. 2002. 'Public Funding and Alternative Spaces.' In *Alternative Art New York 1965–1985*, edited by Julie Ault. Minneapolis, MN: Minneapolis University Press.

Warsza, Joanna, ed. 2017. *I Can't Work like This: A Reader on Recent Boycotts and Contemporary Art*. New York: Sternberg Press.

Weber, Jasmine, A Whitney Museum Vice Chairman Owns a Manufacturer Supplying Tear Gas at the Border, *Hyperallergic*, 27 November 2018, hyperallergic.com/472964/a-whitney-museum-vice-chairman-owns-a-manufacturer-supplying-tear-gas-at-the-border [accessed 10 June 2021]

Weeks, Kathi. 2011. *The Problem with Work: Feminism, Marxism, Antiwork Politics, and Postwork Imaginaries*. Durham, NC: Duke University Press.

White, Harrison and Cynthia White. 1993. *Canvases and Careers: Institutional Change in the French Painting World: With a New Foreword and a New Afterword*. Chicago, IL: University of Chicago Press.

White Pube. 2020. 'The White Pube | Ideas for a New Art World.' The-White-Pube. 3 April 2020. www.thewhitepube.co.uk/ideasforanewartworld (accessed 1 April 2021).

WHW, ed. 2005. *Kollektive Kreativität / Collective creativity*. Frankfurt am Main: Revolver, Archiv für Aktuelle Kunst.

Wójtowicz, Aleksy. 2020. 'Od Września Do Maja. Raport z Roku Antyfaszystowskiego.' Warsaw: Warsaw Biennale.

Wright, Stephen. 2013. *Toward a Lexicon of Usership*. Eindhoven: Van Abbemuseum.

Wu, Chin-Tao. 1998. 'Embracing the Enterprise Culture: Art Institutions Since the 1980s.' *New Left Review* 230: 28–57.

Wu, Chin-Tao. 2003. *Privatising Culture*. London: Verso.

Wuggenig, Ulf, Gerald Raunig and Gene Ray, eds. 2011. *Critique of Creativity: Precarity, Subjectivity and Resistance in the 'Creative Industries.'* London: MayFly Books.

Y

Yúdice, George. 2003. *The Expediency of Culture: Uses of Culture in the Global Era*. Durham, NC; London: Duke University Press.

Z

Zafiropoulos, Hannah. 2017. 'OFF Biennale Budapest — New East 100.' *The Calvert Journal*, 31 October 2017. www.calvertjournal.com/features/show/9150/new-east-100-off-biennale-budapest (accessed 1 April 2021).

Zukin, Sharon. 1989. *Loft Living: Culture and Capital in Urban Change*. New York: Rutgers University Press.